The Next Evolution

The Next Evolution –

Enhancing and Unifying Project and Change Management

The Emergence One Method for Total Project Success

Thomas Luke Jarocki

Brown & Williams Publishing

San Francisco • Princeton, NJ

Published by Brown & Williams Publishing, LLC, Princeton, NJ.
Brown & Williams Publishing offers special discounts on quantity purchases by corporations, professional organizations, academic institutions, authorized training companies, and other organizations. For details, please write to sales@brown-williams.com.

Limit of Liability/Disclaimer of Warranty: While the publisher and author have used their best efforts in preparing this book, they make no representations or warranties with respect to the accuracy or completeness of the contents of this book, and specifically disclaim any implied warranties of merchantability or fitness for a particular purpose. No warranty may be created or extended by sales representatives or written sales materials. The advice, strategies, processes, tools, and techniques presented in this book may not be suitable for your situation. You should consult with a professional where appropriate. Neither the publisher nor author shall be liable for any loss of profit or any other damages. The information contained in the book is subject to change without notice.

"The Emergence One Method" is a trademarke of Thomas L. Jarocki. No person, organization, or other entity may use "The Emergence One Method" within any form of commercial transaction or activity, except for those professionals who have the expressed written permission of Emergence One International, Ltd.

"PMI" and the PMI logo are service and trademarks of the Project Management Institute, Inc. which are registered in the United States and other nations; "PMP" and the PMP logo are certification marks of the Project Management Institute, Inc. which are registered in the United States and other nations; "PMBOK" is a trademark of the Project Management Institute, Inc. which is registered in the United States and other nations.

"SAP" and "AcceleratedSAP" are registered trademarks of SAP AG, Waldorf, Germany. "Oracle" and "Oracle AIM" are registered trademarks of Oracle Corporation, Redwood City, California. All other products and services mentioned throughout this book may be registered or unregistered trademarks of their respective owners.

Cover concept by T. Jarocki
Typesetting and cover realization by Wordzworth.com

Library of Congress Control Number: 2011930157

Jarocki, Thomas Luke
      The next evolution – enhancing and unifying project and change management : The emergence one method for total project success / Thomas Luke Jarocki
            p. cm.
      Includes bibliographical references and index.

      ISBN 978-0-9836678-0-3

1 Project management. 2. Organizational change management
3. Business. I Title

Printed in the United States of America.

Printing Number
10 9 8 7 6 5 4 3 2 1

To my two girls, Madeline and Amélie,
who help me appreciate
the importance of managing daily tasks
within an ever churning sea of change.

Table of Contents

List of Tables and Figures

Preface

On Project Success and Temperamental Relationships

For all practical purposes, there is little difference between projects and change initiatives. After all, projects are created to deliver beneficial change to the organization, and change initiatives require some sort of organized effort (that is, a project structure) if an organization wants to achieve its objectives. As such, projects are the structured implementation of change.

Regardless of how an initiative is labeled, the disciplines of project management and change management are recognized as being critical to the successful planning and execution of any new initiative. These disciplines are indispensible to the success of strategy implementations, technology introductions or upgrades, organizational redesign efforts, process improvement undertakings, culture change initiatives, or any other type of endeavor that will help improve and contribute to the ongoing evolution of a company.

Whether the effort is large or small, "transformational" in nature, or merely an enhancement to an existing organizational component, most experienced project sponsors know that *total project success* is not only about delivering on time, within budget, and according to spec. Total project success also means ensuring that the fruits of the effort are fully adopted by the organization, and that business value realization is achieved promptly and decisively.

Despite the fact that project management and change management often share similar objectives (and as this book will demonstrate, similar activities and deliverables as well), they are often procured, practiced, and managed as separate disciplines.

This separation and sense of autonomy often creates a temperamental relationship between project management and change management. Because each provides its own set of methodologies, project plans, activities, and deliverables, a schizophrenic approach to project execution and change success is often created. Additionally, joint opportunities and interdependencies are rarely identified or realized, and a common vision of success is never fully developed. Despite claims of "integrating" or "complementing" each other, the reality is that an equal, mutually beneficial partnership between project management and change management rarely lasts long.

Rather than complement each other, these two critical project disciplines often wind up competing with each other over roles and responsibilities, project strategy and execution, access to project sponsors and funding streams, and the perceived value of their own work streams. As a result, one side (or both) inevitably discounts the contributions and value of the other and often times change management is marginalized. As a result, organizations struggle to embrace or adopt change, which leads to poor business value realization and a waste of company resources and time. Finally, the project winds up leaving a bitter taste in the mouths of stakeholders and project sponsors.

As Organizations Evolve, So Must Project Practices

Even in situations where roles and responsibilities between project management and change management are somewhat ironed out, many techniques and principles from these disciplines are haphazardly applied. In addition, many assumptions, models, and approaches that project managers and change practitioners rely on are actually decades old and are simply not well matched for many of today's faster-paced companies.

For instance, most project management methodologies were built around managing long-term capital projects and don't account for the rapid introduction of business change into the workplace and its effects on the workforce. Most change management approaches used today were actually developed decades ago for a much more change resistant population than what we have today. For example, today's new-millennium, tech-savvy, Google-driven, Smartphone-happy workforce is much more willing to embrace innovations and new ways of working than were the workforces of previous generations. This does not mean today's organizations don't need change management to help them adopt change and be competent with new requirements; however, it does require us to revisit the methodologies built on a knee-jerk assumption that most modern-day employees have a natural inclination to "resist change."

> *As organizations continue to evolve and integrate more of their processes and practices, so must the disciplines of project management and change management evolve and integrate.*

Most books on traditional project management techniques often pay scant attention to the critical people, politics, and organizational change factors. On the flip side, most books on change management only tout high-level concepts and principles. Most also do not offer enough structure, rigor, or a broad enough adherence to the accurate execution of project tasks to create success. In addition, the focus of so many project management and change management books is on making either the project management or the change management component of a project successful rather than both. *There is a crucial need for a unifying methodology that truly integrates these two critical project disciplines.*

Introducing the Next Evolution

With *"The Next Evolution – Enhancing and Unifying Project and Change Management"* my colleagues at Emergence One International and I hope to update and integrate the project management and change management disciplines.

During my career, I have been fortunate enough to be a steadily employed project team consultant. Over the past 20 plus years, I have logged close to 25,000 hours of direct, on-the-ground project work. I have worked side-by-side with numerous project teams, and sweated it out with fellow team members, day in and day out, on a wide variety of projects and change initiatives.

During this time, I've captured a lot of what went into the thinking that questioned how to make *projects* more successful, rather than simply how to make the project management or change management components more successful. I've captured the methods, best practices, and "real-world" realities that provided tangible and practical solutions. I've pored over hundreds of "lessons learned" documents, employed, tweaked, and validated the various techniques and approaches with esteemed colleagues, and wrapped them all up within a sensible project life cycle framework.

The result is *The Emergence One Method for Total Project Success* and subsequently, the creation of this book.

The Next Evolution – Enhancing and Unifying Project and Change Management provides project professionals with some much needed clarity regarding the importance and role that both project and change management have in facilitating total project success. This book begins by detailing the evolution of the project management discipline and the emergence of the practice of organizational/behavioral change management. This book also details why both project disciplines are critical for project success and provides the complete Emergence One project life cycle methodology. The Emergence One Method is a proven methodology that has enhanced the way projects are managed and executed in Fortune 100 companies both in the United States and abroad.

Rather than treating project management and change management as separate disciplines with redundant or disparate project plans, activities, and deliverables, the Emergence One Method integrates and enhances the best practices of both. This methodology details the essential project tasks for each stage of the project life cycle, while also applying the same rigor to address vital stakeholder management and organizational change needs.

This integration addresses not only the critical human, political, and organizational change issues inherent in all projects, but also the numerous design, development, and project execution issues as well. It also offers business, IT, and project professionals the necessary activities, structure, tools, and real-world insights to optimize both people *and* process within one comprehensive methodology.

The Emergence One Method can be used as a standalone project methodology, or to enhance existing project management and change implementation approaches. Not just applicable to major organizational transformations, the Emergence One Method is fully scalable for use on small to mid-size projects, even when there are minimal organizational changes or end-user impacts.

The Emergence One Method offers:

- An integrated, unified approach to addressing and executing essential project and change management activities and tasks; eliminating the need to procure and manage two sets of project resources (for example, a core project team and an adjunct change management team).
- Clear roles and responsibilities for project managers and change practitioners in order to eliminate overlapping activities, optimize joint opportunities, and form more productive, collaborative relationships.
- A tangible, rigorous, yet practical approach to addressing the numerous human, political, and organizational change issues that can impede project momentum, return on investment, and business value.
- Clear guidance, including real-world insights and helpful caveats, on completing the necessary activities, tasks, and deliverables within each project phase.
- A clear method on satisfying end-user adoption and other stakeholder management issues well before deployment so operational disruptions are minimized and business value realization can occur much sooner.

The result is a business change initiative, strategy implementation, or IT project that is:

- Properly scoped, managed, and supported;
- Efficiently designed and built;
- Conscientiously deployed; and
- Eagerly adopted and sustained by the entire organization so business value can be decisively realized.

The Emergence One Method captures the next evolution of the project management and change management disciplines... a logical and essential merger of these two critical project disciplines into one unified approached focused on achieving total project/organizational success.

Whom This Book Is For:

- **Business Managers in a Project Role** who may have strong functional or operational knowledge, but are unfamiliar with how to best organize a project, properly sequence the essential tasks, effectively manage stakeholder needs and expectations, and successfully move the project forward.
- **Project Managers** who may already have excellent skills with more traditional aspects of project management, but would like more insights on how to seamlessly integrate various change management techniques and approaches into their project plans. This book will also help project managers better understand the complexities behind managing many of the human, political, and organizational change issues of a project, and how the broad skills of an experienced change practitioner will help facilitate project management success at every stage of the project life cycle.
- **IT and Other Technical Project Managers** who may have deep technical and subject matter expertise, but would like additional guidance in managing complex change management and end-user adoption needs that are critical to success.
- **Change Management Practitioners** who may have a strong understanding of "people issues," but would like clearer guidance on how to best integrate that with the nuts and bolts of a project, or how to interweave their change management approaches within a project management methodology. This book will also provide change practitioners with a better understanding of the project execution process and the rigor required to be successful both as change facilitators and as valued project advisors.
- **Program/Project Management Offices** looking to augment or enhance their current project methodology with a scalable and flexible approach to managing project tasks and stakeholder needs and expectations.
- **Business Executives and Change Leaders** who would like to move their company initiatives toward achieving total project success by promoting and optimizing the right balance of people and process.

- **Students** looking for a more forward-thinking, real-world approach to managing people and projects beyond what is typically propagated by academic theories.
- **Anyone else** seeking a more robust understanding of how to seamlessly integrate organizational behavior and change management elements into a project plan.

For more information on Emergence One International, please visit our website at: www.emergenceone.com.

Part One

The Next Evolution –
Enhancing and Unifying
Project and Change Management

Chapter 1

Projects Are the Vehicles of Change

Introduction

During the past several decades, the business world has changed, adapted, and evolved to one degree or another. However, in today's world, organizations within most industries and markets are evolving at a faster pace than ever before. As companies continue to evolve, the methods, processes, and techniques they use to manage their many business initiatives, strategy implementations, IT projects, and change initiatives must evolve as well.

For today's companies, most of the usual suspects such as increased competition, globalization, and the introduction of innovations still factor into an organization's need to change and evolve. However, there are two relatively new innovations that really stand out. They include the introduction of robust IT business applications and the Internet. Both of these developments have particularly influenced and accelerated the pace of change in business today.

While there is an ample literature regarding the impact of the Internet on external operations and other technological innovations that improve operations, little has been written on how the Internet has impacted the *mindset* of those in business operations.

Never before have so many people been able to access such a broad spectrum of information so easily. Information consumers also have the ability to share information with thousands of others in a nearly instantaneous fashion. For those in the business world (and elsewhere), information technology has created a greater *awareness*… a greater awareness of marketplace changes, of real-time positions and progress, of fast changing external situations, and of moves by competitors. It has also stimulated greater awareness of emerging innovations, new technology, and the latest "best practices."

This, in turn, has led to a greater awareness of both operational and competitive deficiencies that might exist within a company or organization. Therefore, companies are now much more cognizant of how they could be quickly left behind if they fail to act fast and implement whatever the latest and greatest improvements may happen to be.

The Acceleration of Organizational Evolution

This heightened sense of awareness regarding new possibilities, new opportunities, threats, and so on has shifted the mindset of many in the business world. Businesses have gone from simply desiring smooth, "stable" operations to seeking ways to constantly tweak, improve, enhance, or even radically transform operations. This greater awareness has brought with it a greater desire to evolve and change at a more accelerated pace than ever before. Combine this with the new reality where even the most established businesses can be usurped by much smaller competitors (who, in today's world, do not need a long history to attract significant investment or launch a widely successful initial public offering), and you have a heightened desire to implement new ideas, new technologies, and new ways of operating.

Since "being nimble" is the new normal, companies are acting on that desire. These companies are continually initiating a variety of new projects and initiatives, whether they are customer-facing or operations-focused, at a pace faster than what has typically occurred in the past. Whether they are called change initiatives, strategy implementations, improvement programs, operational enhancements or upgrades, or simply "a project," the result for the organization is the same... a continuous process of change. These are changes that the company must absorb and extract some type of business value from if it wants to continue to evolve and compete; otherwise, it faces the fate of extinction. Call it "organizational evolution" if you like.

Organizational evolution is characterized by numerous small to mid-size projects being executed concurrently throughout the company, where the whole is greater than the sum of its parts. This new evolution is spurred on by a newer generation of workers who have been exposed to a broader range of new ideas and best practices. This current generation possesses a stronger willingness and a greater openness to embrace change and to try new things than has been seen in previous generations.

No longer can managers and executives make their mark on the company simply by maintaining the status quo. Rather, they make their mark by offering and implementing new ideas – improvements, enhancements, and innovations that will move their company forward at a faster pace than what has typically occurred in the past. Additionally, rewards and promotions no longer go to the apt manager of the status quo, but to someone who makes the effort to contribute to and facilitate the company's continuing evolution.

The Shift to Being More "Project-Driven"

This desire and need to rapidly evolve has caused many companies to shift from being operations-focused to being project-driven. Although operations continue to form the bulk of activities for most companies, operations, along with organizational support services, are constantly being improved, re-imagined, reengineered, transformed, enhanced, restructured, and expanded via numerous project or change initiatives that occur throughout the company.

Where major change efforts or "revolutionary transformations" grab the headlines and attract the academic crowd sensing the next big book, the reality is that today there are multitudes of small to mid-size projects occurring within most companies. While it may not appear that a company is undergoing any major transformation, you can bet that it is evolving some aspects of itself, whether it is enhancing or updating its practices and processes, its technologies, or its underlying infrastructure. Additionally, these projects on their own may not necessarily be revolutionizing company operations or identity, but they are, at the very least, spurring on the evolution required to maintain a competitive edge.

Whether it is in the form of a revolution or a less noticeable evolution, change is always occurring in one form or another, to one degree or another, somewhere in the company. But whether the change is large or small, it must be managed well.

Change Does Not Occur in a Vacuum

In recent years, "change" has become a loaded term, full of earth-shattering connotations. However, it is important to note that change is not always synonymous with transformation. However, whether a change effort is large or small, "change" does not occur in a vacuum; rather, it is often the result of some organized approach or structured effort.

In fact, change might not always be referred to as a "change." Rather, it might simply be called an implementation, an upgrade, a compliance requirement, or just a mere enhancement.

Regardless of the terminology used, three things are certain:

1   Beneficial business, organizational, or IT change requires the support of an organized effort (i.e. a project).
2   All projects will produce changes that will affect people, process, and/or structural elements of the organization (such as the IT infrastructure or organizational hierarchy).

3   Organizations must effectively manage both the project and the associated changes in order to achieve benefits.

Projects Are the Vehicles of Change

Although organizations may use different terms to describe a change effort, the fact that change is organized and given structure (as opposed to being amorphous in nature) qualifies it as being a *project*.

A project may be organized in a highly structured and formal manner, with trained project managers who regularly employ project management software and other tools to help manage the project. Alternatively, a project may be organized in a rough, *ad-hoc* manner with a few people sitting around looking for consensus on implementing a collection of high-level ideas. Regardless of the amount of rigor used, any planned undertaking that produces change in the workplace will take the form of a project.

There are many definitions for the term "project." One that is particularly useful comes from *The Definition Guide to Project Management* by Sebastian Nokes:

> *A project is a temporary endeavor, having a defined beginning and end (usually constrained by date, but can be by funding or deliverables), undertaken to meet unique goals and objectives, usually to bring about beneficial change or added value.*

Notice the last part of the definition "*… to bring about beneficial change or added value.*" Projects are initiated to bring about change; they are the structured implementation of change. Put another way, projects are the vehicles of change.

NOTE:: *"Projects are the vehicles of change" is a variation of a statement originally presented in an excellent book by Englund, Graham, and Dinsmore entitled: Creating the Project Office: A Manager's Guide to Leading Organizational Change.*

The Elusive Nature of "Project Success"

Projects vary enormously in size, scope, make-up, and potential impact to the organization. However, regardless of the size or scope of the project, it, along with the resulting change, still needs to be effectively managed in order to achieve even a modicum of success.

Now that more and more companies are becoming project-driven, project success is more important than ever. Despite this, achieving project success remains as elusive as ever.

What Is "Project Success"?

If one scours business literature for project success rates, he or she will find various statistics depending on the source, date of publication, and type of project or initiative that is being considered.

Here are some examples from different surveys throughout the years that have evaluated the success of large-scale enterprise resource planning (ERP) initiatives:

- 61% of ERP projects analyzed were deemed to have failed (KPMG Canada Survey, 1997).
- 40% of ERP implementations failed to achieve their business case within one year of going live (The Conference Board Survey, 2001).
- 51% of respondents viewed their ERP implementation as unsuccessful (The Robbins-Gioia Survey, 2005).

A more reliable analysis of "project success" comes from the Standish Group. Unlike other organizations that quote various project success and failure rates at only one point in time, the Standish Group is one of the few organizations that has been tracking (IT) project success rates via a similar methodology since 1994. Specifically, the CHAOS body of research published by the Standish Group is the largest ongoing body of research in the IT industry. Further, statistics obtained from this data collection effort are the most widely quoted and most highly regarded amongst industry professionals.

Similar to the perspective of the Emergence One Method, the Standish Group does not consider project success or failure to be an "either/or" issue. To these analysts, the following categories apply:

- *Successful* – The project is completed within the original timeframe, within budget, with all specified functions and features included.
- *Challenged* – The project was eventually completed, but went over budget, was late, or did not include all the functions and features that were originally specified.
- *Failed* – The project was canceled before completion, or the project was never implemented.

When the Standish Group first began conducting the CHAOS study in 1994, "successful" projects were only found in a paltry 16% of cases. Jump ahead to 2003, when the Standish Group found that project success rates of 34%. This means that from 1994 to 2003 there was more than a 100% increase in project success! However, keep in mind that a 100% increase in project success is still a far cry from making a claim that 100% of projects are successful.

Along with this 34% success rate, the "outright failure" rate was 15%. However, the bulk of projects (51%) fell into the "challenged" category which means that the project was over budget, came in late, or did not include all the functions and features originally specified.

While this upward trend in project success looked promising, the Standish Report from 2009 brought an unexpected turn. Specifically, the "CHAOS Summary 2009" report actually found a *decrease* in project success rates, from 34% to 32%. While this might not seem like much, project *failure rates* (as in "outright failure") rose from 15% in 2003 to a very troubling 24% in 2009. This was the highest failure rate reported in over a decade. Clearly, something is amiss.

Why Projects Fail

Despite decades of research and the proliferation of numerous articles, books, and "expert" advice, ideas on how to best achieve project success or how to make a change initiative succeed have only grown more diverse (and some would argue more schizophrenic) over the years. A quick Internet search yields thousands upon thousands of articles, white pages, blog entries, book excerpts, and so forth. These pieces of advice on why projects fail or how to make an initiative more successful are often dished out in "Top Ten" lists (or other numerical variations) offered by consultants, researchers, and academicians. In today's Google driven world, there is no shortage of neat, readily digestible lists from which to choose.

However, if one takes the time to reconcile these lists with one another and find some consistency, they will be in for a frustrating experience. (I should know. I tried.)

The fact is there are literally *dozens of reasons* why a project or change initiative might fail. The list below will provide a good start, but, as we will soon see, this list is by no means comprehensive:

- A poorly defined project scope
- Insufficient requirements gathering
- Ambiguous goals and objectives
- Shortcuts in testing or piloting
- Lack of adequate change control
- Unrealistic timelines
- Poor scope management
- Untested software or other untried technology
- Poor risk management
- Cost cutting or cost overruns
- Competing priorities

- Inadequate project funding or support
- Poor project planning

The Importance of Project Management

To address these issues, organizations have typically turned to the practice of project management for help in accounting for, and mitigating, the above components that can threaten project success. In fact, one of the largest predictors of project success is the appropriate application of commonly accepted project management practices by an experienced project manager (although, as we will see later, often times, more than just project management is required to achieve total project success within the business and IT worlds).

First-rate management of projects and the subsequent change is what separates good companies from poor and mediocre companies; change will never be successful if it emerges from a poorly managed project. *This is one reason why change success depends on strong project management.*

If change emerges from a project that is poorly defined and scoped, or is inefficiently managed, it doesn't matter how great an organization's change deployment efforts are. Either the status quo will remain or the change will have a negative impact on the company.

This is especially important in today's project-driven business world. A poorly managed project can bring down an entire company or, at the very least, the reputation of the project sponsor, project manager, or those on the project team. Additionally, a poorly managed project can damage the company in the long run, since it will lower the company's confidence in its ability to execute change... no matter how badly the change is needed. If this happens, any new "big idea" that might elevate the company to the next level of performance may be dismissed prematurely.

The Importance of Change Management

Despite the fact that project management, as a formal discipline, has been around for several decades, projects continue to fail or fall short of expectations at an alarming rate. The reason for this is that the discipline of project management does not always account for a whole host of other factors that might threaten project success.

These factors include such things as:

- Company politics and power struggles
- Hidden agendas
- Cultural barriers
- Lack of motivation

- Project decision makers reneging on agreements
- Deficient communication
- Insufficient executive sponsorship
- Inability or unwillingness to alter a particular course or direction
- Poor organizational adoption
- Lack of competent or committed project resources
- Disengaged governance or project oversight committees
- Poor or slow decision making
- Ambiguous roles and responsibilities
- Resistance to change
- Poor project leadership

Despite project management methodologies that *mention* the importance of many of the above factors, most project management methodologies are still very much task-focused. For the most part, these methodologies pay scant attention to many of the human, political, and organizational change issues listed above.

Because of this, savvy project sponsors, along with an ever growing number of project managers, have turned to the field of organizational/behavioral change management (which will henceforth simply be referred to as "change management") to augment project management practices.

What Is Change Management?

There are many perceptions and opinions regarding the scope and purpose of change management and some are broader than others. It is the opinion of us at Emergence One, most change management methodologies in use today often have a very narrow "employee transition" or "personal change" focus which offers limited value.

Since projects are the vehicles of change, Emergence One takes the view that the role of change management is to help enable project goals and objectives by giving stricter consideration to the human, political, and organizational change components that are necessary to facilitate project success. Effective change management activities must be anchored to some type of project management plan to be successful. *After all, most "change management" activities are dependent upon the timing or completion of certain project management activities.* Thus, we do not consider change management to be an exclusive discipline independent of project management. Rather, it is a discipline that augments the areas where project management has typically fallen short: chiefly, in the areas of organizational behavior, corporate politics, stakeholder management, and organizational adoption and support. Hence, the goals and objectives of change management are often intertwined with those of project management since the assumption of any project is the adoption and support of the solution by the organization.

Specifically, Emergence One believes that change management contributes to project success in two ways:

A   It helps project management achieve its traditional measures of success (on time, within budget, according to spec) by paying stricter attention to the human, political, and organizational change management factors that can impede project momentum, decision quality, and success.

B   It provides a broad set of stakeholders (not just end-users and employees) with the required skills, understanding, competencies, behaviors, structural support and opportunities necessary to design, promote, and adopt the numerous project-driven changes *that will enable business value realization.*

Adoption of change is required throughout the project life cycle and can include:

1   *Adoption by Senior Leaders and Key Decision Makers* – Senior-level personnel are considered by Emergence One to be "Tier 1" stakeholders. They are responsible for funding the initiative, clarifying and approving of the scope and direction, removing potential barriers, and building organization support. Unless these behavior and responsibilities are adopted, a project or change initiative will never reach the deployment phase.

2   *Adoption by Project Contributors* – These "Tier 2" stakeholders contributes inputs to the design of the initiative, or assist with the execution of the initiative. Unless they too buy-in to the scope, purpose, and objectives of the initiative, and have clear understanding of their roles and responsibilities, their contributions will be minimal and project quality and momentum will suffer.

3   *Adoption by Change Recipients* – These "Tier 3" stakeholders are the end-users and employees who will be directly impacted by the initiative. These impacts may affect their behaviors, attitudes, or just simply some of the structural aspects associated with their job (such as reporting to a new manager or keying in data to a different IT application).

It is important to note that project management also concerns itself with stakeholder adoption. In fact, as we will see in Chapter 4, there are actually quite a number of overlaps between project management and change management.

As stated earlier, the purpose of a project is to "...*bring about beneficial change or added value.*" Essentially, no one would undertake any type of project unless there was some degree of confidence that individuals, teams, and organizations could successfully transition to and support the desired future state. After all, it does the organization little good if something new is introduced to the organization (or if something that already exists is enhanced or upgraded) if it does not adopt the change. It is the adoption of change by affected or targeted stakeholders that holds the key to creating some level of business value and return on investment (ROI) for the organization. But before that can occur, it is critical that senior leaders and other change enablers adopt the project's concept and direction.

How Project Stakeholders Define Success

Not too long ago, I and a few others from Emergence One's consulting unit met with the CIO of a large, international retail company who was looking to implement a SAP ERP system. In the meeting with us were her chief IT project director and a manager from business operations.

Although they all had some familiarity with project management, they were not very familiar with the practice of organizational change management and were intrigued by Emergence One's approach of integrating change management with traditional project management activities.

Before discussing the project at hand, I asked them, as I often do with new clients, about the success they have had with past projects. The first person to chime in was the director of IT who was responsible for overseeing a number of projects. He remarked that most of their projects were successful.

"Wait a moment," chimed in the CIO. "What about that warehouse management system?"

"What about it?" the IT director answered back. "We got it implemented on time and the system works fine."

"That may be true, but we went significantly over budget to hire the additional resources to make sure that we made the implementation deadline," the CIO added.

"Yeah, that's true. But that's because everyone had a different opinion regarding requirements. Once we had the scope nailed down, the costs were in line with an implementation of that size."

"Well, you may have hit the target go-live date," the operations manager jumped in, "but you were so busy fixing system bugs right up until the system went live that you didn't communicate or train any of my people on how to use the system like you should have. It took us several weeks and a lot of pain and frustration until our operations were running smoothly again."

"Oh really?" the CIO remarked. "I didn't hear about that. I thought the system was running fine."

"The system was running fine; there were no bugs as far as I could tell, but the people responsible for utilizing the system really didn't like it at first, nor did they have the right amount of training or understanding of the system beforehand. And, when they finally did get it to work, the overwhelming consensus was that even though the interface was "prettier," it was no better than the old system when it came to running operations. I have a feeling we spent a whole lot of time and money on nothing more than installing a slicker, better looking user interface."

At this point, the conversation was at a standstill. The director of IT thought he did a fine job of implementing the system and meeting the time-line with a bug-free system. The CIO thought the system worked fine, except for the cost overrun, which was only a minor concern since she had contingency money in the budget for that kind of thing anyway. Even the operations manager saw the project as an *eventual* success since it eventually seemed to work fine and was *no worse* than the previous system.

The Various Interpretations of Project Success

During the meeting described above, we heard several different opinions of the success of the project. We heard that the director of IT thought it was unquestionably "a strong success." However, the CIO, who was a little more cost conscious than was the IT director, considered the project to be a "moderate success." In addition, from the operations manager perspective, he thought that, even though things eventually worked out, the project more or less "missed the mark" in terms of providing value for his employees as well as for operations.

Here we had one project, three stakeholders, and three different judgments of "project success" (if you were to throw a change management practitioner or some other business stakeholder into the mix, they might have deemed the project a "total failure" because the organization did not fully embrace the system or realize any business value from its implementation).

As you can see, the term "project success" does not lend itself to a simple yes or no verdict. While it is true that some projects do outright fail, most projects experience different degrees of success or failure. Contributing to how successful a project might be is the applied mix of both project management and change management services.

Developing a shared understanding of "project success" is the first step in taking a unified approach to achieving success. Once a common understanding of project success is achieved, we can then gain a better understanding of how the methods of both project management and change management disciplines can contribute to achieving that success.

When Emergence One meets with clients for the first time, we always ask them about their previous experiences with projects. We are often amazed at how many CEO/CIOs or senior project managers make the claim that many of their previous projects were "successful." When we dive down a bit deeper, we almost always find that their projects fit more into what the Standish Group would refer to as the "challenged" category. For example, managers may have completed the project on time, but they either blew the budget out of the water to get there; the project was implemented a year later than expected; the project did not have all the expected functions or features that the end-users really needed; or the project was "delivered" on time, but was never fully adopted by the organization.

This list can go on and on.

The Emergence One View of Project Success

Emergence One takes a slightly different view of evaluating project success than does the Standish Group. Rather than utilizing three categories of project results (failed, challenged, or successful), we view project success *as a continuum* with project failure (that is, a project being defunded or never implemented) on one end, and *strong* project success (that is, a project that *exceeds* expectations) on the other end.

Between project "failure" and "strong" project success we have projects that may have made it to the implementation/deployment phase, but may have fallen short in one way or another; however, certainly not enough to be deemed a total failure.

The other category between failure and outstanding success is "moderately" successful (meaning the project more or less met its objectives).

The Project Evaluation Continuum

Here is what a continuum might look like when evaluating overall project success:

Table 1.1. *The Project Evaluation Continuum*

Evaluating Overall Project Success			
Project Failure	*Project Fell Short of Expectations*	*Project Was a Moderate Success*	*Project Was a Strong Success*

Now, if we go back to our three stakeholders who were introduced at the beginning of the chapter and asked them where they would rate their warehouse management project, you might get three different responses.

- The director of IT might evaluate the project as being a "strong success" since he delivered a working system on time and didn't seem to pay much mind to the additional resources that were required to complete the project.
- The CIO, who *was* more mindful of the additional costs, would probably term the project as a "moderate success" since it cost a little more than she originally estimated.
- The operations manager may deem the project to have "fallen short" since it did cause some additional chaos for his department without delivering anything new or particularly helpful that may have been worth the disruptions to operations.

"Project Management Success" and "Project Success" are Different

By traditional project management standards, the above project would most likely be deemed a success because it was delivered on time, fairly close to budget, and according to specifications. One project, three different stakeholders, three different opinions of how successful a particular project was.

However, by Emergence One standards, the project definitely fell short of expectations, if it was not a total failure, since it seemed to provide little in the way of business value. The new warehouse management system did not reflect *customer specifications* (system specifications reflected those of the IT manager more so than those of the true customers who, in this case, were the warehouse employees); it was not fully adopted by the organization; and ultimately, it delivered only limited, if any, business value.

This illustrates an important point: *project management* success is not necessarily the same as *project success.*

Traditionally, project managers were simply required to deliver a "product" of one sort or another, whether it was a new IT system, a redesigned process, a new organizational design, etc., within a certain timeframe and within a certain budget. Whether or not the organization or business units actually adopted the product was not the responsibility of the project manager but of the organization. Thus, if a company spent millions of dollars on implementing a new IT system, so long as the project manager delivered the system without any bugs and according to specifications, he or she was thanked for a successful delivery. However, whether the system was actually *used* by the organization, or whether or not there was any business value realized by the implementation, were not criteria that fell into the project manager's review.

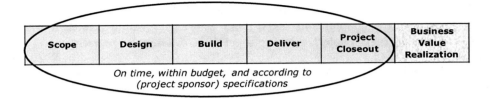

Figure 1.1. *Traditional Project Management "Delivery" Model*

The Five Components of Total Project Success

The Association for Project Management defines project management as *"...the process by which projects are defined, planned, monitored, controlled and delivered such that the agreed benefits are realized."* For our use, we will use the term "business value realization" to capture the latter half of this definition.

Business value realization is often overlooked by project managers who see their role only as a "delivery" person. However, there is no sense in spending the time, expense, and effort on a project unless it provides some kind of business value; the precursor to business value realization is organizational adoption.

Often, the importance of organizational adoption is simply overlooked, or passed on to an adjunct management team to "sell" the change to the organization. Nowadays, more astute project sponsors know that project success and organizational success are inextricably linked.

Emergence One employs five criteria for total project success:

1 **On time** – Refers not only to the final "go-live" or change implementation date, but also to the completion of prior project phases and milestone due dates.

2 **Within budget** – Although cost estimates are usually refined and sharpened as the project progresses, success requires that all project phases are completed within these pre-established estimates.

3 **Meeting customer specifications** – This can sometimes be the most challenging goal to meet for the following three reasons:

    a *According to spec... but who is the customer?* – Very often, projects have multiple customers, all of whom may want "the specs" to be different from what another stakeholder might wish or propose. Reconciling these requests for different specifications can be time-consuming and difficult.

    b *Project teams often do a poor job of engaging the customer* – Project managers, especially IT project managers, are notorious for not properly engaging the customer. Specifically, there is often a pervasive "we know what they need" type of attitude that almost always leads to poor organizational adoption and business value realization.

c   *Customers don't know what they don't know* – Even when there may be agreement on who the customers are, and how to best engage them, customers often "don't know what they don't know." For example, if there is new technology being introduced to the company, end-users might be unaware of the enhanced capabilities that the new system could offer. So, instead of offering specifications that take advantage of this enhanced capability, the customers might instead ask for specifications that simply mirror their current system. While this might help in achieving rapid organizational adoption, it will do little to increase business value.

4   **Adopted by the organization** – Although many project managers and (especially) change practitioners believe that organizational adoption only refers to end-users or other impacted employees, organizational adoption is actually an overlapping three-stage process.

a   *Adopted by senior leaders and key decision makers* – This occurs when decision makers and other key influencers in an organization adopt the project concept, direction, and related costs so the initiative is supported and funded all the way through deployment and implementation. This is a critical (though often overlooked) stage since a large percentage of initiatives (over 30% by some estimates) are either defunded or derailed long before they ever reach the deployment phase.

b   *Adoption by project contributors* – Project contributors refer to stakeholders who can affect design and implementation plans associated with the project. This can include business directors/managers who want to incorporate their own ideas into the project plan; sponsors of other projects who need to concern themselves with potential timing and other integration issues; and internal compliance and regulation departments, such as HR, procurement, legal, health and safety, policy and audit, etc., who may have a say in exactly what can and cannot be done.

c   *Adoption by change recipients* – This refers to adoption by individuals within the targeted group(s) of end-users/employees. Unless there is adoption at the first two levels, there will be no opportunity for adoption at this level. Emergence One uses a fairly simple equation to craft individual adoption plans:

$$\text{Motivation} \times \text{Competence} + \text{Structural Support}$$
$$=$$
$$\text{End-User/Employee Adoption}$$

5   **Business value realization** – Essentially, this refers to the realization of project benefits that are often times documented in the project business case. While many projects are measured in terms of Return on Investment (ROI), there are also many projects that do not produce a clearly measurable ROI. These include projects that may have been initiated to meet some kind of compliance requirement (such as Sarbanes-Oxley) or other types of government regulations.

How a project manager goes about scoping, designing, and building a solution has a direct impact on how well a project is received by the organization and how much business value it eventually achieves. They may come to realize that very few change management teams can facilitate the adoption of a poorly conceptualized or realized product. This is just one of the reasons why the Emergence One Method emphasizes the importance of using change management principles to facilitate project/organizational adoption throughout the project life cycle and not just during project/change deployment.

Simply designing, building, and "throwing it over the fence" to the business has proven, time and time again, to be ineffective. When project managers are not held responsible for organizational adoption and business value realization, the project team does a poor job of factoring in these goals when scoping, designing, and deploying the solution. This failure impedes organizational adoption and lessens the likelihood of true business value realization.

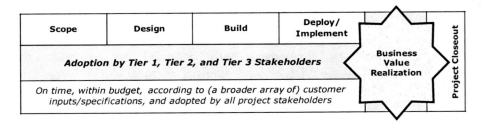

Figure 1.2.   A Model for "Total Project Success"

The Project Success Profile

The "Project Success Profile" is useful in explaining the complexities of determining the perceptions of different decision makers concerning "project success." This profile is also useful in illustrating the importance that different criteria play in contributing to total project success.

NOTE: Depending on whether the change catalyst is a strategy or IT implementation, organizational restructuring, business process change, or some other type of change or implementation/deployment, the wording in each one of the boxes below may be somewhat modified.

Table 1.2.   *The Project Success Profile*

	Failure	Falls Short of Expectations	Moderate Success	Strong Success
Time	Major or multiple project delays	Moderate project delays	Schedule maintained	Ahead of schedule
Budget	Significantly over budget	Moderately over budget	Within budget	Under budget
Meeting Customer Expectations	Few of the required features and functions	Some of the required features and functions	Anticipates features and functionality	Enhances features and functions
Organizational Adoption	Organization rejects the change or used work-arounds	Organization embraces some aspects of the change	Organization operates according to plan	Organization improves on the change
Business Value Realization	Little or no business value	Limited business value	Matches the business case	Exceeds anticipated business value

Emergence One typically pushes its clients to consider the possibility of not simply having a "successful" project, but having a "strongly successful" project: one that exceeds expectations. While clients want to *meet* timelines and stay *within* budget, we try to get them to imagine a project that is so well run that they actually might come in *under budget* or *ahead of schedule*. This can be achieved by adopting a comprehensive approach to project success by *integrating and enhancing* traditional project management and change management approaches.

The View of "Project Success" Impacts Project Structure

A limited view of "project success" held by project sponsors and managers can influence how the project is managed and structured. Further, a limited or narrow view of project success will impede the most advantageous mix of project management/change management practices used on the project.

For instance, if the IT director, mentioned in the story above, was the project sponsor and judged project success via the traditional project management prism of "on time, within budget, and according to spec," then the project team may have placed a heavy emphasis on traditional project management with very little regard to change management. Thus, total project success most likely would not have been achieved.

Table 1.3. *Likely outcome with heavy project management emphasis project management but a light emphasis on change management*

	Failure	Falls Short of Expectations	Moderate Success	Strong Success
Time	Major or multiple project delays	Moderate project delays	Schedule maintained	Ahead of schedule
Budget	Significantly over budget	Moderately over budget	Within budget	Under budget
Meeting Customer Expectations	Few of the required features and functions	Some of the required features and functions	Anticipates features and functionality	Enhances features and functions
Organizational Adoption	Organization rejects the change or used work-arounds	Organization embraces some aspects of the change	Organization operates according to plan	Organization improves on the change
Business Value Realization	Little or no business value	Limited business value	Matches the business case	Exceeds anticipated business value

If, on the other hand, the business operations manager was the project sponsor, the project team may have placed more emphasis on using a *traditional change management* model, which places heavy emphasis on organizational adoption. However, the project may have missed being completed on time and within budget since traditional change management approaches often offer inadequate rigor around project planning and execution.

In addition, even the traditional change management organizational adoption focus area is likely to fall short since it is anchored to a poorly designed/executed project.

Table 1.4. *Likely outcome for heavy change management emphasis but a light emphasis on project management*

	Failure	Falls Short of Expectations	Moderate Success	Strong Success
Time	Major or multiple project delays	Moderate project delays	Schedule maintained	Ahead of schedule
Budget	Significantly over budget	Moderately over budget	Within budget	Under budget
Meeting Customer Expectations	Few of the required features and functions	Some of the required features and functions	Anticipates features and functionality	Enhances features and functions
Organizational Adoption	Organization rejects the change or used work-arounds	Organization embraces some aspects of the change	Organization operates according to plan	Organization improves on the change
Business Value Realization	Little or no business value	Limited business value	Matches the business case	Exceeds anticipated business value

The Use of Two Project Disciplines for One Initiative?

For some, it looks like there might be an easy answer for how to best achieve project success: Why not just use a mix of both project management and change management on the same project/initiative?

Although this suggestion is certainly in the right direction, applying both project management and change management practices to the same project is not as easy as it sounds.

The problem here is that both project management and change management practitioners view themselves as working exclusively on a project. If you review many of the project management methodologies in use today, there is no acknowledgment of change management being a separate discipline that could help balance out some of the needs and challenges projects have. Nor does project management ever outline how to form a collaborative relationship with a dedicated change management practitioner. Instead, this literature offers a nod or two toward the importance of managing the human, political, and organizational change issues on a project. However, this is usually presented only as something the *project manager* has to handle on top of the myriad of project tasks he or she is normally responsible for!

Likewise, most change management approaches virtually ignore the possible presence (or potential benefit) of having a traditionally focused project manager work on an initiative. Therefore, many change models have similar outlines to project management models: "plan the change (project), design the change (solution), make the change, etc..." However, most approaches are void of project management tools and techniques (such as calculating an accurate cost/benefit analysis or creating a work breakdown structure).

The fact that both project management and change management often design, package, and sell their services as if the other does not exist is odd... especially given that the goals of each are not necessarily mutually exclusive. Specifically, project management techniques can contribute to achieving organizational adoption and business value realization just as much as change management techniques contribute to a project coming in on time and within budget.

The Need for a Unifying Methodology

Given that projects are the vehicles of change, and both project management and change management contribute to the overall success of a project, the following questions naturally arise:

- Why is it that many of the models, tools, and approaches used by both project management and change management are so similar to one another, but many project professionals still consider project management and change management as separate disciplines?
- Why is there no unifying methodology for the two disciplines to minimize the common occurrence of project management and change management competing or marginalizing one other?
- Since change management is often sold as an adjunct service to general project consulting services, why must project sponsors procure and manage two sets of project resources?
- Why should an organization manage two separate (or competing) work streams when each frequently interacts with the same overlapping group of stakeholders?

The Emergence of One Comprehensive Approach for Total Project Success

The Emergence One Method satisfies many of the questions and concerns posed above. Further, the E1 Method was born out of a need to focus on what it takes to deliver a seamless approach to achieve *total project success*. The approach avoids creating strict boundaries of "this is project management and that is change management."

Instead, the Emergence One Method applies the strengths, benefits, and unique perspectives of each to the execution and completion of the same project tasks and activities. This integrated approach ensures that all technical, human, and organizational factors are properly addressed. This method also ensures that the final deliverables incorporate the right mix of project management and change management insights and expertise.

The Emergence One Method is neither a traditional project management methodology nor a traditional change management methodology. Rather, it is a comprehensive project life cycle methodology for total project success. The E1 Method represents the next evolution of both disciplines: it is a fully integrated methodology that incorporates and enhances the best practices of each.

Table 1.5. *Likely outcome using the Emergence One Method*

	Failure	Falls Short of Expectations	Moderate Success	Strong Success
Time	Major or multiple project delays	Moderate project delays	Schedule maintained	Ahead of schedule
Budget	Significantly over budget	Moderately over budget	Within budget	Under budget
Meeting Customer Expectations	Few of the required features and functions	Some of the required features and functions	Anticipates features and functionality	Enhances features and functions
Organizational Adoption	Organization rejects the change or used work-arounds	Organization embraces some aspects of the change	Organization operates according to plan	Organization improves on the change
Business Value Realization	Little or no business value	Limited business value	Matches the business case	Exceeds anticipated business value

The Emergence One Method addresses not only critical project tasks, but all the critical human, political, and organizational change issues inherent in projects that can affect project momentum, quality, and ultimately success. Therefore, projects teams who diligently follow the Emergence One Method are likely to exceed initial expectations for project success.

Before we can dive into the details of the Emergence One Method, it would be prudent to first take a step back and understand the evolution of the project management discipline and how it contributed to the emergence of the field of change management.

Chapter 2

The Evolution of Project Management

Introduction

There is a big difference between "project management" and "managing projects."

Project management is a formal discipline that has many commonly accepted tools and techniques. Project managers (those in charge of managing projects) may or may not have any formal training in project management. They also may choose to forgo many of the standard tools and techniques offered by this discipline. However, one of the strongest predictors of project success is having a competent project manager at the helm. Additionally, most competent project managers *regularly employ* many of the commonly accepted tools and techniques from the field of project management.

This chapter will provide an overview of the evolution of project management. Covered in this chapter are a brief history of project management, background on the better known governing bodies behind this discipline, and an overview of common approaches and techniques.

The chapter concludes with a section on current trends and challenges within the field of project management, and how this field has led to the emergence of a similar project discipline generally known as organizational/behavioral change management.

A Brief History of Project Management

Project Management Defined

A definition of project management found on Wikipedia states:

> *"Project management is the discipline of planning, organizing, securing, and managing resources to bring about the successful completion of specific project goals and objectives."*

Project management grew out of several fields, most notably construction, engineering, and large-scale defense projects, and has existed, in one form or another, for thousands of years. There would have been no grand historic feats, such as the building of the pyramids, if it wasn't for some form of project management.

When it comes to the construction of the pyramids and other grand projects, it is suspected that the architects and engineers acted as the project managers. With seemingly unlimited resources of both labor and treasure provided by the pharaohs, it is likely that these engineer project managers did not worry about typical project management constraints such as cost or time. Thus, we can't say for sure that there was much of a formal project management "discipline" (as we now know it) happening during this period. In fact, the birth of project management as a recognized discipline did not occur until the 20th century.

The Birth of Scientific Management

Fast-forward a few thousand years from the time of the pharaohs to around the turn of the 20th century. Frederick Winslow Taylor, a mechanical engineer from Philadelphia, Pennsylvania, began to think that management could benefit from greater applications of both scientific and academic rigor.

Until Taylor, the only method managers had to get more out of their workers was to make them work longer hours. Taylor championed the ideas that if workers worked more *efficiently,* then they would produce more within the same timeframe. What followed became known as "scientific management" (Taylor's tomb in Philadelphia is even inscribed with the words *"The father of scientific management"*).

Two individuals influenced by Taylor's work were Henri Fayol, a Frenchman (who was actually born in Turkey), and Henry Gantt, an America who is the father of the most commonly associated tools of project management, the Gantt chart.

Fayol originally developed six functions of management that included forecasting, planning, organizing, commanding, coordinating, and controlling. Over time, these elements morphed into the commonly accepted project management life cycle of Define, Plan, Organize, Control, and Close.

Likewise, Gantt developed the ubiquitous Gantt chart, which was famously used on such major projects as the construction of the Hoover Dam. He also promoted the idea that industrial efficiency can be achieved only by applying scientific analysis to all components of the work in progress.

The Beginning of a Formal Discipline

While the notion of scientific management emerged at the turn of the century, it was not until the 1950s, a time when most of the world was recovering from the ravages of World War II, that project management started to become a more formalized, independent discipline.

Specifically, during the 1950s, business, engineering, and defense industries saw the introduction of more formal project scheduling, cost estimating, and project control techniques. PERT (Program Evaluation and Review Technique) charts, which represent and analyze tasks, usually in fairly complex projects, were starting to be used in large-scale defense projects. In addition to PERT charts, the Critical Path Method, developed jointly by the DuPont Corporation and the Remington Rand Corporation, was also being used as an important tool for scheduling project activities. These techniques soon proved their worth and quickly spread to wider use in private enterprise.

Project Management Associations

The first organized promotion of project management as a discipline was introduced in Europe by the International Project Management Association (IPMA); it was originally known as the International Management Systems Association, which held its first meeting in Vienna, Austria, in 1967.

Prominent especially in the United Kingdom is the Association for Project Management (APM), which is the largest independent professional body of its kind in Europe, although its membership base is considerably smaller than that of the IPMA.

Better known in the United States is the Project Management Institute (PMI), which was formed in 1967, two years after the first IPMA meeting. Today, the PMI is the world's leading non-profit association for project management professionals and there are over 500,000 members and credential holders throughout approximately 185 countries. As such, PMI standards and credentials are recognized around the world.

The PMI publishes *A Guide to the Project Management Body of Knowledge*. The fourth edition of the *PMBOK® Guide* was published at the end of 2008.

The *PMBOK® Guide* helps promote not only common standards, but also a common vocabulary in which to discuss concepts and share ideas concerning project management. As we will see later, the field of change management has no such advantage.

In the *PMBOK® Guide, 4ᵗʰ Edition*, there are 42 project management processes that fall into five basic process groups and nine knowledge areas.

The five process groups include:

1   Initiating
2   Planning
3   Executing
4   Controlling and Monitoring
5   Closing

The nine knowledge areas include:

1   Project Integration Management
2   Project Scope Management
3   Project Time Management
4   Project Cost Management
5   Project Quality Management
6   Project Human Resource Management
7   Project Communications Management
8   Project Risk Management
9   Project Procurement Management

These nine knowledge areas each contain three or more processes (for a total of 42 processes!) that are required to have an effective project management program.

As you can imagine, it is quite rare to find an experienced, or even a certified project manager who is completely competent in all 42 process areas that branch out from the nine knowledge areas listed above. Even if a project manager is versed in all of these processes, he or she probably would not have enough bandwidth or ability to devote the attention necessary to adequately carry out each process. This is one reason why the Emergence One Method recommends collaborating with a senior change management lead so that many of the people-related tasks can be given the proper amount of attention.

The Rise of the "Accidental Project Manager"

While there are currently fewer than half a million professionals with PMP® certifications or other types of project management certifications, there are perhaps *millions* of projects happening at any one given point in time. This means there are countless projects occurring worldwide that are being managed by people who have very little experience with formal project management tools and techniques. This has given rise to the "Accidental Project Manager," usually an internal business manager or department head who has a lot of experience in operations, but little project management experience.

The Project Management Triangle

The "Project Management Triangle" is an essential concept in project management and was first popularized by Harold Kerzner in his book *Project Management: A Systems Approach to Planning, Scheduling, and Controlling.*

Most projects have certain constraints that the project manager is expected to effectively manage. These constraints are scope (sometimes referred to as "customer specifications" or "spec"), cost, and schedule. Project management is the discipline that provides the tools and techniques to enable the project team to effectively work within these constraints.

Changes to one side of the triangle will inevitably affect the other sides of the triangle. For example, if you increase the scope, you will need to increase the budget (cost) and extend the timeline (schedule). However, if you reduce the budget, you will most likely have to reduce scope, and so forth.

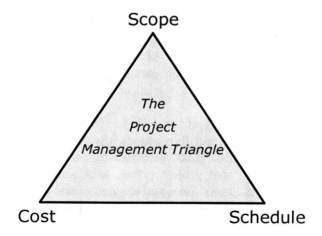

Figure 2.1. *The Project Management Triangle*

Project management success has traditionally been measured by how well the project team can deliver the project specifications while still managing cost and schedule. (This has given rise to a popular project management line regarding project success: "On time, within budget, and according to spec").

Time, scope/customer specifications, and budget are all important and critical measures of success. In addition, because projects typically address a real or potential problem, or exist to take advantage of an opportunity, timing is a critical component of project success. For example, a project that delivers after its scheduled "go-live" date may have arrived too late to mitigate the problem it was trying address, or may have missed the window of opportunity it was aiming for. Additionally, project benefits can easily be nullified if a project's costs end up being much higher than anticipated. Finally, if the project does not deliver what it intends to deliver (that is, customer specifications), then the whole effort is a waste in terms of both time and money.

There have been some enhancements to the Project Management Triangle over the years. For example, some have modified the model by adding in "Quality" as a fourth constraint. The *PMBOK® Guide, 4th Edition* has modified the three-constraint model by overlaying an upside-down triangle on top of the traditional model with three additional constraints: risk, resources, and quality.

Project Life Cycle Methodologies

The Project Life Cycle

Projects can be long and complex affairs. For instance, the typical duration for Emergence One projects is from six months to two years.

Given the complexity and extended timeframes of projects, a common approach to simplifying the management of a project is by following what is known as the project life cycle: a logical sequence of phases from project initiation through completion.

Each phase within the project life cycle has its own unique goals and objectives. By breaking the project into phases, the project manager can focus more clearly on the activities, tasks, deliverables, and resources required for successful completion of that project phase. Additionally, the tasks within each project phase should be rational and sequential and care should be taken to ensure that each task is successfully completed: going back and reworking tasks or deliverables is discouraged.

Different projects employ different project life cycle models. For example, some projects may have as few as three project phases, while others may consist of up to a dozen or more separate project phases. Regardless of the project size, most projects' life cycle models generally have some type of variation on four essential project themes:

Table 2.1. *A common project life cycle model*

Phase 1	Phase 2	Phase 3	Phase 4
Initiating the Project	Organizing and Preparing	Doing the Work	Closing out the Project

Regardless of the exact project life cycle model used, there are some common characteristics and guidelines to follow when working within a project life cycle approach:

- Each phase has a distinct focus that is different from other phases in the project.
- Each phase may require different skill sets; therefore, there may be modifications to the composition of the project team during each subsequent phase.
- Executive influence is higher at the start of a project since these executives are the ones who can decide whether or not to continue to fund the project or pony up the appropriate resources.
- Staffing levels are low in the beginning and typically ramp up with each subsequent phase, before ramping back down once the project is deployed.
- Project team resources work on only one phase at a time; all work must be completed during a phase before moving on to the next phase (however, there are some newer project management methodologies, such as Rapid, that promote overlapping certain phases).
- Before the project can proceed to the next phase, there is a project review or decision point typically known as a "Phase Gate," "Stage Gate," or other comparable term.
- In order for Phase Gates to provide value, the event should offer a critical, unbiased review of the project by *objective* senior-level stakeholders who determine whether or not the project should:
  - Proceed to the next phase (usually an indication that the work to date has been acceptable, the plan forward is optimal and doable, and the business case remains relevant and compelling);
  - Be reworked (usually the result of unacceptable or incomplete deliverables);
  - Be temporarily suspended (most likely due to some kind of timing issue related to an external event or interdependency with another initiative); or
  - Be terminated (usually because the business case is no longer compelling).

The Waterfall Method

The Waterfall Method is a project management approach that is particularly prevalent in the construction and manufacturing industries.

The approach dictates that once a phase is completed, the deliverable is "set in stone" and there is no going back to modify any of the deliverables from the previous phase (mainly because this could prove to be a very expensive proposition in construction and manufacturing environments).

Table 2.2.   Two versions of the Waterfall Method

The Original Waterfall Method	Modified Version for Software Development Projects
1 Requirements specification	1 Conception
2 Design	2 Initiation
3 Construction (Implementation or Coding)	3 Analysis
4 Integration	4 Design
5 Testing and Debugging (validation)	5 Construction (or Coding)
6 Installation	6 Testing (or Validation)
7 Maintenance	7 Maintenance

The Waterfall Method has both its supporters and critics. Supporters contend that the structured approach of this model is needed if a project is expected to be delivered on time, within budget, and according to spec. Critics contend that "perfecting" the deliverable at the end of each phase is unrealistic, and that a better design could be created if information gleaned during a subsequent phase were used to improve the deliverable of a previous phase.

This criticism has led to the rise of Agile and other iterative project life cycle models.

Agile and Other Iterative Project Life Cycle Approaches

An iterative project approach is used frequently in IT system development; however, it can also be used with other types of projects as well. Since user requirements frequently change or develop over time, an initial plan or design should not be etched in stone. By employing various iterations, the solution develops over time, which can better accommodate new or changing requirements.

Table 2.3.   *Example of an iterative project management life cycle*

Iteration 0	Iteration 1	Iteration 2, 3, or more as needed	Iteration *n*
• Project Set-up • Plan	• Plan • Develop and Test • Feedback	• Plan • Develop and Test • Feedback	• Develop and Test • Release Product

Agile is principally known as a software development project life cycle, although Agile principles are starting to be applied to other types of projects as well. Agile was created out of a need to develop software applications quickly, as a variation of an iterative project life cycle. In theory, Agile is supposed to dramatically reduce the delivery time of a product and promotes a strongly collaborative approach.

The Emergence One Method Project Life Cycle

The Emergence One Method also has a six-phase life cycle framework. The six phases in the Emergence One Method, which will be covered in detail in the second half of this book, include:

- Phase 1: Project Initiation
- Phase 2: Assess Alternatives
- Phase 3: Detail Design
- Phase 4: Build and Final Prep
- Phase 5: Deploy/Implement
- Phase 6: Support, Sustain, and Enhance

Structurally, the Emergence One Method looks like a traditional Waterfall method; however, it has the flexibility to take an iterative approach between Phases 3 and 4 when necessary.

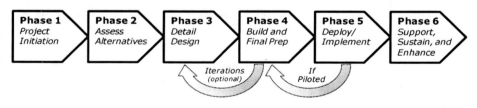

Figure 2.2.   *The Emergence One Project Life Cycle*

Technically, the Emergence One life cycle is not a true *project* life cycle since projects have traditionally been defined as having a definitive end date, while the Emergence One life cycle contains an ongoing continuous improvement phase. However, these phases are critical in order to achieve the key components of total project success that include organizational adoption and business value realization.

More on the Emergence One project life cycle will be covered later in this book.

ERP Implementation Life Cycles

The project phases within the Emergence One Method bear some resemblance to the project management and implementation methodologies utilized by two of the largest ERP vendors in world: SAP and Oracle. (This has allowed Emergence One consultant to integrate aspects of the Emergence One Method quite effectively on some of the large-scale SAP and Oracle implementations we have had the opportunity to work on.)

The SAP project phases come from their ASAP methodology (Accelerated SAP).

Figure 2.3. *SAP ASAP project phases*

The Oracle project phases come from their AIM methodology (Application Implementation Methodology).

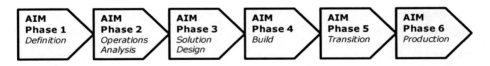

Figure 2.4. *Oracle AIM project phases*

Current Trends in Project Management

As discussed earlier, project management tools and techniques started to coalesce into a more formal discipline to satisfy the needs of major capital projects: the building of the Hoover Dam, the delivery of complex defense systems, etc. Unlike business initiatives, major capital projects do not necessarily introduce change into the workplace or impacts organizational behaviors. It is only when project management started being applied to business settings, where most projects had some sort of change impact on employees' attitudes and behaviors, that organizations started seeing a gap. Project management was no longer about delivering a tall building or a new warship, but about delivering business and organizational *change* that would inevitably effect employees' behaviors and mindsets.

This has created an increase in the need to evolve the practice of project management and has resulted in an increase in several current trends and challenges within the development and practice of this discipline.

Embedding more formal project management methods and competencies within the organization

Many projects within companies were, and still are, overseen by business managers with little or no formal training or knowledge in the field of project management. Additionally, many business and, to a lesser degree, IT projects are managed in an *ad-hoc* manner by company personnel who may have strong subject matter or organizational knowledge, but little project management knowledge. As one can imagine, this has led to a whole host of projects that are poorly managed, leading to cost overruns, missed deadlines, poorly defined project boundaries or deliverables, etc.

Today, many companies, especially fast-growing companies, tolerate these poorly managed projects as long as they are internal projects that do not directly affect the company's revenue stream. This lack of internal project management capability is muted by the fact that many of these companies bring in professional management consulting firms who have strong project management acumen to manage some of the larger, mission-critical projects.

However, more forward-thinking companies, especially larger companies that engage in multiple, often simultaneous, organizational initiatives, have invested in the development of internal project management methods and capabilities. Additionally, some companies have formal project management methodologies that all internal (and sometime external) project managers must follow. And, others have a complete Project Management Office (PMO) to oversee a portfolio of projects and provide trained project managers for many of the company's internal projects.

Adopting a more enterprise-wide "portfolio management" approach

As companies launch more and more projects across their enterprise, it is becoming increasingly important to manage these projects in a cohesive and strategic manner. As such, portfolio management strives to optimize the mix and green-lighting of projects so they align with their organization's long-term visions and strategies.

There are numerous change management issues that accompany a portfolio management approach. Further, in companies that do not have portfolio management, decisions regarding projects are usually made locally by middle management with or without upper management approval.

Using a portfolio management approach, all projects (usually above a certain dollar amount or some other criteria) are reviewed by a centralized governing body that is responsible for overseeing how each project fits into the "big picture." Only when a project is deemed a good strategic fit will funding and resources be allocated. This loss of decision making authority is hard for some to swallow, especially when they are more concerned with their own fiefdom than they are with the overall enterprise.

Despite challenges and resistance from department heads and other executives to green-light their own projects, a strategic portfolio management approach is long overdue. This is especially true for companies that are transforming into more project-based organizations.

Greater emphasis on managing stakeholder expectations and other change management–related issues

Project management is sometimes (rather unfairly) associated with "being all about tools and project processes," while ignoring the numerous stakeholders who can delay or kill a project. Thus, more project sponsors expect project managers to excel at having "people skills" (including skills in conflict resolution and change adoption) as well as the more "traditional" project management skills.

While the PMI and other project management governing bodies have done much more in recent years to address some of the "people and political" issues inherent in project execution, there is quite a bit truth to the criticism that project management focuses more on the process than on the people.

However, teaching someone "soft skills" can take a very long time and even with regular soft-skills training and coaching, there are few overnight transformations. Even when an organization does employ a project manager with excellent people skills, there is also the matter of bandwidth. Very few project managers have both the required expertise and the required bandwidth to adequately manage the myriad of stakeholder needs and expectations. This is especially true when there is an overwhelming number of project tasks that also needs managing.

The Emergence One Method focuses a good bit of its methodology on managing stakeholder needs and expectations and promotes more of a collaborative model between project managers and the change management experts who excel in the area of stakeholder management.

The Emergence of Change Management

Project management is a discipline that grew out of the need to deftly manage capital projects. Project managers were hired to help build something static, for example, as we saw earlier, with something like the Hoover Dam or a new missile defense system. However, when projects are undertaken in the business and IT worlds, the focus is in creating and introducing something more dynamic... something that will cause a *change* to operations and required behaviors.

In addition, the field of project management never really modified its approach to account for this shift into the business world, where changes introduced by a project would influence an actual living, breathing, working individual or a dynamic organizational entity. Further, the discipline did little to enhance or augment its tools, techniques, and methods to account for the people and organizational change factors, but rather continued to focus solely on scope, schedule, and cost.

Although project management is beginning to place more emphasis on such things as better stakeholder management, initiating broader communication efforts, and facilitating organizational adoption, project management has typically done a poor job in these areas. After all, it is still called "project" management and not "people" management.

Unlike those involved in engineering or product development initiatives, what project sponsors in the business world saw were projects that (sometimes) came in on time, within budget, and according to spec, but were not being embraced or utilized by people in the organization.

Something more needed to be done. This need opened the door for the emergence of a complementary (some might argue "competing") discipline generally referred to as "organizational/behavioral change management" to help fill the void left by the doctrinaire application of project management practices.

Chapter 3

The Emergence of Change Management

Introduction

As we saw in Chapter 2, the discipline of project management never really augmented its practices to account for the fact that projects within the business and IT worlds introduce change into the workplace. Project management also has paid scant attention to the "people and politics" elements that can affect project momentum and success prior to the organizational deployment phase. If traditional project management methodologies did adequately account for these factors, then the emergence of organizational/behavioral change management would never have occurred.

While the field of change management still needs to mature and coalesce around more defined descriptions and practices, there is no arguing that the reason why the field even exists is to fill a void left behind by traditional project management approaches.

While there may be debates regarding the exact definition or scope of change management activities, there is also no denying that it has now become a prominent discipline; there are hundreds of books on the topic, graduate school programs dedicated to the discipline, and thousands of gainfully employed change management professionals.

Defining Change Management – A Daunting Task!

Change management is actually a very broad field, although there are many consumers and practitioners of change management who have very narrow definitions and perceptions of its scope and purpose.

Unlike project management, where there is little variation amongst different definitions of the discipline, trying to find an agreed upon definition of change management can be a daunting task because there are many different flavors, practices, goals, and objectives within the practice of change management. Thus, the term "change management" is much more ambiguous and open to a wider range of interpretations than is project management.

Emergence One applies change management principles and techniques in a much broader fashion than many other consulting firms. For us, change management has two purposes:

1   To help project management achieve its traditional measures of success (on time, within budget, according to spec) by paying stricter attention to the human, political, and organizational change management factors that can impede project momentum, decision quality, and scope management.

2   To provide stakeholders with the required skills, understanding, competencies, motivation, and support to adopt the numerous project-related changes that enable business value realization.

What Is Changing?

"Managing change" can refer to many different types of change, including:

- A change to a business process
- A change to an employee's emotional state
- A change to organizational structure, such as a reorganization or merger
- A change in an employee's required behaviors, competencies, or skill sets
- A change to a work group's focus or purpose (such as offering banking customers additional financial products instead of just providing them with account data)
- A change in a mandatory company policy
- A change in strategy or corporate direction
- A change in business tools, such as new machinery or new software applications

Things are further complicated when we consider that change can be major, minor, or something in between. For instance, the word "change" is often used to describe anything from a minor upgrade of a software application to a major organizational transformation.

Who Is Involved in Change?

Although a majority of change management practices take the less effective route of focusing only on the needs of the end-user/employee community, there are actually three essential groups that experienced change practitioners focus on:

1 **Senior leaders/key decision makers of the change** – This includes executives in charge of initiating or championing a change effort. This can also include less visible supporters of the change who quietly work behind the scenes to secure the appropriate funding, resources, and political support needed to initiate or maintain the change initiative.

2 **Contributors to the change** – This includes personnel who design the actual components of the change initiative. Also included in this group are various stakeholders who can influence change designs, from concerned managers to those responsible for maintaining adherence to company policies, standards, and regulations.

3 **Recipients of the change** – Depending on the scope of the initiative, this can include individual employees, work groups, departments, divisions, or everyone else within the organization.

It is also important to note that a more mature, sophisticated practice of change management looks at facilitating more than just the behavioral elements of change. These more sophisticated approaches also consider facilitating changes to other organizational components beyond the people element. This includes modifying company policies or organizational structures to support the goals and objectives of a change initiative.

As we will see later in this chapter, there are some change management approaches that may be geared toward the needs of one group (such as the "Leading Change" principles of John Kotter), while other change approaches take a more holistic view.

Variations on the Term "Change Management"

Because of the wide variety of principles and approaches that fall under the umbrella of "change management," several variations on this term have emerged and include the terms organizational change management (OCM), behavioral change management (BCM), business change management (which also goes by the "BCM" acronym), people/employee change management, organizational readiness, change leadership, change implementation, organizational or user adoption, and transition/transformation management. Nevertheless, it is important to keep in mind that these augmented change management terms are still widely interpreted (or misinterpreted) regarding their exact scope and application.

For instance, not all organizational changes (such as an outsourcing initiative) will require that (remaining) employees make a behavioral change. In this case, *employee change management will require maintaining the status quo as opposed to changing it.* Conversely, an organizational initiative that may require employees to make behavioral changes (such as demonstrating more "customer-centric" service skills) does not necessary mean that there will be any accompanying changes to the organization's structure.

"Change management" can also have a distinctively different denotation depending upon the audience. Within the project management and IT application development fields, "change management" can also refer to the manner in which project or configuration changes are formally introduced and approved. Change management is also sometimes confused with the term "Management of Change" (MOC). This is a facilities operations term to describe the process in managing changes to facilities, documentation, operations, and personnel so that health, safety, and environmental risks are controlled. The exploration of these fields is out of the scope of this book.

An Abridged History of Change Management

Many change management theorists will be surprised to learn that, like the discipline of project management, we can also trace the roots of change management back thousands of years. In fact, change management was also used to a certain degree in the building of the pyramids to get workers to adopt changing work situations. However, managing change back then relied more on whips and beatings than the more benign methods of today.

Throughout history, for the most part, change has been managed in one of two ways:

1   *By decree* – This is where someone in authority simply tells people how they must change. If you are picturing some bearded guy with a puffy shirt and funny hat holding up a scroll while bellowing out of a castle window, you get the idea. "Starting today, the king decrees that all villagers will now go about their work while wearing their underpants outside of their trousers!" Of course, today, managers can forgo the puffy shirt and funny hat and just send out an email announcement with the same directive. However, this is now called "communication" rather than royal decree (though some in the corporate world might argue that there is little difference between the two).

2 *By replacement* – Replacement takes one of two forms:

a ***Replacement of the individual:*** "You, knave, why are you not wearing your underwear outside of your trousers as the king decreed?" "But sir, I am not wearing any underwear at all. For I own no underwear in which to wear outside of my humble trousers." "No matter. Take him! Off with his head!"

b ***Replacement of a work tool:*** "What's this? A shovel you call it? You mean after moving dirt with my hands for 18 straight years you now give me something which can help me move dirt quicker and easier?" (At which point the worker hits the man over the head with the shovel and quickly runs off.). For those of you who perhaps had your software unexpectedly "updated" by IT without any type of training or communication beforehand, I'm betting many of you can see the parallel.

Although "by decree" and "by replacement" are still techniques used today by old-school managers who want to facilitate change, many change historians would say that the roots of many modern theories of organizational change began with the classic Western Electric "Hawthorne Studies" of the late 1920s and early 1930s.

The Hawthorne Effect

Back in the late 1920s, the Western Electric Company maintained a robust factory in Cicero, Illinois, known as "The Hawthorne Works." Management at the plant, like many in American business at the time, was enthralled by the scientific management theories of Frederick Taylor. They decided to undertake a series of studies themselves, the results of which became so influential that they collectively became known as the "Hawthorne Studies."

In one of the studies, management was interested in pinpointing the optimal level of lighting to maximize productivity or, as they so casually put it: "The relation of illumination to industrial efficiency." They conducted several experiments with each containing a "control group" (a group in which no variation in lighting occurred) and a "test" group (the group that was subject to variations in lighting). Neither group knew whether they were in the control group or the experimental group, though all participants knew that they were taking part in a scientific management experiment.

The researchers fiddled with the workplace lighting in several ways with the experimental group and recorded and compared the levels of productivity with both the (supposedly steady) control group and the experimental group. The results, as one reviewer later exclaimed, "…were screwy."

In one experiment, as researchers increased the level of lighting, productivity of the test group increased as well, which probably confirmed someone's hypothesis that increased lighting will increase productivity. However, there was one inconvenient result that accompanied those of the test group: productivity in the control group (who did not experience any changes in illumination) also increased.

In another experiment, when lighting was reduced for the test group, the productivity of both the test group and control group still *went up!* This made no sense to the researchers, who went away with the conclusion that "Nothing of a positive nature has been learned."

It wasn't until many years later that writer Stuart Chase concluded: "There is an idea here so big that it leaves one gasping." What the Hawthorne Studies illustrated was that the workers were not merely simple pieces of equipment that could be predictably manipulated via the adjustment of lighting or some other scientific management "variable." It was the revelation that humans are indeed human; that is, they are social beings that respond to other social beings. The productivity level changes had nothing to do with the lighting in the workplace; rather, it was the presence of other human beings (the researchers) and the workers' knowledge that they were being studied that proved to be the catalyst for the productivity changes.

Up until this time, workers were mainly thought of as another piece of equipment to be turned on and off and optimized through lighting, work design, etc. What was missing was the human element. Once the human element was found, the whole field of organizational behavior, from which the study and practice of change management grew, was born.

The Birth of Organizational Change Management

Out of the field of organizational behavior grew the theories and concepts of organizational development. However, it was not until the late 1960s that the term "organizational change management" started to find a place in academic literature on a more frequent basis. Further, it was in 1948 that one of the foundational principles of change management first made its appearance: the need to overcome "resistance to change."

"Resistance to Change"

Two researchers, Lester Coch and John French, Jr. published an article in the academic journal *Human Relations* where they described their work at the Harwood Manufacturing Corporation. These researchers found that workers at the Harwood plant regularly resisted necessary changes to production methods and jobs, and they set out to test various ways to help employees to overcome this resistance to change.

They found that the "learning curve" (which was characterized by lower production levels) was longer for an experienced worker who had transferred to a new job than it was for a new worker who had just started work at the factory (even when both jobs had comparable levels of difficulty).

Their preliminary theory on the resistance to change, which was confirmed by their experiments, was that skill is a minor factor, and motivation is a major determinant of the rate of production level recovery. Their solutions for overcoming this resistance to change became two of the most fundamental principles for managing change:

1   Management needs to communicate the importance of the change to their workers.
2   Management should involve workers in the planning of change.

Unfortunately, many companies today do not practice either one of these two principles. Some project managers may practice the first principle by inviting in a communications consultant or junior-level change practitioner late in the project life cycle to communicate the change. However, because the second principle is often ignored, trying to mitigate resistance to change by applying only the first principle is of limited value. This is one of the primarily reasons why the Emergence One Method stresses the importance of involving change management throughout the entire project life cycle, rather than making a shallow attempt at trying to mitigate resistance issues by employing "change management" only prior to deployment.

Lewin, Schein, and the Rise of the Three-Stage Change Model

In 1951, one of the father's of social psychology, the great German-American psychologist Kurt Lewin, developed one of the first models of change that was later modified by Edgar Schein in the 1960's. Today, the two models are often conflated with one another.

The first stage, typically referred to as "Unfreezing," is where the conditions for driving the change are developed (note that *the development of the actual change driver*, such as a new IT system, is not part of his model). The second stage is "Move," or "Transition;" moving people from the prevailing status quo to the new state. This stage is characterized by confusion and transition since there is no clear understanding of the new state. The third stage is known as "Freezing" or "Refreezing" is where the change is made permanent.

These three stage ideas form the basis of many change management models today. However, the application of these models usually occur after the core project (involving the creation of a business solution or "change driver) has been initiated, scope, designed, and built. Hence, these three stage models do little to address the numerous change management needs within earlier project phases.

The Dominance of Psychological Theories

There are several schools of thought when it comes to change management. These schools of thought have arisen primarily out of the field of counseling and clinical psychology and thus have taken a very emphatic approach toward working with employees (sometimes to the detriment of achieving project objectives). Though often mislabeled as "organizational change" approaches, they are really approaches to managing an individual's adjustment to change. The fact that these individuals are in organizational settings is almost irrelevant.

Although there are literally dozens of models on how to best manage change, most of the psychology-based theories and models (which account for the bulk of change management practices) fall into one of the following five schools of thought.

1   **Behavioral** – Change is based on what can be observed; people can be motivated to change by linking desired behaviors with extrinsic rewards.

2   **Cognitive** – Internal thought processes affect change; with the right amount of coaching and personal goal setting, change can be achieved.

3   **Psychodynamic** – Emotional states of those experiencing change are the focus under this school of thought.

4   **Humanistic** – Based on the counseling psychology work of Abraham Maslow and Carl Rogers, the humanistic view places heavy emphasis on a person's feelings and developing a positive, facilitating environment.

5   **Hybrid** –The hybrid model acknowledges that there are vast differences between individuals and company cultures. Therefore, finding the right "levers" to facilitate change means reviewing and applying techniques from a whole suite of approaches and schools of thought.

Of the five schools of thought listed above, one school tends to dominate. It steadfastly promotes a model that still finds its way onto the PowerPoint presentations of many novice (and sadly, many experienced) change practitioners. This occurs despite the fact that this model first arose over 40 years ago and was developed in a very non-businesslike setting. It is the psychodynamic model proposed by Elisabeth Kubler-Ross, which was later expanded by others for organizational settings.

Enter *Death and Dying*

Perhaps no other book has been more influential or has done more to separate the change management discipline from the discipline of project management and to move toward a more purely psychodynamic orientation than Elisabeth Kubler-Ross's 1969 book titled *On Death and Dying.*

For this book, Kubler-Ross spent a significant amount of time with terminally ill patients and found that most patients went through a similar emotional process (or stages) when faced with the prospect of dying. These stages include: Denial, Anger, Bargaining, Depression, and finally Acceptance. Recently, Kubler-Ross's model has come under intense criticism, notably from George Bonanno of Columbia University as well as a few others, who have found that her five-stage grief model has no scientific basis.

In a review of this book, the *British Journal of Social Work* had this to say:

> *"All those involved in social work, be they students, practitioners, or teachers should read it; for it concerns loss, and assisting people to deal with losses of one kind or another is the social worker's commonest task. Here is a book that helps them to do this with sensitivity, insight and compassion."*

Clearly, this was not a business book. (As a matter of fact, the subtitle of her book is *What the Dying Have to Teach Doctors, Nurses, Clergy and Their Own Families.*) After all, knowing that you are about to die is certainly a lot different from experiencing a software update at work or hearing that part of your job responsibilities are once again changing. However, that did not stop others from applying her work on death to business settings.

In the mid-1970s, Kubler-Ross's original concept was modified for use in organizational settings by Adams, Hayes, and Hobson and from this, they developed nine stages: *Shock, Denial, Anger, Bargaining, Depression, Acceptance, Experimentation, Discovery, and Integration.* With nine stages, this model was a little difficult to succinctly explain to project stakeholders and, as a result, was simplified by Jaffe, Scott, and Toby to include *Denial, Resistance, Exploration, and Commitment.* Additional variations of Kubler-Ross's work soon followed and included an expansion or renaming of the stages to: Satisfaction, Denial, Resistance, Exploration, Hope, and Commitment; or Stability, Immobilization, Denial, Bargaining, Depression, Testing, and Acceptance.

Regardless of the exact wording of the stages, they have all, more or less, led to the development of the ubiquitous "Change Curve," which illustrates a person's emotional reaction to change and how it affects their productivity level.

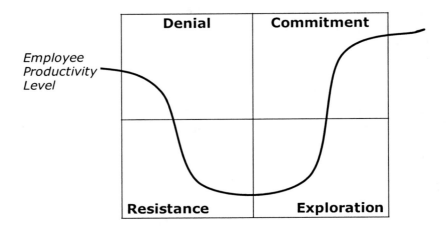

Figure 3.1.   *One Version of the Ubiquitous Change Curve*

The Change Curve

The "Change Curve" has been shown, in one form or another, to thousands upon thousands of managers, businesspeople, and students.

The problem with this approach is that it is purely a psychological point of view and is completely disassociated from any project objectives. Further, it assumes that any type of change, no matter how big or small, will still be met with some sort of predictable response that is a part of all employees' inherent psychological make-up.

This approach also doesn't take into account whether someone is a trendy 25-year-old working for a fast-pace high-tech company in Silicon Valley, or a 60-year-old factory worker in Peoria who has not seen any work changes over the last 30 years. According to the "Change Curve," and the person promoting that concept, both individuals would experience the same emotional reaction to change. Therefore, a change management program would be offered to facilitate these personal emotions through a variation of Kubler-Ross's death-and-dying model, even though it is really nothing more than a (somewhat condescending) assumption on the part of the change management promoter.

When Cutting-Edge Software Companies Send Mixed Messages

Because Emergence One focuses exclusively on project management/change management and doesn't sell software, we often partner with software vendors who want to ensure that their products are successfully implemented and adopted.

We do a lot of market research on software vendors and find many of their websites have a tab or two on the importance of organizational/behavioral change management (which is good) and some information on how they might address these issues (by using some variation of Kubler-Ross's model).

We are usually shocked to find a cutting-edge software company promoting "bleeding edge" technology standing side-by-side with a change model that is more than 40 years old! Don't they understand what kind of message they are sending potential customers?

"If you buy our software, then you'll need to spend extra money on these change management services because your workforce will be either:

A) in denial that you would even consider buying our software, or

B) so angry and depressed that you are buying our software that you simply won't be successful in trying to implement our product… Your workforce won't love and embrace our product, they'll resist it!"

This is not to say that change management would not be needed. But the change management challenges would be focused more on getting stakeholders to agree on the scope of the implementation, engage the right people to agree on the most preferred configuration, and the logistical challenges behind informing and training a large number of geographically dispersed end-users.

The Tale of Two Rogers – Carl Versus Everett

Ask any change practitioner of the work of Rogers and he or she will inevitably start talking about the eminent psychotherapist Carl Rogers, founder of the humanistic school of psychology, and a favorite of the "psychotherapist turned management consultant" change practitioner.

However, it is actually another Rogers, Everett Rogers (no relationship to Carl), who probably has much more to offer in way of facilitating change.

Everett Rogers, born on an Iowa farm in 1931, was a sociologist best known for the theory "Diffusion of Innovations." Although this theory is not an organizational theory *per se*, much of it can be applied to facilitating change in organizational settings.

Diffusion of Innovations covers how and why new ideas and technology spread through communities and cultures. Essentially, it explains the spread of new ideas (which is usually the forerunner to change) through four main elements. This includes the innovation itself (innovation is defined as "an idea, practice, or object that is perceived as new by an individual or other unit of adoption"); the various communication channels available to spread the innovation; the time it takes for the innovation to be "adopted"; and a social system, which is a set of interrelated units.

Rogers's work centers a lot around the concept of "adoption." As a matter of fact, Rogers, along with colleagues from Iowa State University, coined the phrase "Early Adopters," which has become a fairly standard term in change management and IT circles.

Rogers suggested that there is a five-step process that leads to adoption of something new. During the course of his career, Rogers changed the terminology of the adoption process, although the descriptions of each step are virtually the same

Table 3.1. *Rogers's adoption process*

Diffusion of Innovations Adoption Process	
Original Version	**Later Versions**
1 Awareness	1 Knowledge
2 Interest	2 Persuasion
3 Evaluation	3 Decision
4 Trial	4 Implementation
5 Adoption	5 Confirmation

It is important to note that individuals might reject the innovation at any point during the adoption process, even after the fifth step (Adoption/Confirmation). This points to the importance of making sure that change adoption is sustained over time.

Rogers also introduced the concept of "champions": individuals who support an innovation and tackle any opposition that may arise. This is a concept that is again found in many current change management models, whether referred to as a "change champion," "change leader network," "change advocate," "change ambassador," or other similar term.

From "Individual" Change to Organizational Change

With the exception of the later work of Rogers, up to this point, most change management theories and practices have focused on individual or personal change (even if the models are somewhat erroneously referred to as *organizational change* models). However, when considering change in a workplace setting, where there is an organization hierarchical, various policies and procedures, performance metrics, an underlying company infrastructure, etc., change models require a bit more than simply helping employees deal with (the often overemphasized) reaction to change on a personal level.

In the truest sense of the term *organizational* change means more than just facilitating an individual's reaction to the change, but changing other components of the organization as well. This includes a company's policies and procedures, its hierarchical organization, various business processes, support organizations, infrastructure (both physical and technological), overall corporate culture, informal "political" coalitions and alliances, and so forth. *A true organizational change management program will consider all of these components.*

In the 1990s, we saw an important shift in thinking regarding change. While change management was (and to a certain extent, still is) dominated by psychotherapeutic models, new models have begun to arise. Beyond changing individual mindsets, these models of organizational change have also considered the need to address business elements and corporate structures.

W. Warner Burke and George Litwin

A groundbreaking *organizational* change management model was developed by W. Warner Burke (whom I studied with while at Columbia University) and George Litwin. In 1992, they published *A Casual Model of Organizational Performance and Change.*

This model centers on 12 organizational dimensions, how they link to each other, and how the external environment may interact with the dimensions within an organization.

The 12 organizational dimensions include:

1   External environment
2   Mission and strategy
3   Leadership
4   Organizational culture
5   Structure
6   Management practices
7   Systems
8   Work unit climate
9   Task and individual skills
10 Individual needs and values
11 Motivation
12 Individual and organizational performance

Burke and Litwin's work is important because it is more of a true *organizational* model of change rather than simply being a model of personal change.

John Kotter

Another influential change management model comes from Harvard professor John Kotter. Kotter's model was a welcome relief from the models that focus on individual change by presenting a true model for *leading* organizational change.

Kotter proposes an eight-step model for transformational change within corporations. The eight steps include:

1 Establish a Sense of Urgency
2 Form a Powerful Guiding Coalition
3 Create a Vision
4 Communicate that Vision
5 Empower Others
6 Plan/Create Short-Term Wins
7 Build upon the Change/Consolidate Improvements
8 Anchor the Changes in Corporate Culture

Kotter's model is certainly a strong one; however, what many project-centric change practitioners fail to realize is that this model is geared primarily toward advising high-level executives on how to best lead *transformational* change (and as was outlined in an earlier chapter, not all change projects within organizations are necessarily transformative).

As such, Kotter's model is really more of a leadership model than a practical, tangible model for the typical project professional. It can also be overkill for projects that are not transformational in nature, or frustrating for a project change team member to apply when he or she does not have regular access to senior-level leaders.

The Technology Acceptance Model and the Importance of Design

Beginning in the late 1980s, and continuing to today, individuals and organizations have been inundated with the near constant introduction of new technologies. From personal computers, to more sophisticated enterprise-wide IT systems, to Smartphones and PDAs, it is logical that those involved with developing and introducing new technology would also be interested in learning more about how new technology is accepted and adopted. Unfortunately, much of the work that has been done within the Information Systems (IS) community on technology adoption has not been "adopted" by most mainstream change management practitioners.

For the past 20 years, there have been robust opportunities for change management practitioners to work on engagements that involve the introduction of new technology (most of my early experience in change management, for instance, was in facilitating the adoption of complex ERP systems). Even today, "managing change," due to the introduction of new technology into the workplace, is the bread-and-butter work of many change management practitioners. However, since many change management practitioners do not necessarily come from a technical background, much of the adoption work concerning technology continues to be overlooked by change practitioners who are more comfortable with generic, psychology-centric change models.

One of the more influential theories within IS circles is the Technology Acceptance Model (TAM). TAM was originally introduced as part of a doctoral thesis by Fred Davis at the MIT Sloan School of Management in 1985. TAM went through several iterations and soon became one of the leading models in predicting system adoption and use. An extension of the refined model, titled "TAM2," was released by Davis and Venkatesh in 2007.

Rather than starting from a "people have an inherent resistance to change" mindset, which is so common with many change practitioners, Davis postulated that it is the *system's features* that influence the user's motivation or attitude toward using the system.

The two factors proposed by Davis that influence someone's attitude are:

1   **Perceived Ease of Use** – How much an individual believes that there will be minimal effort required.
2   **Perceived Usefulness** – How much an individual believes the system would enhance his or her job performance.

Although TAM, like most theories, has its share of critics (most notably Richard Bagozzi, 2007, and Mohammad Chuttur, 2009), it does show the diversity of thought which could contribute to the important change management objective of adoption. TAM proposes that it is the qualities *of the system* (ease of use, perceived usefulness), not the qualities internal to an individual's psychological make-up, that affect the adoption of something new.

The Emergence One Method incorporates some of this thinking in its methodology by ensuring that design teams understand the importance of end-user "ease of use" and "perceived usefulness," rather than designing something that appeals to the company's deep subject-matter experts and "techies." This is just another reason why a change management perspective needs to be incorporated earlier in the project life cycle and not just during deployment.

Adoption as a Multi-Stage Organizational Process

Building upon the work of Zaltman, Duncan, and Holbeck, from material first presented in their 1973 book *Innovations and Organizations*, other researchers (notably Barton and Deschamps, 1988, and Lucas, Ginzberg, and Schultz, 1990) began to note that there is more to adoption than simply convincing end-users or other affected employees to accept and work with change.

This is because organizational adoption is actually a multi-stage process. Change, whether it is termed a project, a solution, or an opportunity, first needs to be adopted by decision makers and influencers within the organization. If this does not occur, then planning for "end-user adoption" is a pointless activity.

A project or change initiatives goes through several stages of development before end-user adoption is even an issue, and anywhere along the project life cycle, the initiative can be killed, defunded, or road-blocked by any number of executives or other project influencers. This might include senior-level people who control finances and resource allocations, who have the ear of key decision makers, or who hold some kind of trump card in their pocket that could derail a project. In fact, a large percentage (over 30% according to the Standish Group) of projects and change initiatives get shelved long before deployment to the end-user or employee community.

Despite this, there are many change management models in use today (namely the "individual change" mdoels) that focus primarily on getting the end-users/affected employees to adopt the change being thrust upon them by the organization. This usually falls far short of what is actually needed for any type of change initiative. As a matter of fact, in many corporate situations, end-users have few other alternatives available to them outside of adopting what their employer asks them to adopt. *The real change management challenge is to ensure that project decision makers, executives, financial gatekeepers, and other project team influencers adopt the project concept, direction, and related costs.* This is an important objective that most end-user-focused change management practitioners seem to miss.

System Integration Firms and the Development of Rigor

Up until the mid-1990s, the field of change management had many schools of thought and high-level models from which to choose. However, what was missing was a rigorous project-centric methodology that detailed the specific tasks on how to implement "change."

During the 1990s, there were numerous large-scale IT system advancements. The rise of giant, influential ERP firms, such as Oracle and SAP, brought in a completely new phase of organizational change as companies struggled to implement and adopt these monstrous IT systems. Assisting with the implementation (but some would argue *not* the adoption) of ERP systems were many of the large system integration consulting firms such as Andersen (now Accenture), IBM, Deloitte and Touche, Ernst & Young, Price Water-house (now PricewaterhouseCoopers or PwC), KPMG (which later morphed into BearingPoint before the U.S. division was bought out by PwC), and others.

Many of these large ERP system implementations initially failed, went dramatically over budget, or did not deliver the expected benefits. *These enormous failures continued to occur despite the fact that many of these firms have some of the supposedly best and brightest project managers leading the engagements.* After numerous "lessons learned" studies, these firms started to notice that, often times, the "people factor" was overlooked.

This breathed new life into the field of change management as many of these firms scrambled to develop change management practices.

What happened next was initially a mess. As change management practitioners from various backgrounds and schools of thought became part of these highly structured firms, there was great difficulty coalescing around a single methodology or approach. The ERP project managers who brought in their firms' change management consultants never quite knew what they were getting. Were they getting someone who really knew something about the impacts an ERP system would have on the workforce, or were they merely former clinical psychology students whose only focus was on an individual's emotional reaction to "change"? Since it was usually the latter, most change management consultants were often asked to leave engagements once the project started to go over budget (which, as any IT manager from the time could tell you, was a frequent occurrence).

Eventually, these fledging change management practitioners understood the need to become more methodical so they would be taken a bit more seriously by their IT counterparts. Thus, firms started to invest in the development of more rigorous change management methodologies.

With so many models to choose from, and different schools of thought to guide them, the change methodologies that were developed varied greatly from firm to firm. However, they did have one thing in common: they finally had a degree of rigor. As a matter of fact, the Oracle Organizational Change Management consulting practice developed several change management process and task reference handbooks that had a combined page count of over two thousand pages! No longer could these groups be accused of having "nice ideas but no methodology."

However, what appeared to be a promising step forward for the transformation of change management into a rigorously defined field, turned out to be short-lived. Soon, the dot-com bust hit. As firms struggled to simply keep their core strategy and IT consultants utilized, many of these change management practices faded away.

Today, change management services are still a staple within the service offerings of many of the major system integration firms. However, if you peel away the curtain, you would find only a small boutique practice at best. Though most large firms claim they maintain a robust change management practice, in reality, it is often a small group of practitioners who keep some change management templates and marketing materials. A few others make change management a "secondary specialization" for their strategy or education/training design consultants to keep them better utilized. However, the reality is that most mid-size and large firms just manage a short list of contractors whom they call upon to work with clients on an as-needed basis.

One of the reasons for this isn't because change management isn't valuable, but because most change management practices are only 1% to 2% of overall revenue at best. Since the slice of the pie is so small in relation to other services, the change management practices have not always attracted the amount of senior management support required to be sustained or grown within large firms.

> *However, the main reason that change management withered within most large system integration firms is that it was never truly integrated with their project implementation methodologies or practices. Instead, it was always offered as an optional, adjunct service.*

Within the large firms, change management was consistently designed, packaged, and sold as a separate discipline; thus, it had the appearance (to both internal project management colleagues as well as to clients) as being an "add-on" or some type of "up-sell." The fact that the change management practices were often placed in the firms' "Educational Services" business unit or "HR Consulting" instead of being an essential, integrated part of implementation consulting only further separated the practices from where they needed to be.

Today, change management is, for the most part, represented by a vast network of independent contractors and a handful of small boutique change management firms. Even many of the large consulting firms contract to independent contractors or boutique firms rather than keep full-time change practitioners on staff.

For more information...

For more information on how to best secure change management resources, and to learn the pros and cons of different sourcing methods, download the free e-Guide "Evaluating and Securing Change Management Resources" from the Emergence One website:

www.emergenceone.com.

Current Trends in Change Management

Change management is a less mature discipline than is project management, and there are no widely recognized governing bodies, nor is there even much clarity about what actually constitutes "change management." Therefore, the field of change management is paradoxically evolving and "devolving" simultaneously.

It is evolving because, in many cases, businesses are demanding more tangible, less touchy-feely approaches. If change management is to be better executed, it needs to adopt some of the rigor and tangibility that the field of project management offers. Any change program that forgoes essential and established project management practices will flounder during execution.

Conversely, the field is devolving because there are many firms that provide nothing more than basic end-user communication plans, but, either naively or unscrupulously, promote themselves as being robust "change management firms" nonetheless. Project managers, unaware of the robust scope and value of change management, help contribute to this by only requesting "change management" resources to do deployment related training and communications work.

Other notable trends:

Moving change management away from the human resources and corporate education/training departments and into the IT and project/program management groups

A current practice in many large companies that have an internal change management practice is to place the practice in either the human resources department or the education/training department, which may or may not be part of HR. This is usually the result of faulty reasoning on the part of the decision making executive who probably thought, "Change management is about people. HR is about people. Therefore, change management should be in HR."

Change management isn't just about people... it is about successfully implementing project objectives. This may mean going beyond behavioral changes and making policy, procedural, or organizational infrastructure changes as well.

HR departments often times represent the opposite of change. The bulk of the work in most HR departments is about maintaining and supporting the status quo...maintaining employee records and benefits, scanning and storing resumes, making sure everyone follows the same hiring and performance review processes, etc. The culture of HR is more likely to promote *compliance* than it is to initiate change.

Fortunately, more progressive companies understand the need to have change management resources in the business units that are most likely to drive change. This includes the IT department, a project resources department, or a project portfolio management group.

Desire to have change management appear as a more mature, standardized, and "standalone" discipline

There has been some rumbling in the change management blogs about the creation of a governing body to oversee the creation and adherence to "change management standards." This appears to be an attempt to develop a change management equivalent to the PMI.

However, this can be a challenging proposition. Unlike project management, which has mature and universally accepted tools and techniques such as PERT charts, Gantt charts, work breakdown structures (WBS), cost estimating, risk analysis, and so forth, there are no universally recognized tools that are *unique* to the field of change management (common change management activities such as "stakeholder analysis" or communication plan development *are also quite common in project management methodologies*).

Another potential challenge is that, unlike project management, there is a much greater variety behind the different schools of thought or focus areas that make up the field of change management. While some change management models are more popular than others, many of them are still narrowly focused when compared to more robust approaches. For instance, there are some popular change management models that only focus on end-user/employee behavior change during a transition period rather than looking at the broader range of stakeholder needs throughout the project life cycle.

Lastly, the creation of a "PMI equivalent" for change management would further cement the notion that change management is a separate discipline that is distinct from project management. The reason why the Emergence One Method works so well is that it takes an integrated project management/change management approach. We strongly believe that, when project management and change management are treated as separate disciplines (each with its own sets of standards, practices, tools and techniques), it *divides rather than unites* project execution. Furthermore, the development of a separate professional organization will continue to cement the (false) notion that change management is an optional "nice to have" instead of being a critical component to overall project success.

Increased offerings of external change management "certification" programs

Unlike the field of project management, which has several universally recognized certification programs such as those offered by the PMI or the APM (which offers certification in the PRINCE2 methodology, popular in the UK), there is no widely recognized body for change management certification.

However, several organizations are willing to offer change management "certification" for anyone willing to pay, no matter how poorly qualified. Unlike the PMI, which requires that anyone applying for certification must first have either 4,500 hours (for those with a college degree) or 7,500 hours (for those with a high school diploma) of direct project management experience, most change management "certification" programs have few prerequisites for applicants. All you need to do is sit in a class for two or three days, fork over a few thousand dollars and *voilà!*, you are a certified change management professional!

Disclosure Notice Regarding Certification Offerings

Emergence One International, Ltd. does offer certification in the Emergence One Method, which is an integrated project management/change management methodology. However, unlike most training firms in the United States (PMI is an exception), Emergence One does require applicants to first have a substantial amount of verifiable project-based work experience. Emergence One also requires the successful completion of post-training exams and does not grant certification merely because of attendance.

Additional information on becoming an E1 Certified Consultant can be found on the Emergence One website.

Expectations for change practitioners will evolve

Regardless of what the future holds for the discipline of change management, one thing is for certain: the need for quality change management services will continue to increase. Although the field is still somewhat plagued by many non-business or non-project-centric professionals who are looking to make a quick corporate buck, consumers of change management services are becoming savvier at discerning who the stronger change practitioners are. Junior-level professionals who provide little more than PowerPoint slides to end-users will play less of a role along with those who overemphasize the influence of employees' emotions to the detriment of achieving tangible goals and objectives.

Finally, project sponsors and clients will evolve their thinking of change management as being much more than just "communications and training employees prior to deployment." They will begin to look for change management practitioners who can build strong, productive, collaborative relationships with senior level project sponsors, managers, and key decision makers. They will also look for change practitioners that will have strong project-related subject matter expertise, and will be able to identify and mitigate an expansive array of project-related issues throughout each phase of the project life cycle.

Why Change Management Has Failed to Deliver

As was previously mentioned, one of the main reasons why change management has grown to become such a prominent discipline was to fill the void that project management has failed to adequately address: the need to better manage stakeholder needs and expectations throughout the project life cycle.

One would think that with the increased prominence and acceptance of change management over the last decade that this void would have been filled, and that projects would ultimately have experienced a greater degree of success. Unfortunately, from what we have seen in data from the Standish Group and elsewhere, this is not true. Change management has failed to deliver on its promise of balancing out the deficiencies which have existed in project execution and stakeholder management.

There are many reasons for this, including:

Outdated assumptions regarding "change" that simply will not die

Many business people have been taught by "old-school" change management practitioners that people *naturally* "resist change" and thus build an entire change management program around this assumption.

People embrace change all the time… they move, they get married, they try new activities, they increasing use the Internet to replace more traditional processes, and they stand in line on raining days so they can be the first to buy the latest new technological innovation. While this may not be true for everybody, it is certainly truer today than when these change management assumptions were first formulated four or more decades ago. Besides, change in the workplace, whether it is adopting a new process, reporting to a new boss, or utilizing a new IT application is generally not as life changing as descendents of Kubler-Ross's "Denial, Anger, Bargaining, etc." "death and dying" models would have you believe. Especially when it comes to organizational or IT change that is incremental and part of a company's natural evolution... it is just not the same as learning you are about to die!

While there is such a thing as "resistance to change," it is often the result of legitimate business concerns (*"This might not be the best solution for our needs"* or *"I need more training and communications than what they are providing"*) rather that because of an inherent psychological "fear of change." In fact, practitioners of these "psychological hindrance" models can often do more harm than good by dismissing legitimate business concerns as being nothing more than a "typical emotional reaction" to change.

People don't resist change as much as they resist poorly executed projects.

The continued dabbling of non-business-focused professionals

The change management profession has attracted many people who have had a more psychotherapeutic or semi-mystical "new age" background rather than a business or project execution background. Click on any of the change management blogs out there and one will still see change management described as an "art form" or some type of "near-spiritual" exercise where *"Buddhist principles are artfully applied to help facilitate organizational change."*

These practitioners tend to be *overly* empathetic toward employees while eschewing rigor, technical project know-how, or the importance of achieving project objectives. This often does not fly well with more tactical or results-oriented project professionals hoping to see something a bit more tangible. It also makes it harder for change practitioners who do have an in-depth understanding of business operations, project execution, or the specific impacts that new technology can have on the workplace, to get their foot in the door.

The misapplication of change management models

John Kotter's eight-step model is an excellent model for executives who are involved in leading transformation change. But for a standard, incremental change project such as an IT upgrade, the model offers little concrete guidance on the specific change management activities project team members would need to engage in conjunction with other project activities.

Other change management models, especially ones that focus on "personal change" or self-development (that is, individuals learning how to cope with and accept change) are thoroughly ineffective for most stages of a large-scale ERP initiative, such as SAP ASAP or Oracle AIM. Here, the primary change management challenges center on getting executives to reach agreement on scope, minimizing the bias in the solution assessment process, or identifying and mitigating project team performance issues.

Good people skills, but poor project execution skills

Many change management professionals know a lot about the "people side" but very little about the components of actually executing a large or complex change management program that supports project objectives.

It is one thing to know how to theoretically build an individual's awareness and desire for change, it is quite another thing to have the skills sets required to execute the complex logistics involved in communicating and training hundreds or thousands of end-users in various geographical locations. For this type of activity, more "project management" related skills are required.

Having objectives separate from project management

There is a false notion that project management and change management do not share the same goals and objectives. Total project success is not achieved by having one team focusing exclusively on time, budget, and scope while another team focuses solely on "people." "People issues" affect time, budget, and scope just as a project's planning, design, and project execution will affect its ultimate adoption and business value realization.

The Next Evolution of Project and Change Management

Although the field still faces some challenges, change management, when focused on achieving specific project objectives and is executed with a high degree of rigor, can lead to brilliant results. However, in order for this to happen, it must be properly integrated and unified with project management.

This means more than just sprinkling in a few change management-related activities into a project plan. It means enhancing the way both project management and change management is practiced today. This is done by unifying the techniques, approaches, and perspectives of both disciplines to jointly execute the critical project tasks that help achieve total project success. It also means letting go of outdated assumptions regarding the scope, purpose, and practice of each of these disciplines.

The bottom line is this: There needs to be an evolution of both project and change management if we are truly serious about achieving total project success.

Chapter 4

The Next Evolution

Introduction

In Chapter 1, we saw how both traditional project management and change management practices are required to achieve total project success. Chapters 2 and 3 provided us with an overview of the history, evolution, and current trends within each discipline. At the conclusion of Chapter 3, we explored the numerous reasons why change management has typically fallen short when it came to facilitating project success.

Insights and techniques of both project disciplines should be judiciously applied if the organization is serious about achieving *total* project success (that is, on time, within budget, according to customer specifications, adopted by the organization, and providing value to the business). However, trying to incorporate two project disciplines on one initiative has proven time and time again to be challenging at best.

When two project disciplines are employed on the same initiative, they often either wind up subtly competing against one another, or one marginalizes the work (and potential value) of the other. As a result, the initiative becomes divided and disjointed.

Some of the issues which occur when attempting to integrate these two disciplines include:

- Confusion over roles and responsibilities
- Questions over the timing of certain activities and deliverables
- Challenges over methods and perceived value

- Issues around access to key project decision makers and funding streams

Overlaps Between Project and Change Management

Project management and change management are two sides of the same coin. While some may argue that the two disciplines complement each other, to say change management is "all about people" (i.e., "soft skills") and project management "is all about tasks" (i.e., "hard skills") is to take a rather unsophisticated view.

Good project managers need to understand and apply soft skills just as often as change management practitioners need to understand and apply hard skills. Project managers do not simply sit around writing project plans and tracking expenditures to progress. They typically interact with a wide variety of stakeholders – from project sponsors, to executive decision makers, to project team members, and so on. Because of this, they too need to have "soft skills," including in the areas of communication, team building and motivation, conflict resolution, and performance management.

Conversely, most change management practitioners must possess a certain degree of "hard" project execution skills. Especially on large, complex change initiatives, many change management practitioners are not just called in to talk about what constitutes good change management practices, but are asked to draw up detailed plans and execute them as well. It is one thing to know the principles behind good communication or training. It is another thing to be able to create a detailed execution plan and actively manage a complex communication or training initiative – especially if the project calls for reaching out to hundreds if not thousands of geographically dispersed stakeholders who have diverse information or competency development needs. Having the right amount of "hard skills" will definitely be needed in order to keep an initiative like that on time and within budget.

From Flirting to Overlapping?

If one studies many of the project management and change management practices in place today, one will see that the two disciplines not only flirt with each other but downright overlap in most areas.

Take, for example, the PMI *PMBOK® Guide, 4th Edition* (the definitive standard for project management as of this printing). *PMBOK®* clearly states that project management "can enhance and accelerate organizational change." And to support this statement, *PMBOK®* is full of project management processes that would make any change management consultant stand up and say, "Hey, that's my role!"

A few examples:

- "Identifying Stakeholders – *identifying all people or organizations impacted by the project and documenting relevant information regarding their interests, involvement and impact on project success*" *(PMBOK® Guide, pg 46).*
- "Plan Communications – *the process of determining the project stakeholder information needs and defining a communication approach*" *(PMBOK® Guide, pg 251).*
- "Manage Stakeholder Expectations – *actively managing the expectations of stakeholders to increase the likelihood of project acceptance*" *(PMBOK® Guide, pg 261).*

The above examples sounds a lot like what any change management consultant would also propose. While PMI is starting to incorporate many change management tasks into its *project management* standards, the organization has not yet been as bold as its UK counterpart, the APM. The APM states: *"Projects bring about change and project management is recognised [sic] as the most efficient way of managing such change."*

The *PMBOK® Guide* contains many other examples which have a decidedly "change management flavor." Some of these sound like they were pulled directly from change management role descriptions:

- Develop Project Team
- Identify Stakeholders
- Plan Communications
- Distribute Information
- Manage Stakeholder Expectations
- Report Performance
- Identify Risks (including organizational and user adoption risks)
- Plan Risk Responses (including an organizational change plan if necessary)

So if the two fields really overlap, why even bother with change management? Because, despite the efforts PMI is making in this direction, it still falls far short of providing the necessary depth and breadth needed in terms of managing human, political, and organizational change. As discussed in previous chapters, the discipline of change management emerged to fill a void in what project management was offering. *It wasn't that project management was ignoring change-related activities, it was that project management wasn't doing them well enough.*

Table 4.1. *How Change Management Can Enhance Traditional Project Management Activities*

Project Activity or Objective	What a Project Manager Typically Does	How Change Management Can Enhance the Activity
Team building	Invites the team out to dinner so they can "get to know one another" on a personal level	Maps out an ongoing team development plan with short, focused activities around the team's professional interactions and needs so that a high-performance team can be quickly realized
Solution design	Designs a solution given to the project manager by the project sponsor or some other stakeholder	Tests what the human and/or organizational impact of the design will be and provides that feedback to the design team for consideration and possible modifications
User acceptance testing (UAT) and conference room pilots (CRP)	Has the technical team members conduct the UAT and CRP sessions	Utilizes some of the UAT or CRP session to gather more insights into end-user communication needs, solicits input for what the "word on the street" might be regarding the initiative, and identifies particularly enthusiastic participants for possible inclusion in a "change champion" network
Understanding project direction	If mixed directions are received from project decision makers, follows the directions of the executive the PM feels most comfortable with	Periodically tests for executive alignment and clear direction. If misalignment or mixed messages are discovered, facilitates an executive stakeholder session to create better alignment and more consistent messaging
Clarifying roles and responsibilities	Verbally explains roles and responsibilities or presents a high-level outline	Documents roles and responsibilities with enough detail that a verbal explanation is not necessary; augments roles and responsibilities by outlining behavioral expectations.

The Need for Change Management to Adopt Greater Rigor

To be fair, it is not just that project management seems to be incorporating classic change management concepts and activities. In fact, *most change management activities should be anchored by project management tasks.* Any good change management program should incorporate many of the following standard project management processes:

- Direct and Manage Project (or Change) Execution
- Monitor and Control Project Work
- Define Scope
- Define Activities
- Sequence Activities
- Estimate Activity Durations
- Determine Budget
- Manage Project Team
- When applicable, Plan and Conduct Procurements (e.g., training development resources)

Unfortunately, most change management training programs or methodologies never address these critical project management processes. Unlike project management, which grew in part out of the field of engineering, change management developed primarily out of the field of psychology and other social sciences. Thus, the latter attracted a large number of practitioners who were very people-centric but eschewed areas of work that were very technical or detailed. This disconnect has resulted in a legacy effect on the field of change management, in which the shrewd use of tools, technology, and financial metrics are often overlooked in favor of more touchy-feely face-to-face approaches.

Table 4.2. *How Project Management Can Enhance Traditional Change Management Activities*

Project Activity or Objective	What a Change Professional Typically Does	How More Rigorous "Project Management" Techniques Can Enhance the Activity
Create alignment amongst executive stakeholders	Facilitates a discussion session amongst the executives	Calculates what the project "burn rate" (costs) are for each day a critical project decision is delayed; relays that to participants; and then introduces appropriate decision-alignment tools (e.g., "forced choice," "value driver rankings"). Crunches the numbers in real time; displays results on the conference room screen
Plan a change project	Develops a change model using high-level models and concepts	Creates one or two alternative plans and does a comparative cost/benefit analysis of each plan. Chooses the most optimal plan and creates a work breakdown structure that accurately tracks each activity, the expected duration, the resources required, and the associated costs
Promote an enterprise-wide change initiative	Creates a "change champion" network, providing them with key talking points and other supporting materials	Creates an issues database where change champions can input pertinent feedback and areas of concern; configures a work flow so that alerts can be instantaneously pushed to others in the network
Ensure good project sponsorship	Coaches or provides a workshop on the "soft skills" of leading change: how to be sensitive to employee needs, portray confidence, display a sense of importance and urgency, etc.	Provides the project sponsor with solid numbers and reliable cost estimates so that the project can be successfully defended from those who might try to reduce or eliminate funding

Two Project Disciplines, One Initiative... Multiple Problems

Despite the obvious overlap between the two disciplines, project management and change management have been, and in most case still are, sold, practiced, and managed as two almost mutually exclusive project disciplines. Instead of taking a unified approach toward project success, the project is divided between the project management and change management camps instead.

The execution of any worthwhile change management program involves competently executing numerous project tasks. Likewise, project managers need to involve people for the accurate and timely completion of project tasks.

Unfortunately, while many change practitioners say their approaches and activities "integrate" well with project management, this is rarely true.

Project managers do not do the "people" side of projects very well, and that change practitioners, lacking the requisite project rigor, don't do a very good job of managing the nuts and bolts of their change initiatives.

Rather than complementing each other on projects, what happens in many cases is that:

- There is competition over project funding allocation or scope responsibilities
- Critical activities fall between the cracks due to role confusion
- Redundant activities, especially as they pertain to stakeholder management, often occur
- Joint opportunities are never realized
- Access to project decision makers becomes guarded
- Different political alliances begin to form
- There is poor coordinated use of resources
- There is increased finger pointing and blame
- The two teams do not leverage the insights, perspectives, or solutions the other team can offer

Although there are some situations in which a change management practitioner takes charge of an initiative or project, this is rare. In a majority of cases, the project manager is the one driving the project. Sometimes the project manager chooses to let change management ride along in the back seat. Worse than that, there are still some project managers who won't even allow change management in the vehicle.

This situation can best be characterized by the band of desperados' reply to the offering of badges by State Attorney General Hedley Lamarr in the classic Mel Brooks' movie *Blazing Saddles*:

"Badges? We don't need no stinking badges!"

Many project managers have been, or still are, uttering a similar phrase: *"Change management? We don't need no stinking change management! Ha, ha, ha."*

However, when project managers do not completely dismiss change management, they often (either intentionally or unintentionally) limit its scope and influence. This will be explored in the next section.

Common Project Management/Change Management Work Structures

Though some may think that project management and change management "complement" each other, the reality is that this idea often does not last for long. Good intentions aside, applying project management and change management to the same initiative is usually fraught with ongoing challenges. These challenges cause the two work streams to limit their interconnectedness, and the relationship usually devolves into one of the following work structures:

1   The "Go Sell It" Approach
2   The "Project Support" Approach
3   The Silo Approach
4   The Parallel Approach

Since "projects are the vehicles of change" we will use a road trip as an analogy to describe the various project manager/change practitioner working relationships.

A. The "Go Sell It" Approach

With this approach, a project sponsor urges a project manager take a road trip. The project manager decides the route, picks out and tunes up his vehicle, and does most of the driving. It is only when the project manager is finished with the trip that he decides to use a change management person when it comes time to sell the car to someone else. It might not be the type of car the person wants or needs, but the project manager assumes that if the change professional can develop the right selling points and provides the hesitate buyer with a well designed driver's manual, than everything will work out fine.

Unfortunately this is one of the most common approaches to how project managers utilize change management resources. And even more unfortunate is the number of popular change management approaches and change management certification programs promoting this approach.

In this approach, change management plays a role only later in the project life cycle, usually during or immediately prior to the deployment phase. In this work structure, the primary and perhaps only role for change management is to prepare the organization (meaning the end-users/employees only, not the executive decision makers or the heads of critical support organizations) for the impending change. Change management appears too late in the project life cycle to address critical executive buy-in and alignment needs or to build momentum and dedicated cooperation with other project contributors such as project team members, human resources, procurement, etc.

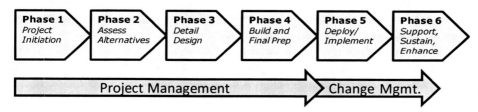

Figure 4.1. *The "Go Sell It" Approach*

Limitations and Disadvantages of the "Go Sell It" Approach

With this model, change management insights and expertise are not utilized in earlier project phases, when numerous issues arise that a good change management practitioner can help mitigate. As Chapter 1 highlighted, organizational adoption is actually a three-stage process. Unless the decision makers in the organization first adopt the solution or opportunity, and other project influencers OK the subsequent project plans, focusing on end-users and other impacted employees is a moot point. By focusing only on deployment/end-user-related issues, myriad other issues are ineffectively managed: executive alignment, effective sponsorship, maintaining project team momentum, organizational impact of different design decisions, stakeholder engagement during testing and review sessions, etc.

Unless change management is involved throughout the entire project life cycle, more likely than not, the project management goals of staying on time, within budget, and within scope (or according to spec) will go awry due to poor stakeholder management and other human/political issues that arise in earlier project phases.

In addition to the above pitfalls, strong change management practitioners are keenly aware of how various components of a project or initiative may have unintended consequences when introduced to the workforce. Therefore, they are a tremendous asset to have on hand when it comes to project scoping or reviewing potential design alternatives that could have varying degrees of organizational impact. After all, the goal of any project is not simply to create change for change's sake but to introduce the *right* kind of change.

Lastly, with the "Go Sell It" approach, change managers are often times put in the difficult, if not exasperating, position of trying to "sell" a poorly scoped or ineffectually designed change to the organization. Thus, when the organization resists the change for purely justifiable reasons (because the employees have legitimately determined that this is an imprudent change, and not because they possess a natural resistance to change), the change is never adopted. In a case such as this, that is probably not a bad thing. However, the change team may be blamed for not having an effective program instead of blame resting with the design team, who created something off-target because they didn't do a proper job of engaging stakeholders.

As the old adage goes: "It's hard to sell a bad idea." And without change management expertise to help with scoping and design, there is a much greater chance that the change will not meet the true needs of the recipients.

B. The Project Support Approach

In the Project Support approach, the project manager will allow a change practitioner to sit in the back seat of the car. He or she will occasionally take directions from the change practitioner, but doesn't really allow change management to be a full-fledged participant in driving toward project success.

I recently read a job description for a change management position within one of the major "Big Four" consulting firms. I was surprised to read that one of the change management job responsibilities was "taking notes."

"Taking notes?" Excuse me?

Project managers, who often have a limited understanding of the role and value of change management as a project resource, often create a docile, subservient role for their change managers.

Within this structure, change managers are denied a "seat at the table" with key project stakeholders. They have limited, if any, access to project decision makers and contributors to hear firsthand of any stakeholder-related or change-related issues or concerns. Instead, the change practitioner works under the thumb of the project manager in a very limited, administrative-like support role.

Junior-level change practitioners, who have limited change management experience, often fall into this position, as do project resource managers who have more of a background in communications than in the much broader field of change management.

Most of their duties consist of putting together slide decks for the project manager to present, or writing and distributing memos to other project stakeholders. They have limited direct access to stakeholders and virtually no role in project planning or decision making.

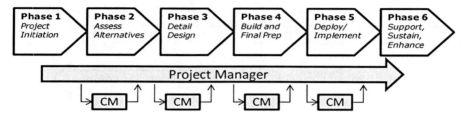

Change management plays an occasional "support only" role to the project manager.

Figure 4.2. *The Project Support Approach*

Limitations and Disadvantages of the Project Support Approach

Although the change practitioner is more in tune with the pace and needs of the project, he or she generally lacks the insights, expertise, and/or authority to play a more substantial role. Instead, he or she winds up boxed in to a shallow support role to a project manager, who limits the former's activities and potential value as well.

C. The Silo Approach

The Silo Approach find the project manager driving along a beautiful stretch of road. Driving somewhere else, usually on another road but in the same general direction as the project manager, is change management. Their roads never intersect, and each only has a vague idea of what the other is doing.

The Silo Approach occurs when there are concurrent project management and change management activities occurring on the same project, but because both teams rarely interact or coordinate with each other, they work in a "silo," away from one another.

Many times, the Silo Approach is results from procuring change professionals who take more of a clichéd or generic approach to change. Since many people on the change management side may not have a strong technical or business background, they are usually quite comfortable with the separation. Most of them "don't quite get" what the project team is doing (and vice versa), so interactions are minimized.

This is a common occurrence when employing psychotherapeutic or other "personal change" models.

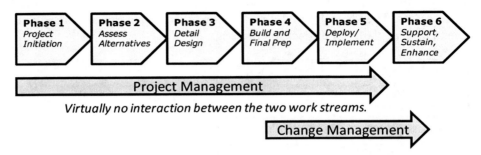

Figure 4.3. *The Silo Approach*

Limitations and Disadvantages of the Silo Approach

The disadvantages and limitations of the Silo Approach are similar to those of the "Go Sell It" approach, but perhaps even worse.

Silos create an "us versus them" mentality, with little sense of having a shared purpose or common vision of success. With the Silo Approach, the managers of each respective half see themselves as mutually exclusive, and there is never any synergy created that would enhance the creation of deliverables or drive the project forward. For the client, to separately source and oversee two separate project teams (the core project team and the adjunct change management team) is burdensome. Also, subtle or overt competition may develop between the two teams for access to additional funding or to senior-level decision makers.

Because the two teams have limited communication, similar or redundant activities are more likely to occur, especially around managing stakeholder needs and expectations. Also, critical project activities may fall between the cracks owing to one team thinking that it was the other team's responsibility.

D. The Parallel Approach

As a somewhat improved variation of the Silo Approach, the Parallel Approach finds both project management and change management, in separate vehicles, driving along the same road. Sometimes they are driving parallel to one another, other times, one or the other may be off in the distance. They occasionally meet up and exchange a few ideas at gas stations and road stops, but their interactions are limited.

Many project professionals mistake the Parallel Approach with an integrated approach; however, there are key differences. The main difference is that the Parallel Approach is characterized more by the *occasional synchronization of activities* than by the joint execution of activities, as found within a truly integrated model.

The Parallel Approach still has an "us versus them" flavor, similar to what is found in the Silo Approach, but because there are occasional touch points between the two teams, activities are somewhat better coordinated. Even so, "project management" tasks and "change management" tasks are still separate from one another, and both the execution of activities and the creation of deliverables are independently managed.

Touch points usually occur around major milestone events. For example, the project team informs the change team that the change designs have been finalized so that the change team can begin crafting the training material. (A better approach would be to have both teams working together designing the change so that critical organizational impacts, stakeholder inputs, and potential end-user reactions are all part of design considerations.)

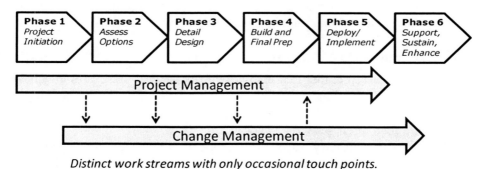

Distinct work streams with only occasional touch points.

Figure 4.4. *The Parallel Approach*

Limitations and Disadvantages of the Parallel Approach

In the Parallel Approach, the two teams still maintain distinct areas of independence from one another. While there may be some handoffs between the teams, there is little synergy created that will result in higher quality, more comprehensive, complete, and accurate deliverables.

Though the Parallel Approach is becoming more and more common (and quite often is falsely characterized as being "integrated"), its disadvantages and limitations are numerous:

- Two sets of project methodologies, plans, and project resources (a functional/technical project team and a change management team) are created instead of one truly integrated team.

75

- There is a high risk that the project team and the change team might develop different political alliances or different interpretations regarding project direction.
- Since deliverables are created by one team or the other, they have a distinctly one-sided perspective and do not possess the insights the other team can offer.
- Opportunities are missed to jointly create and enhance core deliverables which incorporate both project management *and* change management expertise.
- Limits are placed on change management support to help the project team achieve peak performance.
- Change management plans run the risk of being executed without the same level of rigor as the core project team plan (since there is typically less project management expertise and acumen within the change team).
- Wasting time, resources and frustrating participants by interviewing/engaging the same stakeholders for different purposes instead of holding joint engagement sessions

The Best Laid Plans of Mice and Men...

It is important to remember that many of the above work structures may have started out with the best intentions of fully integrating both the project management track and the change management track, but the best laid plans of mice and men often go awry.

There are two primary reasons this happens. One is that, often times, one side does not fully understand or appreciate what the other side can bring to the table. The other reason is that there is no unifying methodology for the two fields. *Because there is nothing concrete holding them together, they gradually drift or are forcefully pushed apart.*

There is a need for a unifying methodology between project management and change management: a methodology that is not characterized by handing back and forth different project tasks but rather by the *joint execution* of project tasks.

The Emergence One Method

With the Emergence One Method, both project management and change management are both driving in the front seat together. They regularly engage each other, share ideas on what the best route to take might be, have a wider skill set between them to navigate road blocks or address vehicle maintenance needs, support each other through long stretches of road, can jointly fight off bands of desperados, and have a shared commitment to reaching their final destination together. And when it comes time to sell the vehicle to the buyer, one is adept as configuring the mechanical specifications to buyer specifications; the other is adept at understanding and promoting the total driving experience to the buyer.

The Emergence One Method recognizes that, because of the many overlaps between project management and change management, there is little to gain by perpetuating a "this is project management, that is change management" mindset. Whether something is labeled a "project management activity" or a "change management activity" is less important than having both perspectives and approaches embedded within most project activities and deliverables.

With the Emergence One Method, task execution is accomplished by utilizing an optimal combination of both project management and change management inputs. It is no longer necessary to separate project management from change management activities and deliverables. Now one set of project activities and deliverables is available to incorporate the tools, technique, and insights from both project management and change management. Both elements are judiciously applied to most projects tasks throughout the complete project life cycle.

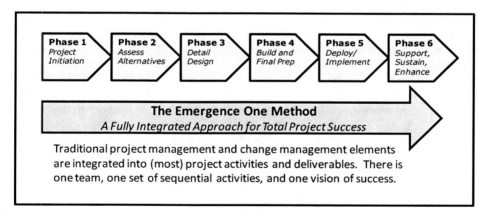

Figure 4.5. *The Emergence One Method, a Fully Integrated Approach for Total Project Success*

This integrated approach allows traditional "change management" tasks to be executed in a more rigorous manner owing to the appropriate application of proven project management techniques. And, by thoroughly accounting for the human variables which may affect task completion and quality, project tasks can be executed with a higher level of assurance.

Since the tools, techniques, and insights of both project management and change management are considered for each task, teams can do away with the labels supporting a "project management versus change management" mindset and simply focus on achieving project success.

NOTE: *In the Emergence One Method, there is less emphasis on project management versus change management activities, but there is still an emphasis on project management and change management roles. That is, a project management lead applies project management know-how and expertise to tasks, while a change lead applies change management know-how and expertise to the same set of tasks.*

One Set of Activities with Two Sets of Inputs

Project momentum, quality, and ultimately, success, depend upon both the deft execution of project tasks and well as the proactive management of stakeholder needs and expectations. These two goals are not mutually exclusive – in fact, they are mutually interdependent. Therefore, on *most* (not necessarily all) project activities, both the project manager and the change lead will offer the appropriate thoughts, insights, perspectives, as well as some of their traditional tools and techniques to holistically address the myriad of needs and potential variables that accompany each activity.

The Emergence One Method is based on the viewpoint that there are two experienced project professionals: a project manager and a change management practitioner, and that rarely can the same person play the same role. There are two reasons for this:

1 *Matter of expertise* – Change management, like project management, is not something that can be learned overnight or by taking a two-day workshop. Because so many people have a narrow definition of change management, they think it is fairly easy to learn. It is not. Anyone who tells you differently probably has a very limited understanding of the depth and breadth of the field.

2 *Matter of bandwidth* – In the rare instances where a project professional has strong expertise in both project management and change management, in most cases, there is simply not enough time to execute both roles adequately. With all the demands that come with being either a project manager or a change lead, at least one, if not both, of those two areas would suffer. There just aren't enough hours in the day to effectively play both roles. (Note: An exception to this rule is a small initiative that has a limited set of stakeholders.)

Building a Collaborative Approach

Peter Block, in his classic book *Flawless Consulting,* expanded upon three types of consulting relationships that were originally introduced by organizational development theorist Edgar Schein. Emergence One has adopted their thinking in defining how the relationship between the project manager and change lead should work.

The three types of consulting relationships are:

1   *The expert role* – The project lead (who is usually the project manager) sees the other as an "expert" and thus allows him- or herself to play an inactive role. This attitude helps to promote a Silo Approach or parallel work structure, as described earlier.

2   *The "pair-of-hands" role* – The project lead sees the other as someone who is there merely to carry out his directions or decisions. This role in effect nullifies the expertise, contributions, and potential value of the other. This relationship often leads to the establishment of the Limited Support Role structure, also described earlier.

3   *The collaborative approach* – In this more integrated system, both parties become interdependent. There is a mutual exchange of ideas, perspectives, and respect for the tools and techniques each party brings to the table.

It is the collaborative approach that exemplifies the desired working relationship between the project manager and the change lead when employing the Emergence One Method. Broadly speaking, the project manager can help add rigor and structure to managing the human, political, and organizational change needed on a project. In turn, the change lead can help the project manager become more aware of how workforce behaviors, stakeholder attitudes, and other organizational elements (e.g., HR policies or corporate culture) can affect project execution and the achievement of project objectives.

Advantages of the Emergence One Method

To recap the advantages of the Emergence One Method, outlined in the preface, the Emergence One Method offers the following:

- An integrated, unified approach to addressing and executing all essential project management as well as change management activities and tasks, thereby eliminating the need to procure and manage two sets of project resources (e.g., a core project team and an adjunct change management team).
- Clearly defined roles and responsibilities for both project managers and change practitioners so that they can eliminate overlapping activities, optimize joint opportunities, and form a more productive, collaborative relationship.

- A tangible, rigorous, yet practical approach to addressing the numerous human, political, and organizational changes that can impede project momentum, ROI, and business value.
- Clear guidance, including real-world insights and helpful caveats, on how to complete all the necessary activities, tasks, and deliverables within each project phase.
- A step-by-step approach on how to satisfy end-user adoption and other stakeholder management goals well before deployment so that operational disruptions are minimized and business value can be realized much sooner.

The result is a business change initiative, strategy implementation, or IT project that is:

- Properly scoped, managed, and supported;
- Efficiently designed and built;
- Conscientiously deployed; and
- Eagerly adopted and sustained by the organization so that business value can be decisively realized.

In the next chapter...

Chapter 5 will present many of the fundamentals and key elements of the Emergence One Method. These include the required project structure, which enables the Emergence One model to succeed, as well as details on Emergence One's Three Stage Organizational Adoption model.

Chapter 5

Elements of the Emergence One Method

Introduction

The Emergence One Method promotes the idea that project managers and change managers are jointly responsible for ensuring that a project/change initiative comes in on time, within budget, according to specifications, *and* is embraced and utilized by all relevant stakeholders throughout the organization. It is this joint responsibility that helps ensure maximum ROI and business value realization.

However, as was detailed in the previous chapter, project managers and change management practitioners often do not build the productive, collaborative, and truly integrated relationship necessary to achieve total project success. The Emergence One Method seeks to rectify this failing by breaking down the distinction between what have traditionally been regarded as project management activities and what have traditionally been considered change management activities. Instead, the E1 Method presents a single set of project activities which, to one degree or another, are jointly executed by those who possess a more task-focused, project management skill set alongside those who possess a more people-oriented, change management skill set.

Therefore, one of the first, and most critical, project activities is to establish a project structure that optimizes the skill sets, experience, and level of influence that an experienced project manager and a skilled change practitioner bring to the table.

Structured for Success: The Collaborative Project Structure

Often times, the project sponsor develops the governance architecture, usually with minimal help from the project manager. The results look like a typical hierarchical structure with little integration of change management.

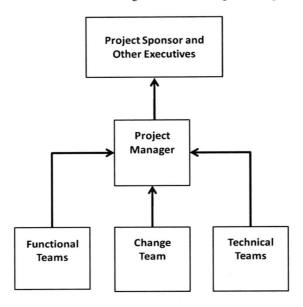

Figure 5.1. *Example of a Less Collaborative Project Structure*

However, it is critical that the project manager and the change lead agree upon a governance structure that will benefit *the project* as opposed to a structure that is simply more convenient or gives more control to the project manager.

It is quite obvious that in the above structure, the position of change lead is not integrated with the role of project manager. Some would argue that it is the project manager's role to integrate the work stream, including change management. While that it true for different functional and business work streams, change management is different for two key reasons:

1 ***Change management needs to ensure that key executives are aligned on project objectives and are willing to visibly support and promote the project*** – It is very difficult for change practitioners to achieve these goals when the project structure puts the project manager between them and the project executives. Access to the project

sponsor and other senior executives will be controlled by the project manager, who will act as a "gatekeeper" to control the flow of information upwards. While this may serve to protect the project manager, by having a "filtering" system in place to limit any inconvenient project team performance or stakeholder issues from reaching the executives' ears, it does not serve the project well. Executive-level project stakeholders need to hear perspectives on the project from people other than the project manager, especially when they involve team performance and stakeholder management issues the project management might not be particularly attuned to. In addition, an experienced change lead should be highly skilled at identifying and addressing both subtle and overt points of contention and misalignment amongst executive stakeholders. Typically, confronting issues of executive team misalignment or insufficient change sponsorship carries less political risk for the change lead than for the project manager.

2   *Change management needs to keep its finger on the pulse* – Because one of the key responsibilities of change management is to assess and mitigate people and process issues as they occur, it is critical that the change management lead keep his or her finger on the pulse of what is happening at all times. In order to be effective, he or she cannot rely on the project manager to decide which issues are "worthy of change management's attention" and then wait for the project manager to get around to filtering down the issues for change management to address. While good project managers do possess some knowledge and insights to the critical "soft" issues, their main strengths usually lie within most of the "hard," technical aspects of the project.

A structure needs to be in place that maximizes the ability of change management resources to do what they do best: i.e., work in a high-touch manner with executives as well as proactively mitigate various project-related people and process issues. Therefore, whenever Emergence One consultants work on consulting engagements, it typically recommends something along the lines of the following structure:

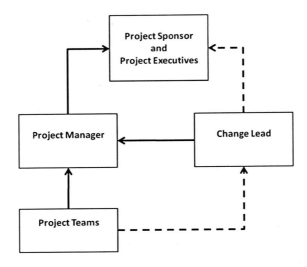

Figure 5.2. *A Project Structure Which Allows for Stronger Collaboration*

As this figure shows, the change lead now has better access to project executives and key decision makers. However, the change lead still reports to the project manager, who is still responsible for overall project success (after all, the role of the change resource is to *augment, not replace,* project management.)

In addition, because the change lead (or change management team, if there is one) depends on many of the outputs of the project team, the project team now has a reporting relationship to the change lead (represented by the dotted line).

For larger projects which have a Project Management Office (PMO), the structure might look like Figure 5.3.

In this structure, the change lead sits with the project manager as part of the PMO. This is an ideal structure because it allows the change lead to keep a finger on the pulse of all the people and process issues that are happening during the project in real time, as well as having unfiltered access to the project sponsor and other project executives. Also, the dotted line between the change team and both the functional (business) and technical teams is significant. Change management often bridges the gap between the business and technical teams, making sure that business needs are being incorporated into technical solutions and ensuring that the technical teams don't go crazy adding bells and whistles to a system that would be of little business benefit.

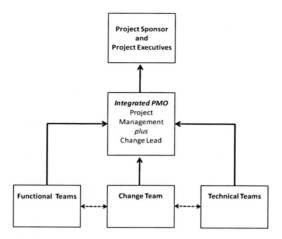

Figure 5.3. *A Collaborative Project Structure for Larger Initiatives*

Fundamentals of the Emergence One Method

Several key elements are fundamental to the proper understanding and application of the Emergence One Method.

All key project activities result in a tangible output

The E1 Method places a heavy emphasis on documentation. Emergence One believes that the knowledge and insights regarding the project, the various stakeholders, the issues, the risks, and so forth belong to the project team and should be available for reference. Information and insights should not simply reside in someone's head, especially given the fact that personnel changes on projects can be quite frequent.

The terms *deliverable* and *documentation* are used interchangeably and may not always mean the creation of a *formal deliverable* that is submitted for client review and approval. Depending upon client expectations and the governance structure of the project, either term may simply mean documentation of the outcome, which in turn can be used as an input to create a more formal or comprehensive deliverable further down the line.

In addition, not every output needs to be overly formalized or detailed. It is not the Method's intent to have projects drown in a sea of paperwork. There is no need to write a 12-page report if a three-page summary will provide all the necessary actionable information. In addition, Emergence One does not encourage the time-consuming creation of overly slick presentations and graphics when the goal is simply to convey required information or updates to internal stakeholders.

Lastly, the thoroughness of the documentation should be scaled to the size and scope of the project. For instance, a $30 million dollar ERP implementation would require a more thorough and in-depth business case than would a small, $50,000 project which is not driving significant change.

The bottom line is that documentation should be steady, efficient, succinctly written, and appropriately scaled to the importance and size of the project at hand. When the documentation goes beyond what is needed, it only burns up precious time and project resource dollars or becomes what is sarcastically referred to as SPOTS – Strategic Plans on Top Shelf.

A strong emphasis on stakeholder management throughout the project life cycle

Besides helping project management mitigate the human and political issues which can hinder project momentum, change management also helps to facilitate organizational adoption by effectively managing stakeholder needs and expectations. However, in order for true organizational adoption to occur, more than just the end-user/employee community needs to be considered.

In order to make stakeholder management more methodical, Emergence One divides stakeholder groups into three tiers:

1   **Tier 1 Stakeholders** – Senior Leaders and Key Decision Makers
2   **Tier 2 Stakeholders** – Project Contributors, those who provide inputs to, or assist with, the coordination and deployment of the effort. (Note: Although Tier 1 and Tier 3 stakeholders can also provide input to the project, since their contributions tend to be mostly ad-hoc, they are technically not categorized as Project Contributors.)
3   **Tier 3 Stakeholders** – Change Recipients

The concept of a multi-stage adoption process was first introduced in Chapter 3. The three-stage model of organizational adoption is outlined below.

Emergence One's Three-Stage Organizational Adoption Model

1   *Adoption by Senior Leaders and Key Decision Makers* – These are generally the major sponsors and supporters of the initiative. The project/change concept, direction, and related costs must first be adopted by key senior leaders and project decision makers, including the financial gatekeepers. These stakeholders are most prominent in the early stages of the project life cycle and are critical not just for keeping the project on time and within scope, but also for laying the necessary foundation for change adoption by the broader organization. Even if a project is expected to have limited impacts on the behaviors and required competencies of end-users/employees, applying change

management principles and techniques is still required to facilitate this critical (and often more challenging) first stage. Adoption is achieved and maintained at this stage through the use of a compelling business case and project metrics, the mitigation of political issues and executive misalignment, and regular updates and project performance reviews.

2   *Adoption by Project Contributors* – Project contributors can be anyone who is involved in providing inputs to, or helping with the coordination and execution of the project. Unless you have the support and cooperation of various project contributors, the initiative will falter. *Project contributors need to adopt the role they will be asked to perform, whether it is one of advisor, provider, coordinator, or supporter.*

This broad stakeholder group includes core and extended project team members as well as those involved in other projects who may have concerns regarding the timing and/or touch points between initiatives. This group also includes those from the affected business and operations areas who want to incorporate some of their needs into the project plans. Lastly, any corporate support or compliance organizations such as HR, procurement, legal, help desk, health and safety, policy and audit. who may have a say in what exactly can and cannot be done fall into this group. Managing these various stakeholder groups through ongoing engagement sessions and the proactive identification of potential issues and risks is critical to preventing project delays and rework.

Many traditional change management approaches exclude this group, one of the reasons why traditional change management approaches are not always effective. For instance, if an organization is implementing something that will result in major process changes, then that change will impact the roles and responsibilities of the affected employees. Therefore, in order to support this change, HR will need to rewrite or approve modifications to job roles, work descriptions, performance measures, and maybe even pay scales and career ladders. If HR is unwilling to accommodate or adopt the changes into what typically falls within their (fairly entrenched) scope of work, then the initiative will not be properly supported. Therefore, HR is a "project resource" who will also need to adopt and make some type of change before deploying the project among end-users/employees.

3   *Adoption by Change Recipients* – If the project succeeds in reaching the deployment/implementation phase (and many projects do not),

the next objective is the adoption of project goals and objectives by the impacted end-users/employee groups or others in the organization. "Adoption" implies, at a minimum, "acceptance." It does not necessarily mean that something is liked or favorably looked upon (although these factors certainly help to accelerate adoption). It does, however, mean that there will at least be an acceptable level of compliance with the new performance expectations.

The reason why this stage tends to be less challenging than the first stage is that often times employees have limited options available to them for not complying with or adopting the change. While in their personal lives many people are free to embrace or reject a change which may come their way, in an organizational setting, the employment contract and prevailing workplace expectations help facilitate (but not necessarily guarantee) the adoption of workplace change. (There are of course numerous exceptions to this.) Another reason may be that the project may have little impact on workplace behaviors or required competencies. For example, something such as a database consolidation effort might not have major impacts on the end-user community but would still require Stage 1 and Stage 2 organizational adoption efforts.

It is important to note the frequent overlaps between these three stages. For example, stakeholders in Stage 1 can decide to kill or defund the project at any point up to and even including during deployment.

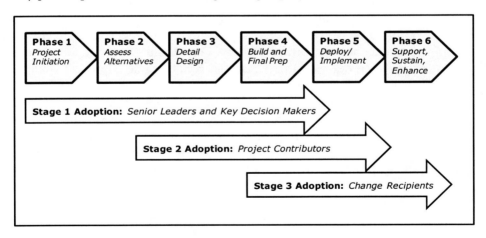

Figure 5.4. *The Emergence One Three-Stage Organizational Adoption Model*

How efficiently and thoroughly adoption objectives are reached in each of the above stages will have an impact on the project timeline, budget, scope, and overall success.

To achieve each stage of organizational adoption, the Emergence One Method focuses on anticipating the needs and expectations of various project stakeholders and addressing these needs and expectations in a timely manner. Depending upon the size and scope of the project, stakeholder needs and expectations will various tremendously. The table below illustrates some of the more common ones.

Table 5.1.   *Common Needs of Project Stakeholders*

Project Stakeholders	Common Stakeholder Needs and Expectations
TIER 1 Stakeholders: Senior Leaders/ Key Decision Makers	• Having confidence in the business case, anticipated ROI, and the potential competitive advantage offered • Remaining aligned as to scope, objectives, costs, and overall direction • Receiving direction on how best to promote and champion the initiative • Having confidence in the ability of the project team to deliver total project success • Ensuring that adequate funding will remain available
TIER 2 Stakeholders: Project Contributors	• Making sure that the initiative does not come into conflict with any corporate policies or government regulations • Having opportunities to offer feedback and recommendations on project designs and ongoing plans • Understanding the potential impact on the organization, the underlying corporate infrastructure, and other projects and initiatives, either ongoing or in the queue • Believing that the resulting change will not negatively impact any of their formal (or informal) political clout and influence

Project Stakeholders	Common Stakeholder Needs and Expectations
TIER 3 Stakeholders: Change Recipients	• Understanding how the initiative will benefit themselves, their department, and/or the broader organization • Being assured that there will not be major disruptions to ongoing operations • Understanding how the initiative will affect their job responsibilities, job security, upward mobility, relationships with colleagues, etc. • Being provided with the proper amount of time, training, and guidance necessary to develop any required new skills or competencies • Gaining awareness of where to get additional help and assistance if needed • Having confidence that they will be supported and/or rewarded for exhibiting any required new skills or behaviors

"Resistance to change" is often overstated or misunderstood

Emergence One believes that employees *sometimes* resist the change impacts that projects produce. However, we believe that resistance is not based upon some organic psychological condition present in most employees, as descendents of the Kubler-Ross "Change Curve" models would like you to believe.

We believe that many times, end-user/employees' resistance to change comes from:

1   A lack of understanding of what is being proposed and how it might affect them;

2   A legitimate apprehension that whatever is being implemented is not the right solution to their needs or concerns; or

3   A fear that they will not be provided with the necessary amount of training or organizational support to be successful and will thus be subject to negative ramifications.

It is not change itself that employees fear as much as it is a lack of confidence in the ability of the organization to successfully execute change. Consequently, we believe that "resistance to change" is a symptom of poor project planning and execution, not a psychological hindrance that most employees carry around with them.

However, even in cases where employees are eager for change (and there are many scenarios where that is true, because they believe a current process or enabling technology is inefficient or ineffective) change still needs to be managed.

This brings us to our next key element.

A practical, easy-to-understand model for end-user/employee adoption

When it comes to achieving the third stage of organizational adoption, "end-user/employee adoption," there are many different schools of thought on this topic... some of which are quite convoluted. Emergence One, in contrast, believes that it all boils down to a very simple formula:

$$\text{End-User/Employee Adoption} = \textit{Motivation} \times \textit{Competence} + \textit{Structural Support}$$

Figure 5.5. *The Emergence One End-User/Employee Adoption formula*

An employee may be motivated to adopt the change, but unless he or she has the necessary skills and competencies in which to execute the required changes, adoption will fall short. Conversely, just because you send employees to a training class in order to develop the new skills and competencies required, they are unlikely to apply these new skills and competencies back in the workplace unless they have the proper motivation to do so. Both motivation and competence must be developed if the change is to be adopted.

The other critical part of the formula is "structural support." (not to be confused with emotional support which falls under motivation). In this case, structural support is a formal change to one or more parts of the organization's underlying infrastructure. This support is critical for not only the initial adoption of the change, but also for *sustaining* the change. As a matter of fact, the whole idea of "employment, where you get paid to work" is already the manifestation of a change management concept: a supporting structure (steady pay and employment) in return for following directions from your boss. Structural support can, and should, manifest itself in many ways.

Some examples include:

- Formally rewriting job descriptions, reclassifying job roles, or creating new career ladders;
- Adjusting the reporting relationships or redesigning the organizational structure to reflect the new operating environment;
- Creating and instituting new performance metrics;

- Embedding new performance expectations into the employee review process;
- Adjusting compensation levels to reflect the changes in job responsibilities; and
- Giving employees access to databases, IT applications, or other sources of information that were previously restricted, etc.

Once upon a time...
How Structural Changes Supported a Call Center Redesign Effort

Emergence One once had a client challenge us to transform a customer service team from one that processed requests for information (for instance, providing credit card balance amounts, due dates, and interest rates) into a team which not only provided information, but also tried to sell customers "value-added" offerings such as balance transfers, mortgage services, or club discount cards.

The team had been trained on the details of these services offerings, and were pumped up and motivated to adopt this exciting enlargement of their job role. However, because they would soon be talking to customers about different value-added services, and not just answering customer account questions, their "call time" was expected to be twice as long as previously.

The call center employees had the motivation and the competence to perform successfully in their new roles. However, what was missing was the right structural support. Their performance metrics and compensation bonuses were still based upon how fast they worked their way through the call queue. What was needed was the necessary *structural support* to reflect their need to spend more time on the phone with customers.

Regardless of how motivated and competent the call center team may have initially been, unless there was a structural change to accompany the individual change, the new behaviors were unlikely to be either adopted or sustained. This is an important point to remember since so many common but less effective change management models focus merely on how *individuals* cope with change, rather than promote a true *organizational* change model that includes modifying structural elements as well.

Project management structures, techniques, and emphasis on rigor are applied throughout the project life cycle

Many times, a project manager may not be secured until the project has already been initiated or a high-level solution path determined.

Whether it is a project sponsor, a change "initiator" (someone who proposes the initial change idea), or a provisional project manager who is playing the project manager role in the early project life cycle stages, the rigor, structure, and techniques from the field of project management should be judiciously applied. These include techniques for developing a strong business case, structured means to test for executive alignment, a rigorous decision making process to evaluate project alternatives, etc.

In addition, project management techniques should be utilized in later project stages after the change may already have been delivered. These include making sure there is someone in charge of overseeing the "Sustain, Support, Improve" phase of the project life cycle, and that the appropriate structure and rigor for managing this phase are applied.

The effort required for task completion can be appropriately scaled back on smaller initiatives

The Emergence One Method can be utilized on any size project, large or small. Since the Emergence One Method is a sequential project life cycle methodology, the outputs of many activities serve as inputs to later activities and deliverables. Thus, it is not advisable to delete numerous project activities on smaller scale projects. However, when the methodology is utilized on smaller projects, the level of effort and subsequent degree of documentation can be greatly reduced. This allows the Emergence One method to remain thorough without burdening the project team with time-consuming activities or weighty documentation.

The E1 Method can be utilized to augment an existing project methodology

The Emergence One Method can be utilized as the main project methodology, or it can be adapted to enhance an existing methodology and to fill in any "holes" within that methodology. It should not be used as a "silo" or "parallel" methodology to one concurrently being applied to the target project.

For instance, Emergence One frequently consults on SAP implementations. Most SAP implementations follow the standard SAP ASAP project methodology: Start-up; Blueprint; Realization; Final Prep; and Go-live and Support. Rather than replace the SAP ASAP methodology with the Emergence One Method, we augment the SAP ASAP methodology with the unique value-added activities found in the Emergence One Method.

Acknowledges the importance of project sponsorship but does not take a "one size fits all" approach

There is ample evidence regarding the importance of project sponsorship. However, what constitutes "project sponsorship" varies tremendously depending upon who you ask.

To some, project sponsorship means merely approving the project funding requirements. To others, project sponsorship may mean standing on the stage at a company-wide "town hall" meeting rallying the troops and evangelizing about the change.

Unlike many other approaches out there, the Emergence One Method does not take a generic, "one size fits all" approach to project sponsors. Experience has taught up that not every executive can stand up and evangelize about a change in direction. They may be extroverts, or they may to prefer to keep a low profile (which is not uncommon for someone sponsoring an unproven approach or tenuous new direction). However, because they have been in the company for many long years, they have built strong, solid relationships throughout the organization. When it comes to removing potential barriers or project roadblocks, an effective sponsorship role for this person may be to simply pick up the phone and ask for support or assistance from his colleagues.

The Emergence One Method holds that sponsorship, whether it is a formal or informal role, usually has many players. For that reason, we closely assess and monitor a range of key project executives and overtly or subtly steer them into various sponsorship or "change champion" roles. Some may be effective sponsors for the entire organization; others may prove to be more legitimate sponsors or champions to a particular department or work group. Some can be better at generating enthusiasm and motivation; others are more effective working behind the scenes to make sure things get done and there are no politics or hidden agendas slowing down the project team.

This process starts with a stakeholder analysis and engagement plan. Once we understand some of the key needs and issues for each of the key stakeholders, we can then determine how to engage them and steer them toward fulfilling a key sponsorship need.

Table 5.2. *Executive Stakeholder Analysis Plan Example*

Stakeholder Analysis and Engagement Plan: Phase 2					
Stakeholder	**Position**	**Influence**	**Support**	**Concerns, Issues, and Comments**	**Engagement Strategy/ Sponsorship Ideas**
Lisa J.	Senior VP of Operations	5	5	Can articulate what this is about, can be a strong sponsor of project.	Set up events and have PM provide talking points for Lisa to voice her support and enthusiasm for the project.
Carlos R.	Senior VP of Finance	5	3	Wants to be more actively engaged; thinks this project is a good idea but still wants more information. Would like to have more efficient tools to comply with Sarbanes-Oxley.	Forward project overview deck; have VP of IT follow up with a phone call to answer any questions; afterwards, have main project sponsor provide the business case for additional project funding.
Donna K.	VP of Human Resources	4	4	Key conduit back to the Human resources group whose support will be needed for organizational design work. Would consider a more streamlined approach to updating relevant Master Data to be a win.	Prefers face-to-face meetings over emails; has good relationship with change lead; ensure change lead arranges periodic meetings; ask for assistance in thinking through potential organizational barriers and how she can help mitigate those barriers.

Stakeholder Analysis and Engagement Plan: Phase 2					
Ramesh P.	IT Group	5	1	Does not see why we have to decommission legacy systems (which he helped to design). Believes patches and add-ons will suffice. If project went away, he would shed no tears.	Need his support since he has a lot of influence with other critical IT people. Invite him to be part of the steering committee or solution team to develop a sense of ownership for the project (may also challenge any prevailing groupthink). He can help build a bridge between IT support and the project team.
Yen C.	Business Manager	2	4	Does not have a lot of influence with senior executives but is well liked by end-users. Will have more of an influence during the deployment phase of the project.	Keep in the loop for now, but involve her more heavily in later project phases to evangelize the need to change.

Takes a project-centric approach to change rather than focusing solely on the individual

For instance, a common project activity is to conduct a "change impact assessment." This is a critical activity needed to determine the adjunct project activities that will help facilitate organizational adoption and business value realization.

Change practitioners, who come from more of a therapeutic, "new age" background, may push for a plan which focuses more on the feelings of the change recipients rather than on what they need to do in order to play a role in helping the organization achieve total project success.

For instance, they may ask several generic questions such as:

- How well do you generally cope with change?
- In the past, has the organization done an adequate job when it comes to introducing change to the workplace?
- Do you feel that your concerns are always understood?

Emergence One believes that assessments that center around feelings and general statements may provide "nice to have" information but generally do little to promote the project objectives toward achieving total project success.

On the other hand, those with a project management background are likely to compare the current state with that of the future state, note the differences between them, and call that a change impact assessment. This assessment is also likely to produce only "nice-to-have" information unless the next step is taken.

Emergence One Method builds upon the identified changes between current and future state and then asks another set of questions that pertains directly to our change adoption model, which equals *Motivation X Competence + Structural Support.*

- Will the initiative clearly benefit the impacted individual, or does it provide more of an esoteric organizational benefit which is less likely to motivating?
- Does the change require a major shift in required competencies or skill sets, or will it be fairly easy for the impacted employee to pick up?
- Will the initiative call for any required or recommended changes to structural elements, such as organizational design, corporate policies, job roles, or performance management systems to support and sustain the change?

Stresses accountability to achieve business value realization

There is a well-known concept in social psychology circles; that of "Diffusion of Responsibility." The essence of this concept is that the more people who are present or involved in an activity, the less likely they are to take the appropriate actions to correct a problem or situation – primarily because they believe someone else will. Thus, their sense of responsibility is diffused amongst the various bystanders.

This idea can be applied to projects which affect a large number of stakeholders who are collectively responsible for achieving some degree of business value realization with the changes being thrust upon them. If nobody feels it is their responsibility to be accountable for business value realization, then the likelihood of it happening will be diminished.

The Emergence One approach recommends that various project and business value realization metrics be formulated throughout the project life cycle (and not after implementation) and assigned to appropriate owners. It will be the responsibility of these owners to ensure that business value is achieved. When responsibility is assigned this way, these owners will do a stronger job at keeping their people accountable for ensuring that they adopt the necessary behaviors and minimize or eliminate the use of work-arounds.

Additional Details on the Emergence One Method

The next chapter will provide an overview of the Emergence One project life cycle phases. Part Two of this book provides details on the Emergence One Method. One chapter is dedicated to each phase of the project life cycle. Each of the key activities and subtasks is listed, along with an explanation regarding the execution of each task. Real-world insights and appropriate caveats are also provided when required.

Chapter 6

Overview of the Project Life Cycle Phases

The Emergence One Project Life Cycle

A project life cycle is a sequential series of phases, each with its own unique objectives, which extends the full duration of the project. A project life cycle provides a distinct framework for the orderly sequence of tasks and activities so that the right resources can be applied to the right tasks at the right time.

The concept of the project life cycle was previously introduced, but it is useful to highlight some of the key characteristics and principles again here.

- Each phase has a distinct focus that differs from other phases in the project.
- Each phase must be satisfactorily completed in full before proceeding to the next phase.
- Success in one phase will breed success in the next phase; conversely, poor execution or deliverables quality in one phase will only be amplified in subsequent phases.
- One should only do the work that will drive the completion of that phase – for instance, do not work on Phase 3 activities if the project team is still in Phase 2.
- In regards to stakeholder management, one should focus solely on the needs and expectations of the project stakeholders which are critical for achieving the objectives of that phase. A common mistake

many change practitioners make is to prematurely engage the end-user/employee community long before than when it is necessary.

- Executive influence is higher at the start of the project since upper management can decide whether or not to continue to fund the project or pony up the appropriate resources.
- Each phase may require different skill sets; therefore, the composition of the project team may need to be modified in each subsequent phase. For example, since there will be considerable interaction with senior level executives during earlier project phases, junior level project professional may be better utilized during the middle and latter project phases.
- Before the project can proceed to the next phase, there is a project review or decision point typically known as a "Phase Gate," "Stage Gate," or similar term. The purpose of this session is to review the thoroughness and quality of the execution process and to test whether a coherent plan for the next phase is in place (see below for more on this).

The Six Phases of the Emergence One Project Life Cycle Model

The Emergence One Method is a six-phase project life cycle model. This model differs from most project life cycle models in that there is a post-deployment phase (Phase 6 – Support, Sustain, and Enhance). Although this step violates the traditional understanding of a project as having a defined end date, it is necessary for the continuation of the adoption process and to promote the realization of business value.

The Emergence One project life cycle also differs from many purer change management models. Less effective change management models tend to center mainly around end-user/employee deployments instead of addressing the human, political, and organizational change challenges that occur throughout the entire project life cycle. A high percentage of projects are killed or defunded long before they were ever scheduled to hit the end-user/employee community.

The six phases of the Emergence One method are as follows:

- Phase 1: Project Initiation
- Phase 2: Assess Alternatives
- Phase 3: Detail Design
- Phase 4: Build and Final Prep
- Phase 5: Deploy/Implement
- Phase 6: Support, Sustain, and Enhance

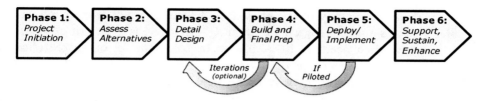

Figure 6.1.   The Emergence One Project Life Cycle

Each phase of the project life cycle is separated by what is often termed a "Phase Gate." The Phase Gates are critical, unbiased reviews of the project team's work and their major deliverables, and a recommended path forward for that phase.

The project review team considers the arguments and supporting materials presented, and then determines whether to:

1   **Proceed** to the next phase (usually an indication that the work to date has been acceptable, the plan forward is doable, and the business case remains relevant and compelling);
2   **Rework** the phase (usually the result of unacceptable or incomplete deliverables);
3   **Suspend** the project (the project is not canceled, just put on hold due to the lack of available funds or support, potential impacts of an external event, or an interdependency with another organizational initiative);
4   **End** the project (usually because the business case is no longer compelling or achievable).

Project Life Cycle Phase Descriptions

Each phase of the project life cycle has a primary goal, along with several key objectives... many around stakeholder management.

When reviewing the descriptions for each of the phases below, note that there are specific task-related challenges (for example, the need to develop an objective and rigorous solution assessment and evaluation process) as well as human, political, and/or organizational change challenges ("Key executives need to be aligned on the business case, understanding the potential benefits and risks, perceptions regarding the strategic fit...").

Phase 1 – Project Initiation

As the avant-garde musician John Cage once said, *"I can't understand why people are frightened of new ideas. I'm frightened by the old ones."*

The primary objective of this phase is to determine whether there is a particular business opportunity worth pursuing, or if there is a current or potential problem which needs to be addressed by some sort of organized effort (usually in the form of a project).

There are many reasons why companies have to change, and they are based as much upon internal needs as they are on external threats. However, most change initiatives and projects are usually undertaken within the business world for one of the following four fundamental reasons:

1   *To provide a solution to a real or potential problem* – These can include external problems or threats, or internal problems. Examples of external problems or threats could be increased competition, poor customer satisfaction, changes in the way the company does business with vendors or suppliers, etc. Internal problems may include outdated technology which is not scalable or flexible enough to meet growth needs; clunky processes which put the company at a competitive disadvantage; inadequate controls that create unnecessary waste or open the door for fraud; or aging equipment or poor maintenance and testing procedures which can negatively impact operations.

2   *To realize an opportunity* – Realizing are opportunities helps make a good company a great company. Opportunities may cover a wide range of initiatives to increase market share, lower operating costs, provide for better, more efficient operations, etc. They may also mean launching some sort of "green initiative," community relations program, or customer outreach project. These are all things that can help a company evolve.

3   *To meet external or internal compliance regulations or mandates* – These motives can include initiating or standardizing processes to comply with local, state, or federal governmental regulations, including regulations regarding financial reporting or environmental practices. Or it can mean adopting processes to gain some type of certification, such as ISO, LEED, or some other type issued by an external governing body. Change can also be brought about because of new union demands or contracts. Or it can reflect internal, corporate directives or mandates such as the introduction of, or changes to, standard business practices, company information retention and protection practices, procurement of goods or services, human resource policies, enhanced health and safety procedures, etc.

However, there is another big reason for introducing a change project within an organization – one that you don't often hear about in business school.

There are projects or change initiatives which have little to do with meeting any of the goals cited above, and usually have more to do with meeting the ego needs of the project champion. We at Emergence One International refer to this as "image-driven" change:

4   *Image-driven change* – Unfortunately, at times projects become active that have little to do with providing a solution, realizing an opportunity, or complying with a regulation or mandate. They usually launch when a new executive or manager takes over a department, division, or an entire company. The new boss cannot articulate an objective need or case for change but feels he must "do something" to either demonstrate authority or differentiate himself from his predecessor. Because he has enough power or autonomy in the new position, he can usually forgo the formality of developing a business case for change, since no one would either think of, or dare, question it. Though this type of change rarely benefits the company, it does enable this person to satisfy some ego-driven need to exert power and influence.

If an idea or proposal is worth pursing, then the first step is to determine project scope. Key executives need to be aligned on the business case, understanding of the potential benefits and risks, perceptions regarding the strategic fit, timing of the initiative, and general acceptance of the associated costs. The Emergence One Method provides specific tools and techniques for testing executive alignment.

Provided that the above occurs, then the project proceeds to Phase 2. If not, then the project, for whatever reason, may not be deemed worthy to proceed at this time.

Phase 2 – Assess Alternatives

The objective of this phase is to make sure that all viable options (alternatives) are considered before committing to one predetermined course of action. In essence, at the end of this project phase, the project team will tell the project review board that: "We have assessed numerous options (alternatives) for this project, and we feel that choice (x) is the recommended solution for the following reasons...."

This phase is critical since many project stakeholders have a tendency to jump immediately into pursuing one "solution" rather than considering other viable (and better) options that may be available. Often times, there is a good deal of subtle or even overt corporate politics which come into play in this phase, as various project stakeholders try to push their preferred or favored options. Therefore, designing an objective evaluation process than can withstand the scrutiny of the most strident critics is a key task of this phase. In order to achieve objectivity, not only does a rigorous assessment and selection methodology need to be devised, but the right balance of stakeholder needs and inputs must be gathered and factored in.

Since estimated costs and anticipated organizational impacts are further refined in this phase, the main risk at this phase is that the organization begins to get "cold feet," once people understand the full impact of the initiative. Another big risk is that there may not be uniformed alignment amongst key executives as to the option selected, causing turf wars and clashing egos to bring the project to a standstill.

Note that when assessing alternatives, it is usually necessary to develop only high-level project design plans. A detailed design of the chosen option occurs in the next phase.

Phase 3 – Detail Design

If alignment and support for the option are achieved, the project will soon find itself in Phase 3 – Detail Design.

Since Phase 2 provided project stakeholders with only high-level designs, the main idea behind Phase 3 is to develop and get buy-in on the detailed designs before committing to the time and expense necessary to realize these designs. After all, you would not want to start buying the materials and building a house if there were still debates regarding the design.

Part of the challenge of this phase is securing the appropriate subject matter expertise required to produce designs that can achieve project objectives in a cost-effective and efficient manner. In addition, in larger organizations, there are numerous corporate compliance policies and procedures that need to be understood and taken into account.

Perhaps an even greater challenge, though, comes with stakeholder engagement. Designs that are created in isolation, away from the broader organization, often miss their mark when it comes to satisfying the needs and expectations of those they are trying to satisfy. However, developing superior designs through greater stakeholder involvement comes at a price. Managing "scope creep," resolving incompatible requirements, dealing with various levels of resistance, and determining what is best versus what is easiest or most popular are all challenges which affect time, scope, budget, stakeholder adoption, and the potential ROI.

If most of the stakeholder management issues are adequately addressed in Phase 3, then Phase 4 should be fairly smooth sailing.

Phase 4 – Build and Final Prep

The main goal of this phase is to build out the designs from Phase 3 into something more tangible, testing or verifying their integrity, and ensuring that everything is ready and set for the deployment/implementation stage. Some professionals believe that "Final Prep" also refers to preparing the workforce for the impending change. It is not. In the Emergence One Method, it is the final preparation of all deployment related materials as well as the final preparation of the solution itself that occurs.

Here, once again, the human factor can severely impact the scope, time-line, and budget of a project. Once recipients of the change get a more complete picture of what it is they will be receiving or how much of an impact something will have on them, then the trepidation, the second-guessing, and the requests for postponements or deferrals start to filter in.

There needs to be a rigorous method for handling scope-change requests, as well as a comprehensive, well structured deployment plan that accounts for all the human, technical, and organizational support elements. In addition, the Build and Final Prep phase is often times one of the longest, most labor-intensive phases. Therefore, developing an efficient, high-performing project team that has clear goals, objectives, and roles and responsibilities is paramount.

Phase 5 – Deploy/Implement

Since the organization has already significantly invested in the design and build of the change, chances are good that the project will proceed to the Deploy/Implement phase. The primary goal of this phase is to deploy the solution, along with the required support components, for the intended audiences. The second half of this phase is to monitor the success of the implementation so that appropriate remedial actions can be taken if needed.

Within this phase, even the best intentioned, most beneficially designed change programs can be rejected by the organization solely out of frustration with deployment and implementation-related issues.

Deployment plans and support materials should have been created and tested toward the latter half of Phase 4. But because so many teams typically get caught up in scrambling to meet deadlines around the build of a solution or design, testing and deployment planning often gets shortchanged. Therefore, it is not uncommon for the deployment and implementation phase to be more chaotic than expected.

There are two primary reasons for this chaos. One is that what may have looked sound in a lab or on a conference room whiteboard does not work as intended when deployed to the real world. This is especially true with more ambitious projects, where it is often difficult to factor in all the dynamics that a living, breathing organization can present. Therefore, the project team needs to make sure there are efficient means to evaluate the progress of an implementation and have contingency or back-up plans available if things go awry.

However, even if there is solution integrity, the organization can still reject it if there is a bungling of the deployment plan. The key to a successful deployment/implementation centers around the timing and coordination of several key components. These include logistics, training and competency development, the appropriate level of stakeholder communication and engagement, and the deployment of peripheral support, such as readily available reference materials and a ready and able help desk.

Many initiatives typically make the mistake of wrapping up and closing out the project soon after deployment and implementation. But as our "total project success" model indicates, the goal of a project or change initiative is not simply to deploy and implement something new, but to decisively realize a business benefit or value from the change. This is why the Emergence One Method has a sixth stage known as "Support, Sustain, Improve."

Phase 6 – Support, Sustain, and Enhance

If the components of a project or change initiative are not properly supported, then it is doubtful whether the change, and the subsequent business value, can ever be sustained. And unless the change is sustained, it can never be enhanced or improved upon to create additional business value.

One of the main risks of omitting this phase is that many who are involved in the project – from project sponsors down to the project team – becomes a little too eager to get to the finish line. As a result, they don't take the necessary steps to sustain the change or put in place the components required to fully realize the business benefits the initiative was designed to elicit.

There is also risk that the organization, after "trying out" the change, becomes disappointed with its perceived value or finds that utilizing workarounds is more efficient. After all, old habits die hard. Therefore, support to maintain the change needs to be provided in both a tangible manner (such as adjustments to compensation and performance rewards) as well as through more informal methods (for instance, encouragement and praise from management). Support can also take the form of corporate policies and compliance mandates, as well as consistently enforcing the appropriate consequences for non-compliance.

Phase Execution: *Key Principles and Caveats*

The Emergence One Method, provided in Part Two of this book, details all of the necessary instructions to utilize the method effectively. There are, however, several requirements and caveats that will improve the execution of the Emergence One Method.

Work One Phase at a Time

The E1 Method may seem overwhelming upon first glance, but team members should just work each concentrate on one phase at a time. For instance, if the team is in Phase 2, they should not be working on the activities or addressing the needs of a subsequent phase such as what may be found in Phase 3 or Phase 4. "Jumping ahead" puts the team at high risk of rework since, in most cases, the completion of one activity serves as an input to the next activity. Subsequent activities will be executed much more efficiently once previous phase activities have been completed.

All Steps Are NOT Mandatory

Each project phase has its own set of key activities and, in certain cases, subtasks as well. One of the first steps of each phase is to plan out the exact set of activities and tasks needed to achieve the objectives of that phase. *Therefore, depending upon the size and scope of the project, not all activities will apply to all projects.* In its purest form, all activities provided in the unadulterated version of the Emergence One Method are strongly recommended in order to achieve project objectives. If the nature or scope of a particular project renders some of these activities irrelevant (or a "nice to have" as opposed to a "need to have,") they should be considered candidates for deletion. Do not execute an activity just for the sake of it. Only execute the activities that will add value.

Dedicated Project Management and Change Management Resources

While the approach assumes a Project Manager will have a Change Management counterpart and vice versa, a particularly experienced project professional can play both roles (with some occasional assistance), provided he or she has the breadth, depth, *and bandwidth* to manage both project disciplines. However, this is rare and is not always feasible in mid-size or large projects.

Role Descriptions Are Recommendations Only

The E1 Method provides recommendations for who does what on a project. For example, it assumes that a competent project manager can add value in certain areas, and that a competent change lead can add value in complementary areas. *These are recommendations only,* based upon typical competency profiles of project managers and change practitioners. It is up to the individuals on the project to decide who is best at doing what.

Adding Activities

Depending upon the nature and scope of the project, additional activities may be required. If supplemental activities are being included, be sure that those activities include inputs from both the project manager and the change lead if appropriate.

Taking Shortcuts

Activities should be skipped only if they are not relevant, not because there isn't enough time to complete them. Taking shortcuts will lessen the effectiveness of the Emergence One Method. Teams tend to take shortcuts when they are scrambling to meet deadlines, or conversely, when a project is running extremely well and the project team thus starts to cut corners.

Sequencing Activities

There is also a recommended sequence of activities since the output of one activity often (but not always) serves as an input to the next activity. There may be minor variations in the sequencing of activities depending upon the project and critical path needs. For example, the Emergence One Method calls for engaging executive stakeholders immediately after the creation of the initial project scope so that the scope can be tested with them. In some cases though, project team members may rather prefer to interview that set of stakeholders prior to the creation of the initial scope rather than test their reactions afterwards.

Organizing Tasks into Subtasks

Within certain activities, the Emergence One Method provides some of the more obvious subtasks. Depending upon the preferences of the project professionals involved, many of the activities listed within each phase of the project life cycle can be further broken down into subtasks for more precise project planning.

Incorporating Other Tools

The Emergence One Method does not provide details on how to execute many tried-and-true project management or change management tools and techniques such as PERT (Program Evaluation Review Technique), RACI (Responsible, Accountable, Consult, Inform) charts, financial or resource allocation formulas, organizational readiness assessments, or developing a Work Breakdown Structure (WBS). Not all projects require these tools or techniques. Where the employment of these tools or techniques would be beneficial, there already exists ample literature.

"Deliverables" versus "Documentation"

Most activities will have one or more outputs or deliverables attached to them. As discussed previously, the term *deliverable* may not always indicate a formal deliverable that is submitted for client review and approval. It may refer to simple, informal documentation for use as internal project team reference material.

Being Flexible about Titles and Naming Conventions

There is great confusion and differences of opinion regarding the titles of project documents and deliverables. For example, some consider a "project charter" to be a one-page document assigning authority to a project manager, while others consider a project charter to contain the project scope, objectives, deliverables, and so forth. Similarly, to some people an "organizational readiness assessment" may mean measuring the workforce's emotional readiness to accept change, while to others it may be a "Go/No Go" checklist covering logistics, technical readiness, etc., just prior to go-live. The description of the document or deliverable is more important than the title.

Do Not Let Project Documentation Hinder Project Momentum

It is important that project documentation or the creation of deliverables not hinder project momentum. The level of documentation should be appropriately scaled for the task at hand. How much granularity is required of project documents and deliverables needs to be established among project stakeholders. The goal is not to create documentation that is so detailed or overwritten that it will inhibit the appropriate stakeholders from reviewing or utilizing the material. Likewise, there is no need to create overproduced deliverables by adding in over-the-top graphics and illustrations which do more to dazzle than to inform.

In Part Two of the book...

Part Two of the book will present the Emergence One Method. There are six chapters, with each chapter covering one phase of the methodology.

Unlike traditional methodologies that simply explain what to do and when to do it, the Emergence One Method often explains the reasoning behind each activities as well as real-world insights and caveats to help increase execution quality. At the conclusion of each phase, information is provided on where the reader can download additional tools and templates relating to the Emergence One Method.

Part Two

The Emergence One Method
for Total Project Success

Version 2.0

A Comprehensive Project Lifecycle Methodology
That Integrates and Enhances All Essential Project Management
and Organizational Change Management Tasks

Chapter 7

Phase 1: Project Initiation

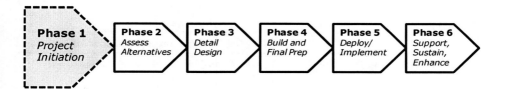

Introduction to Phase 1

There are many people who want to change the world. This is an important thing to keep in mind whenever we take the first steps to initiate and define a project. However, many people, whether they are project sponsors looking to shake up the company, project managers looking to expand the scope of their project as a way to boost their reputations, or technical people looking for all the bleeding-edge bells and whistles, often look to do more than is truly needed.

Then there are "the others": those in the organization who look at the potential organizational impacts and associated project costs and who will try to minimize or kill the project. While some in the change management field might accuse these individuals of being "resistant to change," this phrase is rather condescending and dismissive of what may be very legitimate concerns. There is such a thing as moving too fast or changing too much, as there is risk in not changing at all. This is why it is so critical to develop a strong business case, develop a scope that incorporates the perspectives of numerous stakeholders, and execute a process in which the opportunity will be evaluated in an objective, cross-functional manner. The main objective of this phase is to convincingly answer the question, "Do we have a potential, viable project here that will create a worthwhile opportunity or address a pressing company need?"

Although every phase in the project life cycle is important, it is absolutely critical to get Phase 1 right. A common mistake is to have the project stakeholder jump into creating solutions without really knowing what they are trying to accomplish and why. Unless the project is properly defined, one will never achieve stakeholder alignment, secure the right project resources, or efficiently work through the subsequent project phases. Phase 1 lays the foundation for the subsequent project phases.

Phase 1 – Project Initiation			
#	Activity		Subtask
1.01	Establish the Project Triad	1.01.00	None
1.02	Begin Initial Scope Development	1.02.01	Gather initial project inputs
		1.02.02	Review lessons learned
		1.02.03	Draft preliminary scope and business case
		1.02.04	Create project stakeholder map
1.03	Conduct Phase 1 Startup Activities	1.03.01	Identify prominent Phase 1 stakeholders
		1.03.02	Draft Phase 1 plan/approach
1.04	Determine Team Charter/Protocols	1.04.01	Develop project charter
		1.04.02	Determine information management protocols
		1.04.03	Determine project team communications protocols
1.05	Select and Align Phase 1 Project Resources	1.05.01	Select and align project team resources
		1.05.02	Select and align Project Review Board members
1.06	Gather Inputs from Phase 1 Stakeholders	1.06.01	Conduct an executive stakeholder analysis
		1.06.02	Gather input from project contributors
1.07	Define Business Case and Scope	1.07.00	None
1.08	Develop Project Roadmap	1.08.00	None

Phase 1 – Project Initiation			
1.09	Develop Stakeholder Communication and Engagement Strategy	1.09.01	Determine communication and engagement strategy
		1.09.02	Embed key communication/engagement events into the project roadmap
1.10	Initiate Risk Management Process	1.10.01	Determine risk methodology
		1.10.02	Risk Identification
		1.10.03	Risk Assessment
		1.10.04	Risk Mitigation Approach
		1.10.05	Risk Control
1.11	Prepare for Phase Gate 1	1.11.01	Refine business case and project scope
		1.11.02	Vet/test Phase Gate deliverables with stakeholders
		1.11.03	Assess Phase Gate readiness
		1.11.04	Design the Phase Gate 1 event
		1.11.05	Create and distribute pre-read
		1.11.06	Conduct a Phase Gate 1 preparation session
1.12	Conduct Phase Gate 1	1.12.00	None
1.13	Communicate Outcomes/Next Steps	1.13.00	None
1.14	Phase 1 Wrap-up	1.14.01	Document lessons learned, pertinent observations, and outstanding needs
		1.14.02	Celebrate!

Activity 1.01 – Establish the Project Triad

The "project triad" is the foundational structure of the Emergence One Method. It consists of three of the most critical roles that will be present throughout the entire project life cycle. These three roles will also have the most interaction with one another during the project life cycle.

115

The roles include:

1 ***The Project Sponsor*** – is an executive who will be sponsoring the change initiative. This role is critical since the sponsor will champion the project throughout the organization, have the authority to solicit and allocate funding for the project, and help remove obstacles which impede progress. Sometimes the project sponsor will delegate a portion of his or her role to someone from the business who will act as the project lead (but not as the project manager). Even if this is the case, the project sponsor must be accountable for the success of the project. In order for that to happen, it must be a person of sufficient authority who can make the decisions and allocate the necessary funding to make things happen.

2 ***The Project Manager*** – will be responsible for the day-to-day operations of the project, as well as crafting and delivering the solution that will realize the project vision. The project manager is responsible for integrating all of the deliverables and inputs from the various project work streams.

3 ***The Change Lead*** – will be responsible for anticipating, identifying, and mitigating most of the human, political, and organizational change factors which can inhibit project momentum, quality, and success.

All three members of the Project Triad should understand that they need to work in conjunction with one another in order to achieve each of the five elements of total project success: on time, within budget, according to specifications, adoption throughout the organization, and realization of business value.

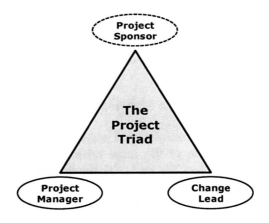

Figure 7.1. *The Project Triad*

Generally, the one role within the Project Triad that is most likely to falter is that of the project sponsor. Despite a spate of articles, tools, and workshops addressing the importance of project change sponsorship, sponsors have consistently proven to be fickle at best when it comes to adhering to any preconceived notions of their role.

There are a number of reasons for this:

- *Sponsors are corporate executives first, project sponsors second* – Corporate executives have numerous responsibilities beyond project sponsorship.

- *Project sponsors may take a "wait and see approach"* – This can occur if the project does not yet have any political momentum behind it.

- *Access is difficult* – You have an executive sponsor who is open to developing change sponsorship behaviors. You have a senior-level change practitioner who has the skills and perceived credibility to offer these services. You have the calendar of the executive sponsor, which shows just one hour of free time, four months into the future. Enough said.

- *It is difficult to change someone's nature* – Effective project change sponsorship requires the sponsor to exhibit certain behaviors – for instance, the ability to show a lot of enthusiasm and to rally people to the cause or display a willingness to challenge the status quo. The problem is that some executives are introverts and have a reserved nature. It will take a lot more than a workshop or a few coaching sessions to change the personalities of these project "sponsors" and turn them into revolutionary cheerleaders.

- *The ego is big* – Executives are often times in senior level positions because they have a track record of success. Many of them already think they know what it takes to successfully sponsor a project (whether they do or not) and don't recognize their need to improve in this area.

- *Too much status differential between a sponsor and a change sponsorship advisor* – I meet with lots of eager, budding twenty-something change management consultants who tell me they would love the opportunity to work with senior executives on change strategy. The only problem is that the desire isn't mutual.

As John Kotter states in his classic 1996 book *Leading Change:* "No one person, even a monarch-like CEO, is ever able to develop the right vision, communicate it to large numbers of people, eliminate all the key obstacles, generate short-term wins, lead and manage dozens of change projects, and anchor new approaches deep in the organization's culture." Kotter then recommends the creation of "guiding coalitions" to help with the change effort.

The Emergence One Method incorporates and expands upon this concept. We do not assume one sponsor can "do it all." Therefore, one person is given the official title of "Project Sponsor," but numerous organizational leaders are asked to engage in various sponsorship-like behaviors, depending upon their position and innate strengths.

In the end, we construct a Project Triad which is supported by a Project Support Network made up of other key executives who support the project by *augmenting the project sponsor's role and responsibilities.*

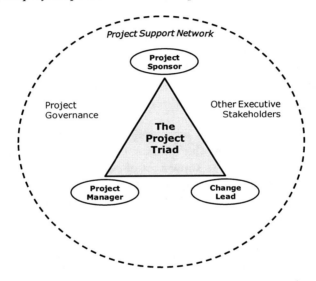

Figure 7.2.   *Project Support Network*

1.01 Outputs/Deliverables

-   Roles and responsibilities for the project sponsor, project manager, and change lead

Activity 1.02 – Begin Initial Scope Development

Before officially starting up Phase 1 activities, the members of the Project Triad should gather the required information necessary to begin initial scope development.

1.02.01 Gather initial project inputs

Projects are generally initiated to provide a solution to real or potential problems, realize an opportunity, or comply with either an internal or external mandate or compliance regulation. The project sponsor should have a grasp of the reasoning, and the change lead should probe to make sure that the reasoning is valid (since project managers generally follow the directions of the project sponsor, the change lead is usually in a better position to probe). Any additional project inputs, including ideas on scope, timeline, and the thoughts of other stakeholders, should be gathered and used as inputs for the initial scope development.

1.02.02 Review lessons learned

Review any available "lessons learned" documentation from previous organizational projects. The information contained in those documents can be a potential treasure trove of valuable insights and caveats.

1.02.03 Draft preliminary scope and business case

At this point, there should be enough information to draft preliminary scope and business case documents. Inputs for a more formal scope and business case document will be provided later on. For now, it is sufficient to get a rough idea of what is most likely in scope, out of scope, or a possible "Undecided" element of the project. For creating the preliminary business case, some talking points on what the business need and expected benefits of this project are should suffice.

1.02.04 Create a project stakeholder map

Many change practitioners and other project professionals conflate a stakeholder map with an executive stakeholder analysis. A stakeholder map looks at all the *departments or groups* the project will need to intersect with, whereas an executive stakeholder analysis looks at the influence and support of influential key *individuals*.

(Note – As discussed in Chapter 6, terminology for various deliverables and documents vary amongst practitioners and organizations. For example, the term *stakeholder map* can have numerous interpretations. Focus more on the description and content of a deliverable or a document than on its title.)

Identifying and managing stakeholders can be made more efficient if stakeholders are divided into three major groupings, or tiers, based upon their relationship to the initiative. Each of these stakeholder tiers can then be further subdivided if it has more than one subgroup within it (for examples, managers and employees may be listed as two separate groups even though they both may be change recipients).

Table 7.1.   *Example of a Project Stakeholder Map*

Relationship to the Project/Initiative	Likely Candidates
TIER 1: **Senior Leaders and Key Decision Makers** – Those who may visibly champion the project or who provide the necessary resources and high-level support to keep the project moving forward	• Executive team • Project governance • Those who control project funding • Those who control access to other project-related resources
TIER 2: **Project Contributors** – Those who will provide inputs or assist with the coordination and deployment of the effort	• Core project team members • Extended project team members • Customers engaged in providing requirements/design feedback • Corporate governance committee (which promotes adherence to company standards, policies, and procedures) • Relevant support organizations (e.g., HR, procurement, corporate communications)
TIER 3: **Change Recipients** – Those who are directly impacted by the change	• End-users/employees • Other impacted individuals, groups, or departments • External stakeholders, such as those involved with the supply chain

The project sponsor can typically give insight into what groups this project will impact. The project manager, who generally has the most technical expertise of the three, can provide input on any groups with which the project may need to integrate or that govern certain standards (such as the IT infrastructure group). The change lead can think about how best to manage the needs and expectations of these different stakeholder groups.

Generally, Tier 1 stakeholders, such as senior leaders and other key change enablers, are most instrumental to project success from Phase 1 through Phase 4; Tier 2 stakeholders, such as the various project contributors, are key players during Phase 2 through Phase 5; and Tier 3 stakeholders, who are the change recipients, are the most influential in Phases 5 and 6. Therefore, most of our Phase 1 stakeholder management activities will center on Tier 1 stakeholders: the executives and other key decision makers.

The project stakeholder map will be an iterative document that will be updated as the project's scope becomes further refined.

1.02 Outputs/Deliverables

- Documentation of project inputs (which includes thoughts and ideas not yet captured)
- List of "lessons learned" that can be applied to this initiative
- Preliminary, high-level scope and business case (internal working document)
- Initial stakeholder map

Activity 1.03 – Conduct Phase 1 Startup Activities

The Emergence One integrated approach recommends a standard set of startup activities for each of the project phases. Depending upon the phase, the startup activities will vary somewhat between phases.

With a project life cycle approach, it is necessary to concentrate only on the needs of the current phase execution. The Emergence One Method takes this same approach with stakeholder management, by looking at who the prominent stakeholders are for each phase so that it can target those stakeholders who have immediate needs. It holds off on addressing the needs of stakeholders who do not have impending needs.

Since one of the main goals of stakeholder management is meeting the needs and expectations of the phase-related stakeholders, this activity must be completed before finalizing the approach for that phase.

1.03.01 Identify needs/expectations of Phase 1 stakeholders

Referring to the Stakeholder Map, created in the previous activity, identify the prominent *individual* stakeholders from each of the three main stakeholder groups who may be relevant to achieving Phase 1 objectives.

Because most of the activities in Phase 1 will center on the viability of the project/change opportunity, our most prominent stakeholders deserve our attention. They are the executives involved in reviewing, approving, and supporting the project launch. They may also include any corporate departments that are responsible for ensuring that certain standards are followed or policies adhered to. Mandated standards and policies often affect project scope.

A later step will determine how best to engage these stakeholders, test out the understanding of their needs and expectations, and take the necessary course of action to address those needs and expectations. In the meantime, the project sponsor should be able to provide enough insights to get the process started.

Listed below are some common examples of needs and expectations of Phase 1 stakeholders. This list is not comprehensive.

Table 7.2. *Examples of Stakeholder Needs and Expectations for Phase 1*

Major Stakeholder Groups	Stakeholders Prominent in Phase 1	Common Needs and Expectations During Phase 1

TIER 1 Stakeholders:
 	
Senior Leaders/ Key Decision Makers
	Company Executives	• Is this the right initiative to fund and support at this time?
		• Will this initiative conflict with other projects or the strategic direction of the company?
		• Do we have the right people in place sponsoring and managing this initiative?
		• As the project progresses, how do we know there will be "no surprises" regarding project direction, scope, or estimated costs?
		• Is there is a compelling business case for change that:
		  ○ Aligns with strategic intent,
		  ○ Aligns with organizational values, and
		  ○ Benefits the business?

	Project Sponsor	• Will this project be a career-maker or a career-breaker? • Are there any hidden political agendas that might undermine support for this initiative? • Besides helping to secure funding, how else can I effectively sponsor this initiative? • How will I be kept in the loop about the project team's progress? • Are there qualified and committed Project Review Board members who will do more than just "rubber stamp" the team's work?

Major Stakeholder Groups	Stakeholders Prominent in Phase 1	Common Needs and Expectations During Phase 1
	Project Review Board Members	• What is my exact role as a Project Review Board member? • Why was I recruited for this role? • Do I have the requisite knowledge and insights to provide valuable feedback and make strong recommendations?
TIER 2 Stakeholders: Project Contributors	**Phase 1 Project Team**	• Am I joining a winning initiative that will increase my visibility and help my career? • Will I be able to contribute and stand out?
	Corporate Governance Representatives	• Does the project team understand any corporate standards, policies, or procedures they must comply with? • Will we have an opportunity to review the project scope document to ensure there are no areas of concern?
TIER 3 Stakeholders: Change Recipients	N/A	N/A

NOTE: This is a generic assessment of stakeholder needs and expectations. Depending upon the scope and nature of the project, as well as the overall structure of the company, other major stakeholder groups could also be involved in Phase 1.

The Emergence One Method is built around managing the typical needs and expectations that are most pronounced in each project life cycle phase. The change lead, in consultation with the project manager, needs to make sure that these needs and expectations are addressed when finalizing the Phase 1 approach in the next activity.

1.03.02 Draft Phase 1 plan/approach

The Project Triad should agree upon and draft the approach for completing Phase 1. Although the Emergence One Method can serve as a blueprint, the project manager, with inputs from the change lead, may prefer to develop a more detailed project plan and schedule that modifies the exact regiment prescribed by the Emergence One Method.

While a project plan discusses the overall approach regarding how activities will be managed and conducted, a project schedule is the series of tasks and their expected duration (including start and end dates) arranged in a logical, sequential manner. Compared with other phases, rigorous project planning may not be as important in Phase 1 as it will be in later phases, especially Phases 3, 4, and 5; however, that should not be an excuse to apply rigor too lightly in Phase 1.

It is important that the change lead not develop a different project plan or schedule of activities from the overall project plan. Nor should a separate "change management" work stream be set up within the project plan or schedule. After all, an important principle of the Emergence One Method is that there is no separation between project management activities and change management activities. Instead, there is only one set of activities, comprising both project management and change management inputs. (This principle will be further illustrated in many of the activity descriptions listed throughout each project phase.)

1.03 Outputs/Deliverables

- Stakeholder management documentation
- Phase 1 approach

Activity 1.04 – Determine Team Charter/Protocols

NOTE: In Phase 1, in relation to other phases, the project team is likely to be fairly small. Therefore, it may make sense to either do an abbreviated version of this activity or push this activity out to subsequent phases.

What should be contained in a project charter will vary amongst organizations and practitioners. The idea behind a project charter is for the team to understand what its purpose is, how it will operate, and what the project's deliverables are. Since there are also behavioral components to team operations, the project manager and change lead should work jointly in executing this activity.

Because information management and team communications are such critical areas for a project team's success, these two areas are called out separately. Establishing protocols early in the project life cycle will contribute immensely to having an organized, well-run project.

1.04.01 Develop Project Charter

The Project Charter may include the following:

- **Purpose** – What is the overall purpose of this project team, and what are the immediate Phase 1 goals the team needs to focus on?

- **Decision Making and Governance** – Will the team make decisions by consensus, majority rule, or a more authoritative approach like allowing the project manager to decide?
- **Issues Management** – What is the issue management process going to look like? Who will be responsible for identifying, recording, and following up on issues? Will issues be tracked in a specific issues database, or will they be tracked in a more informal, ad-hoc manner? What will the process for escalating issues that are not effectively resolved?
- **External Communications** – What will be the standard protocol for handling information requests from people who are external to the project team? How can various team members represent the project in a consistent manner?
- **Meetings** – How often should team members meet? How should they prepare for a meeting, for instance, when team members complete a status or progress report template beforehand? What will be the standard meeting structure?

1.04.02 Determine information management protocols

Project documentation has a way of quickly building up, even on relatively small projects. One driver of project momentum is having commonly understood and adhered-to practices for information management.

Information management concerns itself with how project information will be organized, stored, retrieved, shared, and retained. Projects that lack predetermined information protocols run the risk of version control problems, deleting older work which may contain important baseline data or historical information, creating nonsensical file names, and having a disorganized file structure (making the timely retrieval of key documents difficult).

In order to avoid the above risks, as well as to facilitate the efficient management of information, the project manager, change lead, or other designated team member needs to develop the parameters for information management:

- Who will have access to what documents?
- Should there be a policy on what documents team members can download to thumb drives or other external devices that can be easily lost or misplaced?
- What will be our storage standard (repository) for project documents?
- What will be our file structure?
- Should we utilize standard naming conventions?

- How will we maintain version control?
- What will be the document retention strategy?
- What corporate information management policies must we comply with?

1.04.03 Determine project team communication protocols

Project communications typically come in two flavors:

1 **Project Team Communications** – facilitates communication standards and expectations within the project team.
2 **Organizational Communications and Engagement Activities** - target stakeholder groups outside of the immediate project team. These activities usually have the goal of informing, aligning, and mobilizing project stakeholders who are not part of the immediate project team.

Since there is limited information to distribute to the broader organization at this time, Activity 1.04.03 will concern itself with intra-team communications.

Project team communications should be solidly in place prior to the on-boarding of additional project team members. Although the change lead typically manages intra-team as well as organizational communication, it is important that the project manager establish his or her expectations regarding communication protocols.

Some of the decisions that need to be made are as follows:

- What project information needs to be documented? What can remain as undocumented thoughts and opinions?
- If someone outside the project team requests information, should a particular person be responsible for providing that information so that information consistency can be achieved?
- How often will team members provide progress reports or status updates to the project manager? What form should these reports or updates take?
- Should there be standard expectations developed that will dictate how quickly a voice mail or email will be returned?
- Should team members utilize certain templates to document or communicate information?
- For larger projects, how much information needs to be shared amongst the various work streams?

1.04 Outputs/Deliverables

- Documented project team charter/team protocols

Activity 1.05 – Select and Align Phase 1 Project Resources

In Phase 1, the project sponsor, project manager, and change lead will need to expand beyond the Project Triad structure and begin to involve more people in the project. They will most likely need to gather project team resources as well as recruit members for the critical Project Review Board.

Activity 1.05.01 Select and align project team resources

Since different project phases have different goals and objectives, the composition and skill sets of project resources will likely differ from phase to phase. For Phase 1, the Project Triad will need project team resources who can further build out the project *opportunity* and present their case to the Project Review Board at the end of Phase 1. Generally, a large team is not needed, nor is a full-time commitment always required. Therefore, finding appropriate resources for this phase may not be as challenging as it will be for subsequent phases.

Some things to keep in mind when selecting project planning resources:

1   The change lead may be able to offer the project manager some additional ideas on what sort of behavioral characteristics or personality attributes would be beneficial to have on the Phase 1 team.
2   One should determine how long the resource will be needed for. For example, in Phase 1, the time commitment is usually briefer than in other phases.

After you have selected the project resources, get them up to speed on the project: align them on the initial scope and objectives, the protocols and charter developed in the previous activity, as well as the initial stakeholder map.

1.05.02 Select and align Project Review Board members

The Project Review Board is a small group of usually no more than five or six key executives. They are responsible for reviewing the project at Phase Gate meetings and deciding whether or not the project should terminate, be suspended, be reworked, or advance to the next phase. An alternative role is for the Project Review Board not to render a decision, but instead make a recommendation to the project sponsor (or other executive decision maker) or project governance committee, who will then make the final decision. (Project governance is listed as a Phase 2 activity but may be brought into this phase if necessary.)

Identifying the right individuals for the Project Review Board and securing their commitment are critical activities. The time commitment to being a Project Review Board member is fairly minimal, but the responsible is great. After all, he or she will be deciding whether or not the organization should be investing precious time, money, and other resources in an unproven initiative.

Project Review Board members should be credible, senior-level people within the company whose decisions regarding project team Phase Gate recommendations will be respected throughout the organization. You do not want others to second-guess the decisions of the Project Review Board. It can be beneficial to have the Project Review Board comprise executives from other business units who do not have a direct stake or personal bias in the solutions being proposed. They will be less prone to political influences.

Project Review Board members need to commit to attending every Phase Gate session, thoroughly review any pre-read material that is sent out beforehand, and be available for informal vetting sessions with team members on an as-needed basis. They should also have the skills and ability to accurately assess the quality of project phase execution and the resulting deliverables.

1.05 Outputs/Deliverables

- Phase 1 project team resource commitments
- Project Review Board commitments

Activity 1.06 – Gather Inputs from Phase 1 Stakeholders

It is important that the scope of the project not be defined solely by those on the immediate Phase 1 project team. To develop a more accurate scope, it may be necessary to reach out to certain project stakeholders, identified in previous activities. These include executive stakeholders, whose ongoing support will be critical throughout the entire project life cycle, and project contributors who are needed to provide inputs on project scope and other parameters.

1.06.01 Conduct an executive stakeholder analysis

A stakeholder analysis is a common technique in project and change management. It is used for understanding the needs and level of support of those who can either influence the success of and/or will be impacted by the project.

The executive stakeholder analysis provides foundational information to allow for planning engagements, aligning executives, mitigating political issues, and designing project support strategies going forward. It also serves as the foundation for leadership action plans and sponsorship plans (remember

– this approach believes that successful projects have a coalition of sponsors, not just one). The analysis is likely to contain highly sensitive information and should not be placed on any project shared drive or collaborative work space.

Like many deliverables, the exact format of the executive stakeholder analysis will vary amongst practitioners or service providers. Since this is not a formal deliverable that will be shared or submitted for approval, the change lead need not worry about having a fine-tuned, aesthetically pleasing document. However, it should contain a sufficient amount of actionable information. After all, there is no sense in doing an executive stakeholder analysis unless it will contribute to useful action.

Table 7.3. *Excerpt from the Emergence One Executive Stakeholder Analysis Tool*

Stakeholder Name	Level of Influence 1 - 5	Level of Support 1 – 5	What Are Their Key Needs, Issues, and/or Concerns?
For larger projects, may also list the stakeholder's title or department	Rate level of influence on project success from 1 (low) to 5 (high)	Rate level of support for project goals and objectives from 1 (low) to 5 (high)	
Stakeholder A			
Stakeholder B			
Stakeholder C, etc.			

Because *executive* stakeholders are usually pressed for time, and most don't necessarily like to be "analyzed," Emergence One typically combines executive stakeholder assessment activities with other engagement activities, such as gathering inputs for project scope or providing a debriefing from one of the Phase Gate meetings.

For Phase 1, the stakeholder analysis can be completed by meeting with executives first, gathering their inputs and feelings regarding the potential initiative, and filling out the stakeholder analysis tool afterwards.

1.06.02 Gather input from project contributors

Depending upon the output of Activity 1.03.01, there may not be many people from the project resources stakeholder group who can provide inputs to the business case and project scope at this time. Remember, the objective of Phase 1 is not so much to determine *how* we should execute the project, but *if* we should execute the project. Future-state needs within this phase should still be at a high level.

If the project is large and complex, though, there may be corporate standards, policies, and procedures to adhere to. If that is the case, then the appropriate project team resource should contact the governing organization to see what they are and then incorporate them into the project givens in the next activity.

1.06 Outputs/Deliverables

- Relevant inputs to business case and project scope documents
- Updated Phase 1 approach

Activity 1.07 – Define Business Case and Project Scope

NOTE: There are many different opinions on what should be contained within a business case or project scope document. It is usually best to follow the advice of the client organization and to precisely meet their expectations.

If a project manager and a change lead have been assigned to a corporate initiative, there is a good chance that a compelling opportunity for some sort of change exists, at least in some people's eyes. However, just because a senior manager or executive sees a compelling opportunity does not mean that others will view the opportunity as equally compelling. Therefore, there is a need for a business case and other supporting materials that make the case for change.

Building on the preliminary business case and scope developed as part of Activity 1.02.03, the project team can start developing a more formal business case and scope document.

A business case justifies and sets forth the reasoning behind a project or corporate initiative. Generally, the more expensive, time-consuming, and/or transformational a project or initiative is expected to be, the more formal the business case document needs to be.

At a minimum, a good, solid business case should include most of the following:

1. **Executive Summary** – Generally, this should be written last, and should be no longer than a page or two in length.
2. **Vision and Purpose** – The vision and purpose should answer the essential questions of "what we are trying to accomplish and why."
3. **Objectives** – The more measurable the objective is, the better. A common approach to writing objectives is to use SMART: specific,

measurable, achievable, realistic, and time-bound. Project objectives should also be aligned with the strategic direction of the company.

4   **Value Proposition and Business Benefits** – This section includes what the initiative hopes to achieve in terms of business benefits, and how these will be measured. Expect any financial analysis provided in this section to be heavily scrutinized. Below are some of the categories business benefits fall into:
   - *Company growth* – increased market share or revenue growth
   - *Cost savings* – a decrease in the costs of operating, procurement of goods, etc.
   - *Cost avoidance* – a benefit that would reduce future costs, such as the growth of overhead expenses
   - *Increased customer satisfaction*

5   **Project Scope** – At this point in the project life cycle, the scope should be defined in high-level terms and should include what is in scope, out of scope, and still "Undecided." It is important that change management–related areas, such as items around stakeholder alignment, organizational adoption, competency development, be included as well. It is also helpful to list any assumptions or known "project givens."

6   **Critical Success Factors** – Although both the project sponsor and project manager will likely write this section, it is important that the change lead add in success factors around organizational/end-user adoption, visible sponsorship, adequate training, and other change management–related factors.

The business case is an iterative document that will be refined several times over as the project team further defines the project scope and delves into potential solutions.

When inviting more people to comment on and refine the scope, be aware of any personal agendas someone may have. The change lead (who should also be a skilled facilitator) would probably be the best one to facilitate a business-case-refinement work session, thereby allowing the project manager to participate alongside the others.

Table 7.4.   *Project Scope Example*

Scope Document	
Selection and Implementation of a New Financial Records Software Application	
In Scope	**Out of Scope**
• Selection of a new financial software system through an objective vendor evaluation and selection process • Customization of the system to fit current business processes • Implementation of system in all US locations • Creation and deployment of management action plans (MAPs) to help facilitate end-user adoption • End-user training material • Changes to policies and procedures to support new behaviors and processes	• Business process reengineering • Organizational redesign • Implementation of system in European locations • Delivery of end-user training (responsibility of the business, not the project team) • Ongoing support and maintenance of system

Undecided
• Implementation of system in South American locations • Modification of HR for Finance Department policies relating to the operation of the new system

Givens and Assumptions
Project Givens: • System will comply fully with all financial controls, including Sarbanes-Oxley • System will comply with all corporate information security standards • System will be able to integrate with field-based financial systems
Project Assumptions: • New system will not require any major changes to current IT hardware infrastructure • System will conform to existing company processes • Subject matter experts from finance will be available for system development and testing • Project sponsors will visibly support and champion the project • Adequate resources will be made available to properly prepare the organization for change

1.07 Output/Deliverable

- Initial business case and project scope document

Activity 1.08 – Develop Project Roadmap

One of the project planning team's main tasks is to develop a high-level project roadmap. It is important to note that *a roadmap is not the same as a project plan*. A roadmap is often a high-level visual representation of how to get from Phase 1 through to Phase 6. It is used to show project decision makers what the general approach will be going forward, as well as to orient the team members to the "big picture."

There are many different formats for a project roadmap. Check first to see if there is a common format in use within the organization and, if appropriate, modify it to reflect the six-phase Emergence One project life cycle model.

Regardless of format, most project roadmaps contain several of the following features:

1   An overview of the project life cycle methodology being used. Will it be the six-phase Emergence One model, or will the E1 Method be used to augment a standardized approach already in use?
2   Key activities and major outputs or deliverables those activities produce
3   Key decision or review points (usually at the end of each phase)

Often times, change practitioners come up with their own "change management roadmap." This is fine and may provide the level of detail necessary to help align a large change management team. However, there is no reason why the project should have one roadmap which contains the project management structure, technical, architectural, business, etc. milestones and deliverables but *not* the change management milestones and deliverables. Such a process would separate the change management team from the other project teams and make the change team look like mavericks who don't want to, or know how to, integrate with everyone else.

1.08 Outputs/Deliverables

- Project roadmap

Activity 1.09 – Develop Stakeholder Communication and Engagement Strategy

Before getting into the creation of the communication and engagement strategy, it is important to differentiate between what is considered to be "communication" as opposed to what is considered "engagement." Even experienced communication practitioners sometimes get the two confused.

Communication, within the context of this approach, is considered to be primarily static, unidirectional messaging. On the other hand, engagement activities are dynamic interactions between two or more individuals.

Table 7.5. *Examples of Communication Activities Versus Engagement Activities*

Communication Activities	Engagement Activities
• Emails	• Meetings
• Videos	• Interviews
• Memos	• Focus groups
• Handouts	• Work sessions
• Intranet postings	• Town-hall meetings
• Posters and flyers	• Phone conversations
• Voicemail messages	• "Lunch and learn" events
• Bulletin board postings	• Small-scale conference calls
• Large-scale conference calls	• Unscheduled office "drop-bys"
• Presentation materials	• Informal hallway conversations

1.09.01 Determine communication and engagement strategy

Now that the initial project approach has been laid out in the project roadmap, the change lead (working in consultation with the project manager and project sponsor) is ready to draft the high-level communication and engagement strategy.

This strategy should *outline* (not detail) the general communication and engagement events for each key stakeholder group during every project phase.

Table 7.6. *High-Level Stakeholder Management Communication/Engagement Strategy*

	Phase 1	Phase 2	Phase 3	Phase 4	Phase 5	Phase 6
TIER 1 Stakeholders Senior Leaders/ Key Decision Makers	Engage one-on-one to test project scope and business case	Engage one-on-one to vet solutions and related costs	Comm. progress; engage one-on-one regarding risks	Provide change readiness update; engage via coaching sessions	Provide org. adoption updates	Provide information on business value realization
TIER 2 Stakeholders Project Contributors		Build project awareness; engage to understand compliance requirements	Provide project updates; engage in requirements gathering	Engage in testing/ feedback sessions	Comm. deployment progress; engage to ensure standards are being followed	
TIER 3 Stakeholders Change Recipients			Build project awareness; engage in requirements gathering	Provide more specific information; engage in testing	Provide guidance on why/how to adopt change; engage in training	Provide information on additional opportunities /resources; engage in improvement efforts

It is important to remember when developing this strategy that key messages should be is based upon the project phase. For examples, if end-users are the targeted audience, the key messages in the earlier phases of the project need only be "informational" in nature since the communication objective is to build awareness and nothing more. As the project matures, so will the informational needs of your audience. Therefore, after building some basic awareness, communications can convey to the audience a broader and deeper "knowledge" of the project and anticipated change impacts. And then, prior to implementing the change, more motivational and inspirational "We can do this!" kind of messaging is appropriate.

1.09.02 Embed key communication/engagement events into the project roadmap

Given the importance of communication and engagement activities, the project roadmap should have at least some of the major communication and

135

engagement events embedded within. How much detail should be added depends upon the actual structure and design of the roadmap. Certain key events, like town halls or company-wide information distributions, should definitely be included in the roadmap.

1.09 Outputs/Deliverables

- High-level communication and engagement strategy
- Updated project roadmap with embedded communication /engagement events

Activity 1.10 – Initiate the Risk Management Process

Project risk management is a critical iterative process throughout the project life cycle. Most professional project managers are familiar with risk management processes; however, they often do not consider change management issues to be part of the risk management scope. This is a mistake since change practitioners are keenly aware of the many human and organizational change risks that can impede project momentum or threaten success.

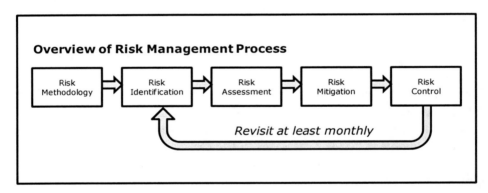

Figure 7.3. Overview of the Risk Management Process

1.10.01 Determine risk methodology

The risk management methodology Emergence One recommends is quite similar to the one espoused by the Project Management Institute.

- **Agree upon roles and responsibilities** – The Emergence One Method recommends that the change lead facilitate the risk management process. Since many (but certainly not all) risks involve people or politics, the change lead can play a central role in identifying and developing mitigation strategies which will help the project stay on time, within budget, according to spec, and on the path to total project success.

- **Agree upon timeline** – It is important for there to be an ongoing process of risk identification and mitigation, and not just a one-time "snapshot" of project risks. All teams need to agree on how often the risk process is revisited.

1.10.02 Risk Identification

Before conducting a risk identification session with the project team, it must first be determined what types of risks will be identified as part of this process.

Risks can fall into a number of different categories, including human/political/organizational risks, process risks, and technology risks.

It is important that risks related to decision making are not included as part of this process (for example: "Vendor A presents these sets of risks; Vendor B presents another set of risks). This risk management process is for project execution risks only.

Brainstorm potential risks. Once a list of risks is created, eliminate duplicates and record risks onto the risk management log. Be sure that the team does not conflate issues with risks, which is a common occurrence.

Table 7.7. *Differences between Issues and Risks*

Issues	Risks
• A *present* problem	• A *potential* problem
• Requires a decision to be made or specific action to be taken	• Requires a mitigation strategy to be developed
• A one-time event	• Can occur multiple times
• Gets resolved	• Gets managed

The risk management log can take a variety of formats, depending upon the preferences of the project professionals involved. Emergence One offers a risk management log template along with instructions that can be downloaded from www.emergenceone.com.

1.10.03 Risk Assessment

Now that risks have been identified, it is time for the team to assess them in terms of both probability (likelihood) and impact.

- *Likelihood or Probability of Occurrence* – On a scale from 1 (low) to 3 (high), what is the likelihood or probability of this risk occurring if the project team were to do nothing?
- *Potential Impact on the Project* – On a scale from 1 (low) to 3 (high), what would the potential impact be on the project if this risk fully manifested itself?

After the initial risk assessment is complete, have the team reevaluate the risks. What may have seemed like a "high-likelihood, high-impact risk" may now appear to be closer to a "medium-likelihood, medium-impact risk" in light of the other risks that have been identified.

1.10.04 Risk Mitigation approach

In this portion of the risk management section, the next three columns of the risk management log need to be considered. With the exception of the "Risk Owner" column, the mitigation approach and strategy can be created off-line and do not necessarily have to be part of the team's risk identification session.

- *Overview of the Mitigation Approach* – What mitigation strategy or approach will the risk owner take? This should only be a summary, and not the actually strategy or plan.
- *Risk Owner* – Who will be responsible for ensuring that the risk is mitigated? Note that the risk owner has ultimate responsibility for the risk but may delegate some of the risk mitigation activities to someone else. There should only be *one risk owner* per risk.
- *Contingency Plan Needed?* – Generally, if a risk has both high probability and high impact, it should have some sort of contingency plan if the original risk mitigation approach fails.

1.10.05 Risk Control

Risk control occurs after the mitigation approaches have been developed. It involves implementing the risk mitigation strategies and monitoring any progress. Risks which are high likelihood but lower impact are more likely to affect project timeline and budget. Risks which are high impact but lower likelihood are more likely to affect project completion.

It is recommended that the risk management log be updated on a regular basis (at least monthly) as well as prior to any Phase Gate meeting.

1.10 Outputs/Deliverables

- Documentation of the risk management process
- Team training material for the risk management process

- Risk management log (updated monthly)
- Risk summary snapshot (updated in conjunction with the risk log)

Activity 1.11 – Prepare for Phase Gate 1

1.11.01 Refine business case and project scope

In Activity 1.07, the first iteration of the business case and project scope was created. Now that the team has had more exposure to the project and various project stakeholders, it is usually beneficial to refine the business case and scope prior to the Phase Gate meeting. This is especially important in Phase 1 since the business case and scope will be the main deliverables for this phase.

1.11.02 Vet/test Phase Gate deliverables with stakeholders

The project review team generally comprises company executives. Executives hate surprises. Therefore, if anything in the business case or project scope documents may be unexpected or potentially controversial, it is best to informally test out this material beforehand by vetting with key stakeholders.

1.11.03 Assess Phase Gate readiness

The first step in preparing for the Phase Gate is for the team to honestly assess whether or not they are ready for a Phase Gate decision. In order to avoid an "End" or "Rework" verdict, the project manager and change lead should really push the team to honestly answer the following questions:

- Is our business case strong enough, or do we need more information?
- Did we identify and appropriately involve all the right stakeholders?
- Is all of our data reliable? Did we utilize credible sources for our information?
- Have we maintained our objectivity in developing this opportunity, or have we let personal biases or agendas into the development process?
- Have we challenged each other to think independently, or have we been swayed by groupthink?
- Do we have a viable plan for how we will go about Phase 2?

1.11.04 Design the Phase Gate 1 event

Meeting logistics include the structure of the meeting (formal presentation or a more informal discussion group), the scheduling of the meeting, and the meeting roles.

As far as roles are concerned, generally, it is the project manager who takes center stage. The change lead facilitates the session by making sure key thoughts and ideas are periodically checked for understanding, any points of contention are captured, and the meeting maintains momentum instead of getting bogged down in details irrelevant to the phase decision.

1.11.05 Create and distribute pre-read material

This should be done no less than five days prior to the Phase Gate meeting so that participants will have ample time to review the material. The change management resource can take the lead on this.

The pre-read package should contain:

1   A cover letter outlining the structure and objective of the meeting (a decision on whether the project should be ended, suspended, reworked, or approved to proceed to Phase 2).

2   The project background: who is on the project team, what the opportunity is, and a high-level gap analysis showing a view of the current state, the desired future state, and a "solution" (very high level) for getting from the desired state to the future state.

3   The project scope and the business case (often times, the business case will make more sense if the scope is introduced beforehand).

4   Recommendations on any outstanding scope issues ("Undecided" items)

5   The plan for Phase 2: this includes deliverables, the project management/change management plan, resources required, and the Phase 2 costs.

6   Cost estimates (within a range usually determined by the project sponsor or organizational standard) for the entirety of the project.

If the pre-read material is to contain any sort of "surprises" (executives hate surprises), make sure that prior to sending out the pre-read, it has been vetted by the appropriate Project Review Board members beforehand.

1.11.06 Conduct a Phase Gate preparation session

After the pre-read materials are distributed, the project planning team should gather in a room and brainstorm a list of potential questions, challenges, or concerns that the project sponsor or Project Review Board might have during the Phase Gate session. In order for the project manager to actively participate in this activity, it is usually best if the change lead facilitates this session. When conducting this session, it is best to have team members think about the different personalities that will be in the room – their reputations, styles, hot-button issues, etc. (e.g., the "Finance person" will probably want to know how certain figures were calculated) and use that as a springboard from which to develop questions.

After the questions have been gathered, the team should work on how best to answer the questions, challenges, or concerns. The change lead can gather everyone's thoughts and, after the session, go about fine-tuning the responses.

The change lead can then prepare a Phase Gate meeting preparation document that contains convincing responses to the questions, concerns, and challenges discussed in the prep session. The change lead then distributes this document to the rest of the team.

1.11 Outputs/Deliverables

- Refined business case and project scope
- Phase Gate 1 meeting agenda
- Phase Gate 1 pre-read package
- Phase Gate 1 presentation and meeting material
- Phase Gate 1 project team preparation material

Activity 1.12 – Conduct Phase Gate 1 Session

Although a project can get killed at any point during the project life cycle, the most common time for this to happen is during the Phase Gate 1 meeting.

The goal of the Phase Gate meeting is to make one of four possible decisions:

1   **Proceed** – The opportunity and business case look strong enough so that the project should proceed to Phase 2.
2   **Rework** – There may or may not be an opportunity worth pursing here. The team needs to provide us with more information before we can reach a decision.
3   **Suspend** – The opportunity *may* be worth pursing, but we need to put a temporary hold on it until we have resolved some other issues which are external to the project.
4   **End** – In light of the current business environment or other projects the company is considering, the opportunity and the business case are *not* strong enough for us to continue.

In reaching one of the above decisions, the Project Review Board or decision maker will have several questions and concerns swirling through his head during the meeting:

- Do we really want to start down this path? How will the rest of the organization react?
- Is the business case strong enough, and will it hold up over time?
- Is the information they are presenting accurate, or is there some bias or massaging of data?
- Are they missing anything or not factoring in other concerns? (May lead to recommendation of "Suspend")
- In light of other projects we may be considering, do we really want to approve funding for this opportunity?
- Do we agree with what they have planned for Phase 2?
- If I recommend that the company proceed with this project, will it come back to bite me?
- Are we really the right people to be making the decision?

The goal of the Phase Gate session is to have the key decision maker in the governance structure render a decision at the end of the meeting. In order for them to do so, they have to be comfortable with the rationale (and the numbers!) behind the business case, as well as with the plans and propositions for Phase 2.

In order to have a successful Phase Gate which will most likely lead to a decision to "Proceed," the following questions need to be answered:

- Has all the work been completed in a satisfactory manner? Are we confident we won't have to rework anything?
- Do we have alignment on the scope/purpose/objectives for the next phase of work?
- Is there still a sufficient business case for proceeding?
- Do we have the right resources in place for the next project phase?
- Are there any concerns about the high-level plan for the next phase?
- Do we need to modify our governance structure/project processes for the next phase?

After the presentations are over and the questions and concerns addressed, it is time to ask the Project Review Board members for their decision or recommendation. Remember, the expectation that they will be rendering a decision or a recommendation at the conclusion of the meeting has already been raised.

Table 7.8. *Excerpt from the Emergence One Phase Gate Documentation template*

Phase Gate 1	End	Suspend	Rework	Proceed	*Reasoning*
Project Review Board Member A					
Project Review Board Member B					
Project Review Board Member C					

If you want to move the project forward, it is critical to achieve consensus at this meeting. You cannot have a naysayer or two leaving this meeting telling others "Well, they decided to proceed with the project even though I disagreed." This negativity will spread like a virus and only cause more dissension and skepticism down the line. If the project is going to move forward and be successful, it is important to build on the momentum that only a united Project Review Board can establish.

If complete unity cannot be achieve despite a majority opinion, it is best to put the project in "rework" status so that the team can develop a stronger business case at a later date to try to sway the dissenters. This is a better way to go than using the other executives in the room to pressure the minority dissenters to change their vote then and there. By going into "rework" mode, the minority dissenters will have a chance to reevaluate the project based upon *additional information*, not peer pressure. This process will help guarantee longer-term support.

From this point onwards, which actions to take naturally depend upon what type of decision was rendered on the project:

- **Proceed** – This is actually the most common decision because the Phase 1 process outlined in this chapter has numerous touch points with project decision makers and influencers. If the team was heading in the wrong direction, there were ample opportunities to correct their course. Nevertheless, if the team does get to proceed, they should go celebrate!
- **Rework** – This is generally a tough judgment for a project team to swallow. It usually means that the team did an inadequate job for the Project Review Board to recommend proceeding. The options in this case are either to send the team back to the drawing board and do a better job at executing Phase 1 activities, or put together a new team which can, hopefully, create a more compelling business case by utilizing different perspectives.

- **Suspend** – A suspend judgment usually means that the change opportunity and business case were indeed compelling, but outside factors are preventing the team from being asked to proceed.
- **End** – Make sure that the Project Review Board decides or recommends to end the project because it firmly believes the business case is not strong enough, *not* because the project team may have done a poor job in formulating or presenting the information. If the latter, then put the project in "Rework" and look at the opportunity from another perspective.

Soon after the meeting concludes, the team should debrief in order to document any concerns, recommendations, or outstanding items.

1.12 Outputs/Deliverables

- Documentation of Phase Gate project recommendations

In contrast with other project life cycle methodologies, which generally conclude the initial phase at the end of the Phase Gate meeting, the Emergence One Method contains an additional activity which is quite important – especially if the project is given the green light to proceed.

Activity 1.13 – Communicate Outcomes/Next Steps

Before wrapping up Phase 1 activities, the change lead should communicate the outcome of the Phase Gate 1 meeting to any stakeholders the project team had significant interactions with. Especially if the Phase Gate was successful and the opportunity to proceed into Phase 2 was granted, this will be a good opportunity to thank stakeholders for their contributions and outline any next steps. The change lead should meet with project team members to determine whether any of these stakeholders will be required to give inputs in any Phase 2 activities. If so, this need should also be woven into the communication.

For higher-level executives, the project sponsor may wish to personally deliver the results of the Phase Gate meeting in a face-to-face meeting.

Since the project still has not taken on a distinct shape, it is generally too soon to broadcast any news to the wider organization.

1.13 Outputs/Deliverables

- Communication regarding outcome of the Phase Gate 1 session, including an outline of expectations for Phase 2

Activity 1.14 – Phase 1 Wrap-up

Before officially closing out Phase 1, two more activities should occur:

1.14.01 Document lessons learned, pertinent observations, and outstanding needs

Anything which can benefit the execution of the next phase, or outstanding issues which need to be addressed, should be documented. This may include:

- **Pertinent observations** – Was any aspect of how something was executed during Phase 1 good to keep an eye on or monitor to some degree going forward? For example, maybe the project team discovered that the project sponsor did not communicate as effectively as they would have liked. If so, this is a factor the team needs to be mindful of going forward.
- **Lessons learned** – Were any specific lessons learned from the execution of Phase 1 that need to be captured in one of the iterative documents (such as the executive stakeholder analysis) or elsewhere? If so, make sure not only that they are documented in the appropriate place but that any relevant lessons learned *are applied* in the next phase or beyond.
- **Outstanding needs** – Does something need to be addressed or completed before continuing into Phase 2? For example, is there an executive who is requesting some additional detailed information from the team? Or maybe there is a document not currently in the project information repository that needs to go in there.

1.14.02 Celebrate!

If the team succeeded in getting the next phase of the project approved, they deserve to go out and celebrate! (Keep in mind, though, with a phase-based approach, technically only the next phase of the project has been formally approved, not the entire project. The project still may get shelved at the end of any one of the next four Phase Gate reviews.)

1.14 Outputs/Deliverables

- Documentation of lessons learned, pertinent observations, and outstanding needs

Conclusion of Phase 1

For more information...
Templates, detailed examples, and process tools relating to Phase 1 of the Emergence One Method can be downloaded for free (though some material may require a small licensing fee) from: **www.emergenceone.com**

Chapter 8

Phase 2: Assess Alternatives

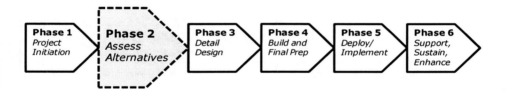

Introduction to Phase 2

Phase 2 represents the start of the "real" project. Whereas Phase 1 was more about assessing whether or not a worthwhile opportunity even existed, Phase 2 begins the process of assessing project alternatives and putting a little more detail into what the solution (which can also be referred to as the "change driver"), will look like.

The main goal of this phase is to convince the Project Review Board that the project team has thoroughly assessed all the options on how to get from Point A to Point B, and that this is the best path forward.

Once the process gets to this point, however, it is at one of the most politically charged of all the project life cycle phases. There will be many champions and naysayers of the various alternatives being considered, so reconciling these conflicts and aligning the different parties on a common path forward can be a challenge. The Emergence One Method builds in many activities around stakeholder engagement, management, and alignment to help with this challenge.

Besides the human and political elements, there are numerous process challenges. Another main focus for the project manager and change lead is to develop a rigorous evaluation and assessment process that doesn't play favorites and can be defended against the most ardent critics.

It is important to note that many projects get shelved during this phase. Once stakeholders get a taste of the costs and impacts associated with the initiative, they start to get cold feet. To address this resistance, some project teams agree to whittle down the project scope, which may in turn limit the amount of benefits the organization will receive.

On a positive note, if the project team succeeds in making it through this phase, the chances are good (but not guaranteed) that the project will eventually be deployed.

Phase 2 – Assess Alternatives			
#	Activity		Subtask
2.01	Conduct Phase 2 Startup Activities	2.01.01	Identify needs/expectations of Phase 2 stakeholders
		2.01.02	Update/review iterative documents
		2.01.03	Finalize Phase 2 plan/approach
2.02	Design and Align Project Governance	2.02.01	Select governance/steering committee members
		2.02.02	Determine scope of governance oversight
2.03	Engage/Align/Mobilize Key Stakeholders	2.03.01	Engage key stakeholders
		2.03.02	Align key stakeholders
		2.03.03	Mobilize key stakeholders
2.04	Identify and Secure Project Resources	2.04.01	Determine project resource needs
		2.04.02	Request project resources
2.05	Kick Off the Core Project Team	2.05.01	Design the kick-off event
		2.05.02	Conduct the event
		2.05.03	Institute processes to build high performance
2.06	Conduct Current State Analysis	2.06.01	Gather requirements
		2.06.02	Refine business case and scope
2.07	Gather High-Level Future State Requirements	2.07.00	None

Phase 2 – Assess Alternatives			
2.08	Generate and Refine High-Level Alternatives/Options	2.08.01	Generate alternatives/options
		2.08.02	Refine alternatives/options
2.09	Conduct Organizational Impact Analysis	2.09.01	Complete a current state/future state gap analysis
		2.09.02	Determine the effect of change impacts on the organization
2.10	Select Recommended Solution Option	2.10.01	Evaluate and compare alternatives
		2.10.02	Choose the recommended solution option/alternative
		2.10.03	Test for decision quality
		2.10.04	Vet the recommendation with key stakeholders
2.11	Prepare for Phase Gate 2	2.12.01	Refine/update critical project documents
		2.12.02	Assess Phase Gate readiness
		2.12.03	Design the Phase Gate 2 event
		2.12.04	Create and distribute pre-read material
		2.12.05	Conduct a Phase Gate 2 preparation session
2.12	Conduct Phase Gate 2	2.12.00	None
2.13	Communicate Outcomes	2.13.00	None
2.14	Phase 2 Wrap-up	2.14.01	Document pertinent information
		2.14.02	Celebrate and acknowledge the team

Activity 2.01 – Conduct Phase 2 Startup Activities

2.01.01 Identify needs/expectations of Phase 2 stakeholders

In Phase 1, most of the activities centered on determining whether or not there was a project opportunity for the company. Therefore, the primary stakeholders for Phase 1 activities were the company executives and project governance members.

In Phase 2, because it begins to refine the future state picture and to choose the best path to get there, *primary* stakeholders for Phase 2 will be business directors and department heads as well as the project governance members. Now that the business opportunity has been green-lighted, and the project is on its way, executives who are not *direct* project stakeholders are no longer considered to be primary. While the project may keep these executives informed, the focus of targeted engagement activities should be business directors and project governance members. Updates to the stakeholder map can be made at this stage.

Table 8.1.   Common needs/expectations of Phase 2 stakeholders

Major Stakeholder Groups	Stakeholders Prominent in Phase 2	Common Needs and Expectations *During Phase 2*
TIER 1 Stakeholders: Senior Leaders/ Key Decision Makers	**Company Executives and Project Governance Members**	• Was the best solution for the organization chosen amongst the several viable alternatives? • Did bias or political influence taint the selection process? • When choosing the solution, did the team show sensitivity to cost? • Does the chosen solution meet or exceed the original business case? • Do we have the right people in place sponsoring and managing this initiative? • Hopefully, there will be "no surprises" regarding project direction, scope, or estimated costs. • Is the trade-off between business benefits and organizational impacts acceptable?

Major Stakeholder Groups	Stakeholders Prominent in Phase 2	Common Needs and Expectations *During Phase 2*
	Project Sponsor	• What can I do to make sure the project will continue to receive the proper level of funding and attention? • How do I make sure "analysis paralysis" does not occur? • How can I be a more effective sponsor? • Will I be consulted prior to any key decisions? • How can I help the governance and Project Review Board members remain committed?
	Project Review Board Members	• Will the project team incorporate any feedback given to them? • When will Phase Gate 2 occur, and what do I need to do beforehand? • Am I the right person to provide the necessary feedback and insights to the project team?
TIER 2 Stakeholders: Project Contributors	**Phase 2 Project Team**	• Am I joining a winning initiative that will increase my visibility and help my career? • Will I be able to stand out on this team? • What is my exact role, and how can I best contribute?
	Corporate Governance Representatives	• Does the project team understand any corporate standards, policies, or procedures they must comply with? • Will we have an opportunity to review the project scope document to ensure there are no areas of concern?

Major Stakeholder Groups	Stakeholders Prominent in Phase 2	Common Needs and Expectations *During Phase 2*
	Business/Process Owners	• Is this a change that will benefits the areas I am responsible for, or is it something just for the higher-ups? • Will the project team understand the needs of the business? • Will the impacts to operations be tolerable?
TIER 3 Stakeholders: Change Recipients	N/A	*There is still a long way between Phase 2 and the start of Phase 5, when this initiative will start impacting change recipients (if it ever gets that far – remember, a project can get canceled or suspended at any point in the project life cycle prior to deployment). In most cases, this stakeholder group will still have minimal needs at this time.*

NOTE: *This is a generic assessment of stakeholder needs and expectations. Depending upon the scope and nature of the project, as well as the hierarchical structure of the company, there may be other stakeholder groups, or other needs and expectations, involved in Phase 2.*

Understanding these needs and expectations will help drive the specific activities of Phase 2.

Remember, these are high-level needs and expectations. More specific needs and expectations can be discerned through various engagement meetings.

2.01.02 Update and review iterative documents

In Phase 1, a number of documents were created that are iterative in nature. Although iterative documents can, and should, be updated as soon as there is applicable new information, the start of a new phase is a great checkpoint to make sure that this has happened.

The iterative documents from Phase 1 which should be reviewed and updated (if required) are as follows:

- *The Business Case and Project Scope Document* – Did anything come out of the Phase Gate 1 meeting that would justify a change in the business case and scope?

- *The Stakeholder Map* – Have there been any new stakeholder groups identified since the stakeholder map was last updated?
- *The Project Roadmap* – Now that the project team has received feedback on the project approach, does the project roadmap need to be changed in any way, shape, or form?
- *The Lessons Learned Document* – Were there any lessons learned from Phase 1 that can be applied to the subsequent project phases?
- *The Executive Stakeholder Analysis Document* – Do we need to add or delete any names on the list? Are these stakeholders more influential on project success during the execution of Phase 2 activities than they were during Phase 1?
- *The Risk Management Log* – The risk assessment log should be reviewed and updated prior to the start of any phase.

Once the documents have been updated, they should be combed for potential inputs to other documents that will be completed in Phase 2.

2.01.03 Finalize Phase 2 plan/approach

Regardless of how much rigor there was in the Phase 1 plan, the activities of Phase 2 demand that there be a rigorous project plan in place. The reason for this is that activities and required stakeholder interactions for Phase 2 are generally much broader than they were for Phase 1.

Within the project plan, there should be more specific guidance on several points:

- **Procurement or request for proposal process** - If the project team will be evaluating product vendors or utilizing service vendors, there needs to be a request for proposal (RFP) process put in place. This activity might need to be coordinated with the procurement department.
- **Quality assurance** – The project team will be assessing and recommending a solution which could have major financial, operational, and organizational impacts on the company. This is no time for poor quality work. Project tasks should never be "check the box" activities. The more robust activity execution is, the stronger the end result will be. Initiating various quality assurance (QA) or quality control (QC) checks along the way will help ensure that this happens.
- **Financial/cost management** – The organization is expecting the project team to be responsible stewards of company resources. There should be a plan in place to adequately track and control project expenses.

153

- **Organizational communication** – Since the initiative is still in the assessment phase and there is not yet an approved path forward, there will most likely not be a lot of communication, if any, going out to the broader organization (Tier 3 stakeholders). However, for initiatives that, despite being in an exploratory phase, have created a certain degree of buzz amongst potential change recipients, organizational communication activities may need to be planned.

Other important processes, such as managing issues and risks, project communications, stakeholder management, and reviewing lessons learned, were introduced as part of Phase 1 and should be continued into this project phase as well.

The project manager should align project team members (whether they are currently on the team or will be joining the project team later in this phase) on goals, objectives, deliverables, and sequence of activities. The change lead may want to check for alignment with other project team members since, many times, overeager project team members may begin working on project activities prematurely.

2.01 Outputs/Deliverables

- Updated stakeholder map
- Documented list of needs and expectations for key Phase 2 stakeholders
- Updated business case and scope
- Updated project roadmap
- Updated lessons learned document
- Updated stakeholder analysis
- Updated risk management log
- Phase 2 project approach and schedule

Activity 2.02 – Design and Align Project Governance

NOTE: Project governance involving the Project Review Board has already been discussed in Phase 1. In Phase 2, depending upon the size and scope of the project, there may be a need for additional governance structures.

Within the Emergence One Method, project governance is responsible for how decisions get made, issues escalated, and problems resolved. This role differs from that of the Project Review Board, whose essential function is to determine (or make a recommendation to project governance) whether or not the project should proceed to the next phase.

Since the design of the governance process often involves defining roles and how people relate to one another, we often recommend that the change lead, working with the project sponsor, be the primary architect of the project governance structure.

Project governance should be separate from any other governance structures that may exist in the organization. Embedded governance structures usually exist to maintain standards, whereas *ad-hoc* project governance structures exist to help guide change.

2.02.01 Select project governance/steering committee members

Project governance/steering committee members should be chosen with great care. Members should be chosen for their ability to regularly contribute to project direction and execution quality, not because of "political reasons" or as an avenue through which they can "stay informed."

It is sometimes beneficial to provide heavily impacted stakeholder groups with representation on a governance committee. However, it may make more sense to retain these representatives as extended project team members who can provide input and feedback to design requirements and plans.

2.02.02 Determine scope of governance oversight

Once all of the project governance stakeholders have been identified, it is necessary to determine how the governance processes will work. Involving the affected stakeholders in crafting these decisions will go a long way toward accelerating acceptance of the final governance document.

These activities may include:

- *Deliverables Review and Approval* – Which documents and other outputs will the governance committee want to review? How much detail and granularity is expected? Will there be a formal deliverable review and approval process? If so, who should be involved? How long should the approval process take? Three days after submission? One week? Two weeks?
- *Phase Gate Decisions* – Going forward, will Phase Gate *decisions* be the responsibility of the Project Review Board (see Activity 1.05.02), or should the Project Review Board simply make a recommendation to the governance/steering committee, who will in turn make the final decision? Or should the decision of whether to proceed to the next phase be given to the project sponsor or another executive decision maker?
- *Funding* – How is the decision to fund the project going to be made? Will the project sponsor or Project Review Board have the authority to grant funds, or will they need to solicit funds from another source

within the organization? If so, what kind of financial rigor and other justification would that person or department be looking for in order to release the funds?

- *Issue Escalation* – If issues affecting the process cannot be mitigated at the project level, what would be the escalation process for bringing them up to the executive level for some type of resolution?
- *Scope Changes* – Although good scope management hopefully continues throughout the project life cycle, what is the best way to handle a major scope request coming in from a determined stakeholder? What type of scope changes can be approved at the project level versus those that must be approved by executive stakeholders of the project?

While many of the above are standard activities one may find in most projects, the change lead can further underscore the importance of change management by embedding several change behavior activities into the formal governance process. These may include:

- *Communication* – Who needs to sign off on project-related announcements that go out to the broader communication? Who decides what the parameters are for putting information out on the company intranet?
- *Championing the Project* – What will be the sponsorship strategy of the project? Who will visibly support and champion the project? Are there stronger or higher-level people in the organization beyond the project sponsor who might make better champions of this initiative?
- *Team Performance Reviews* – Should regular, methodical reviews of team performance (team "health checks") be conducted? If so, who should conduct them and how should the results be reviewed?

Once the governance structure has been completed, it is important to share the governance document with all parties who are playing a role in the governance process to make sure there is agreement and alignment with what is put forth.

2.02 Outputs/Deliverables

- Project governance document outlining roles, responsibilities, and processes
- Completed project directives measurement tools
- Documented agreement on project directives

Activity 2.03 – Engage/Align/Mobilize Key Stakeholders

For Phase 2, the change lead can leverage the need to debrief other key executive stakeholders on the Phase Gate 1 meeting outcomes in order to secure engagement meetings with them. Prior to engaging these stakeholders, however, the change lead can develop Phase 2 debriefing material for use in the executive engagement sessions.

2.03.01 Engage key stakeholders

Determine which executive stakeholders to schedule a one-on-one session with by referring back to the updated stakeholder map and the executive stakeholder analysis document. The Project Triad should decide amongst themselves who should see which person.

- For executives rated either a 4 or 5 for influence, try to meet with these stakeholders in person.
- For executives rated a 3, consider phoning them if that is an acceptable means of communication, considering the dynamics of the organization.
- For executives rated a 1 or 2, an email update should suffice, but be sure to provide them with an opportunity to contact the project manager with any needs or concerns.

After meeting with the high-influence stakeholders, update the executive stakeholder analysis document with any relevant information or changes to their perceived level of support. Remember, this is a confidential document. Take care in keeping it that way.

Immediately address any outstanding issues that may have come out of the engagement sessions.

2.03.02 Align key stakeholders

It should never be assumed that those who are providing input and direction to the team will always give clear, unambiguous direction. Often times, a project manager receive contradictory directions from different decision makers and other project influencers. If these mixed messages are not identified and addressed, it puts the project team at high risk of working on the wrong things or allows misalignment and dissension to fester and grow amongst key project stakeholders and supporters.

Project managers are human beings. And sometimes it is human nature to ignore mixed messages: what Emergence One refers to as "directional dissonance."

Emergence One approach recommends facilitating a work session in which all of the stakeholders who have a say in helping to define project direction and priorities can come together to reach alignment.

The first step toward aligning key stakeholders is to identify those elements about which there is obvious misalignment as well as other potential elements that can affect project direction and execution.

These may include:

- Budget
- Solution quality
- Timeline
- Degree of functionality or complexity
- Scalability
- Degree of organizational impacts

There are a variety of means for capturing and aligning trains of thought on the above issues. While some project managers or change practitioners will merely facilitate a discussion, Emergence One prefers to utilize tools to measure the participants' desires and goals.

For example, Emergence One consultants might distribute a measurement tool, such as the one below, and have participants complete it. The next step would be to consolidate and plot the results, and project them on an overhead screen to show the project advisors where they are in alignment and where they are not.

Table 8.2. *Example Project Alignment Assessment*

Project X					
Level of Importance: Project Team Design Considerations					
Rate the following elements below based on the following scale:					
1 – Low Importance 2 – Medium Importance 3 – High Importance					
	Staying Within Budget	Solution Quality	Timeline	Degree of Functionality	Scalability	Limiting Organizational Impact
Project Advisor A	3	3	1	3	2	2
Project Advisor B	3	3	2	3	1	1

Project X Level of Importance: Project Team Design Considerations					
Project Advisor C	3	3	1	3	1	3
Project Advisor D	3	2	1	1	1	3
Project Advisor E	2	2	2	1	1	1
Mean	2.8	2.6	1.4	2.2	1.2	2.0

Looking at the above example, we can see a few interesting results. Let's look at each column separately:

- **Staying Within Budget** – This factor appears quite important to most members, and there is a high degree of alignment.
- **Solution Quality** – This element also appears to be quite important; it also has a high degree of alignment among participants. However, "Solution Quality" has the same rating as "Staying Within Budget." Sometimes it is difficult to achieve both, a point that will be discussed later.
- **Timeline** – In relation to the first two elements, this element does not appear to be much of a priority. Therefore, if the project team becomes short on time, they should not skimp on developing a quality solution just to meet a deadline.
- **Degree of Functionality** – Although the mean score is pretty much in the mid-range, notice the lack of alignment between the project advisors A–C and project advisors D and E. This discrepancy shows a lack of alignment and needs to be addressed.
- **Scalability** – Here there is fairly strong alignment showing that this should not be a priority for the project team.
- **Limiting Organizational Impact** – The scores on this factor are all over the map. It may mean that respondents have very different feelings on how important this is, or it simply might mean that this area is not commonly understood. This is an area for the change management lead to address with the group.

The goal of the meeting is not to simply accept these ratings but to understand the areas where there is a lack of alignment among project advisors. The change lead will need to facilitate a discussion to understand the reasoning behind some of the ratings and work to see whether greater alignment can be achieved.

NOTE: *This activity may need to be repeated at any point in the project life cycle when there are indications of mixed messages or executive misalignment.*

2.03.03 Mobilize key stakeholders

The purpose of mobilizing key stakeholders is to make sure that they become actual contributors to total project success, as opposed to merely providing lip service or taking a passive approach. As originally stated in the description of Activity 1.01, effective project sponsorship should not all depend upon one individual who may, or may not, have what it takes to properly support and champion a project. It takes a coalition of key executives and other influential project stakeholders to make a project successful.

It should never be assumed that key stakeholders know what is expected of them when it comes to contributing to project success. And, even if they do know some of the expectations, they might not know what specific behaviors or actions are required to meet those expectations. For instance, how exactly does one "create a sense of urgency"?

Emergence One has had great success with the use of leadership action plans (LAPs). A leadership action plan identifies the key dimensions that make for project leadership and then provides specific recommendations on how to realize these dimensions. Each LAP is customized for every relevant stakeholder based upon their inherent strengths and position within the organization.

For instance, for someone who is very personable and extroverted, E1 may recommend that they do the following:

- Communicate and promote the initiative
- Exhibit/build confidence in the initiative

For someone who may be more introverted, but is well connected with other executives, the following dimensions may be more appropriate:

- Resolve issues, facilitate alignment
- Remove barriers or roadblocks

But rather than leave them to their own devices, to figure out how to do this, we also provide specific examples of how they may be able to realize the above dimensions.

For example, for someone who is being asked to "communicate and promote the initiative," the following recommendations might apply:

- *Champion clearly and forcefully the vision and goals of the project, the need for change, and the benefits for all – at staff meetings, informal gatherings, and company events.*
- *Utilize the standard slide presentation to educate your own organization and obtain feedback to ensure people understand project goals.*
- *Take an active role in the upcoming team demonstrations; display your enthusiasm and confidence in front of the participants.*

2.03 Outputs/Deliverables

- Phase Gate 1 debriefing material
- Measurement tools for determining alignment
- Phase 2 leadership action plans
- Updated Phase 2 approach and schedule (if necessary)

Activity 2.04 – Identify and Secure Project Resources

Picking the project team is one of the most crucial tasks of this phase. There tends to be more "permanence" attached to choosing your team resources than for completing other project tasks. In other words, while it is possible to redo or improve upon deliverables, it is often a very time-consuming and disruptive process to let go of a project team resource.

The act of picking project team members has traditionally been done by the project manager, sometimes in consultation with the project sponsor. However, because project managers tend to have more of a "hard skills" focus, many project managers evaluate potential project team resources based only upon their subject matter expertise. While this can work in some cases, the project manager runs a high risk of creating a project team who may not communicate or work well together.

The change lead, who likely has a background in organizational behavior, should help the project manager round out the role descriptions by making sure that appropriate personality traits and behavioral characteristics are factored into the selection process.

However, the most difficult part of this activity is not identifying resources but securing them. Especially when utilizing internal resources, most managers do not want to give up their best people to join a project for several months.

2.04.01 Determine project resource needs

It is usually beneficial for the project team to be composed of representatives from several of the most heavily impacted groups.

The project manager should have some good ideas on what technical and functional skills are required. The change lead can also provide input into what "soft skills" would benefit the functioning of the team, e.g., the ability to work collaboratively or offer creative, out-of-the-box ideas. The change lead can also enhance this activity by adding rigor to the resource identification process.

When the resources should start their new jobs and how much of a time commitment will be required of them should also be noted. Keep in mind that a project team may not need (or want) all of the project resources to start at the same time.

2.04.02 Request project resources

The following actions are recommended as a means of securing internally sourced project resources. For externally sourced resources, most mid-size and large companies should have a standard staff augmentation process for this.

Develop and utilize a "recruitment pitch"

When trying to secure internal resources, be sure to have well-formulated talking points:

- What this project is and why it is important to the company.
- What the challenges are and why so-and-so would be an important asset to the project team.
- What kind of reward or recognition the project team member will likely receive: increased visibility in the company; being on the forefront of the new company direction; possibly fast-tracked to a promotion.
- What is in it for the manager of the resource – gratitude (generally appreciated but not enough), a chance to repay favors, or the assurance that he or she will now have direct representation to express needs and concerns to the project team.

Be prepared to negotiate for the right project resource

One should be wary of managers who offer up resources because "it will be a good developmental opportunity for them." Managers hate to give up good resources, making it a challenge for the project manager to secure quality internal resources.

A few tactics that have proven effective in helping to secure a "borrowed" resource:

- *Determine who from the Project Triad is the best person is to do the asking.*
- *Anticipate and be prepared to address any key concerns they may have* – Since the manager will now be short a working resource, that inevitable question will arise: "Well, who is going to do her job when she is working on *your* project?"
- *Be able to offer something in return* – Though an executive project sponsor may be able to offer something tangible, the project manager is usually able to offer only intangible benefits. This line has brought much success: "By lending us this person for the project, your specific solution-related needs will probably get more attention than if these requests came from a manager who does not have representation on the project."
- *Offer to co-develop a "backfill" plan with the manager* – When seeking a project team resource who has a critical position in the company, it may be necessary to have that person's job role given to someone else in the organization, if their job responsibilities cannot be divided up piecemeal.
- *Expand the donor network* – If the project is still having difficulty finding qualified internal resources, revisit the stakeholder identification list to see whether the project can expand its network of potential resource donors.

The Practical Practitioner:
Utilizing the "Lika" Approach

I first heard of the "Lika" approach around 2003, when Emergence One was working with a project manager to secure project resources for a Back Office IT design project. Rather than ask directly for the targeted resources, the project manager took a less direct approach by saying: "Now that you've heard about the importance of the project, we really need your help in securing someone *like a* Linda Johnson to be on the project team."

Knowing that Linda Johnson was a highly valued direct report of her manager, this was a way of asking for Linda in a less confrontational manner. This helped to avoid an immediate knee-jerk reaction from her manager of "Whoa, you can't have Linda; she's one of my best employees."

After discussing several people who were "lika Linda Johnson," the project manager softly asked: "Well, is there any chance that Linda would be available?"

By that point, Linda's manager had already warmed up to us and had a more thorough understanding of our needs. To make a long story short, Linda was on our project team the following week.

Don't forget that someone from the Project Triad may also have to sell the idea of joining the project team to the prospective project resource as well. Joining a project is a big change, and it can be a major change-management challenge to get them to agree to join up. The project requires committed project resources. A person is not going to be fully committed to the project with concerns like the ones listed above floating around in his or her head.

2.04 Outputs/Deliverables

- Project job descriptions
- "Recruitment" pitch
- Resource backfill plan (if needed)
- Documented project resource commitments

Activity 2.05 – Kick Off the Core Project Team

The Emergence One method isn't so much about simply "kicking off" a project team as it is about *jump-starting* a project team to reach optimal performance levels within the shortest possible time.

Now that project resources have been secured, it is time to plan for and kick off the core project team. While most project managers feel that kicking off a project team is a fairly straightforward activity, those with a background in change management know that there is much more to this activity than typically meets the eye. Most project managers fail to understand all of the change management issues inherent in forming a project team, such as the following:

- Internal resources experience a major change in work routine by being taken out of their normal day-to-day jobs and placed on a project team.
- A project team may comprise representatives from many cross-functional departments who have never worked with one another, each of whom is unfamiliar with the others' processes. Coalescing as a single functioning team will be a major change management challenge.
- The project team may also be made up of individuals who are both internally *and externally* sourced. Again, coalescing two sets of project resources, most of whom likely have very different work styles, perspectives, tools, and techniques, can present numerous change management issues.

Mitigating these issues will lead to high performance. High-performance teams have been shown to be more productive, more likely to complete deliverables on time (or even early), produce higher-quality solutions, and come up with more innovative and cost-saving solutions.

2.05.01 Design the kick-off event

In developing and designing the kick-off agenda, several elements need to be addressed:

- **Whom to invite** – Besides the obvious candidates, such as project team members, it is usually quite impactful if the project sponsor or some other senior-level executive kicks off the meeting.
- **Room setup** – Traditional theater-style or classroom seating arrangements work best only when there is a very large team who will spend most of the day listening. U-shaped setups or chairs arranged around several small tables will help to facilitate greater interaction amongst participants.
- **Determine Roles** – There are several key roles that different people can play within a kick-off meeting. Be sure each of them is defined.
- **Determine Topics and Activities** – For a Phase 2 kick-off, the objectives for the meeting usually include having the project team:
  - Develop a shared understanding of the purpose, vision, importance, etc., of the project.
  - Understand and be able to articulate the business case.
  - Understand the project team charter and work standards.
  - Start building rapport, trust, and a working relationship with one another.

The change lead should be able to develop any of the required presentations to support the above objectives.

- **Promote the Concept of Total Project Success** – Many project resources see their role simply as developing some sort of new process or product. It is essential that they understand the "big picture," which includes the importance of organizational adoption and business value realization, as laid out in Chapter 1.
- **Design a Team Development Activity** – The Emergence One Method recommends *structured* team development activities. These are designed so that team members do not simply get to know each other on a personal level but learn how they will function on the team (beyond what is already documented in the project charter and the roles and responsibilities).

2.05.02 Conduct the event

For a kick-off meeting, it is important to follow the agenda accordingly. It sets a very bad precedent if, on the first day, topics are not appropriately covered or sufficiently timed and does nothing to build confidence among the participants that this will be a well-managed project. Having a good facilitator (the role the change lead typically plays) will help. Be aware that some team members like to use the kick-off meeting to showcase their knowledge and experience by preemptively delving into problems or advocating "solutions" that are generally beyond the scope of the kick-off meeting.

It is important to observe how team members interact. The change lead and project manager can note any potentially inappropriate or unhelpful behaviors that may negatively impact the team if left unaddressed.

These include:

- A team member dominating the conversation and not soliciting input from others.
- A team member being dismissive or disparaging of an opinion or suggestion another team member offers.
- Someone not participating owing to lack of interest (could be a sign of a deeper motivational issue), lack of knowledge (could be a sign that the wrong resource was picked for the team), or lack of assertiveness (could be an indication that coaching may be needed in this area).
- A team that quickly reaches consensus on a solution (may be prone to groupthink and unwilling to make the effort to explore other options).
- A team that cannot reach agreement (may be a sign there are competing egos or the team lacks the ability to organize its work or make decisions, etc.).

If the project manager or change lead notes any "yellow flags" in someone's interactions or working style, he or she should address these concerns in a sensitive manner. This might include having the change lead follow up with individuals on a one-to-one basis for a little coaching.

2.05.03 Institute processes to build high performance

It is important to remember that building a high-performance team takes time. Change management practitioners are quite knowledgeable and often eager to address human behavior and team performance issues. The change lead (in conjunction with the project manager) should monitor and recommend additional activities and interventions that will continue to propel the team down the path of high performance.

2.05 Outputs/Deliverables

- Project team kick-off agenda
- Pre-read materials
- Relevant project on-boarding information consolidated into a master presentation
- Change management primer
- Outline and instructions for the team development activity

Activity 2.06 – Conduct Current State Analysis

NOTE: Depending upon the size and scope of the project, this deeper dive into assessing the current state may not be necessary. An initial high-level current state summary should have been conducted as part of Phase 1's business case and scope development.

Before the project team can determine where it is going, it needs to have a firm grasp on the organization's current state. How to go about conducting the current state analysis depends upon the nature of the project and the anticipated areas of project impact.

A current state analysis is sometimes overlooked by both project managers and change practitioners. One of the reasons is that they believe they have a general sense they "know what the current state is." The other reason is that the activities behind designing and building the future state solution is where project resources get to strut their stuff and show how cleaver and innovative they can be.

However, by not taking the time to do a proper current state analysis, the project will be at risk for:

- Designing a solution that cannot take advantage of, or build upon, the existing organizational design, technical infrastructure, business processes, etc.
- Being unable to determine what the change impact of the future state design will be since there will be no common understanding of the current state with which to compare it.

Whereas the project manager generally establishes the direction for this activity, the change lead can look to enhancing and documenting the process in such a way that the assigned project team members have a clear understanding of the tasks required.

When doing a current state analysis, the main objectives are to:

- Understand what is not working well. This can be addressed when designing the future state (note: this will be a more detailed analysis than was created for the business case in Phase 1).
- Understand what is working well or is a "best practice," something the team may want to maintain in the future state.
- Understand what simply "is." This could be something (a process, a design, etc.) that may be fairly neutral (neither a best practice nor a hindrance) but needs to be understood if the project is going to impact it, build upon it, or integrate with it.

Below is a standard approach for conducting a current state assessment:

1   ***Determine the scope of the current state analysis*** – For example, if the project is a process improvement initiative, there may be impacts on job roles and responsibilities. Determine if reviewing job roles should be within project scope.

2   ***Data-mine and review existing documentation*** - Some organizations are very good at documenting current state processes, job roles, etc.; others are not. Before investing the time, energy, and resources in developing current state documentation, be sure to mine for any existing documentation the organizational may have that could prove useful.

3   ***Assess documentation gaps and create plan to gather additional information*** – In many cases, the organization may not have all the complete information the project team requires to assess the current state. Therefore, a plan must be created to gather whatever additional information is required, beyond what was gathered in the data-mining activity above. Additional information can be gathered by conducting information interviews or focus groups with knowledgeable individuals.

NOTE: If conducting interviews or focus groups, it is important that a change management resource be engaged. This way, these individuals are not contacted without some sort of project messaging that properly positions both the activity and the project.

At the conclusion of the current state analysis activity, the change management resource should send an email to the participants, thanking them for their time and promising to keep them updated or engaged in the process going forward.

2.06 Outputs/Deliverables

- Project team training and promotional material in support of this activity

- Current state assessment report
- Communication material to participants

Activity 2.07 – Gather High-Level Future State Requirements

Before generating solution alternatives, it is critical that the project team solicit future state requirements from stakeholders other than those from the (Tier 1) Senior Leaders/Key Decision Makers group; this time, they should tap into the (Tier 2) Project Contributors group as well. The Tier 2 group typically represents business managers and directors from the impacted departments.

The goal of this activity is to get more specific information on what these stakeholders would consider to be an improvement over current operations. In Phase 2, the teams are still gathering higher-level needs and requirements that the department or business units may have so that potential solutions can be generated and assessed. Exact configuration requirements and detailed solution designs will be undertaken in Phase 3.

It may be important to once again engage (Tier 2) stakeholders from any departments involved in maintaining corporate standards or policies, such as the IT architecture group, information risk management group, human resources, or legal department.

It is often helpful for the change lead to draft guidelines for these engagement sessions in order to maintain consistency in gathering the high-level requirements. Also, the change lead may want to consider having a standard set of "talking points" for engagement participants to walk away with that explains the general scope, purpose, timeline, and benefits of the initiative.

Once this activity is completed, the project business case and scope document should be updated.

2.07 Outputs/Deliverables

- Future state requirement gathering guidelines
- Documented inputs on desired future state
- Project talking points

Activity 2.08 – Generate and Refine High-Level Alternatives/Options

The "solution," sometimes referred to as the "change driver," is what will transition the organization from its current state to its future state. The solution, more or less, becomes the "change driver." Some people confuse the "solution" with the "future state." For instance, implementing and running an ERP solution like SAP or Oracle Applications is *not* the desired state. SAP or Oracle is the solution (change driver) that will help achieve the company's future state. The future state consists of having an integrated platform that facilitates process efficiencies, reduces costs, provides easy access to more comprehensive data, etc.

Coming up with more than one *viable* solution forces the team to consider alternatives, some of which may prove to be more cost-effective, efficient, or easier to implement than the original solution. Alternatives force the group to break away from any groupthink that may be occurring.

Some project team members, and even the project sponsors, may (and usually do) already have "what the solution should be" in their heads. Changing their minds from their favorite option and getting them to seriously consider others is a change management task.

2.08.01 Generate alternatives/options

The change lead can facilitate a brainstorming session (allowing the project manager to be a subject matter participant) to develop a variety of solutions. Since the team is generating only high-level solution options, it should avoid getting bogged down in the weeds of the particulars of any one solution.

Right now, the team is tasked only with generating (feasible) alternatives, not refining them or evaluating them. The change lead can document the alternatives in such a fashion as to facilitate evaluations and comparisons of the alternatives at a later point.

2.08.02 Refine alternatives/options

Now that several alternatives have been generated, the project team should pick three or four of the more promising ones and refine them. The team should consider only viable options that do not violate any of the project givens or company standards and policies.

If the project team will be evaluating product vendors or utilizing service vendors, then they may need to have an RFP process in place. If so, that process should be started earlier rather than later.

The amount of detail that should make it into this preliminary solution design should be only enough to make comparisons amongst the options. For projects that are technical in nature, testing may be required to determine scalability and reliability.

How the project team will go about refining and testing the recommended solution will vary depending upon the nature of the project. The main thing to keep in mind is that the process should contain some rigor and that the results of the testing should be valid.

In this activity, the change resource will have an important role to play, ensuring that there are no rumors circulating as to what the potential change driver is or is not. The change lead will also keep busy communicating with key stakeholders, reassuring them that they can trust in the testing and selection process. In order to do this, the change resource will need to summarize the testing and selection process in an easy-to-understand presentation geared to a general audience.

2.08 Outputs/Deliverables

- Three or more feasible project alternatives/options
- A rigorous testing process (if required)
- Overview presentation of the solution options under consideration
- Communication material (as needed)

Activity 2.09 – Conduct Organizational Impact Analysis

Now that three or more high-level solution designs have been created and refined, the high-level impacts of that design on the organization can be determined. While the project manager will no doubt be focusing on many of the potential technical aspects of the various solutions, it is up to the change lead to determine how the solution/change driver will affect the organization. This will help the team determine the scope of the remaining organizational adoption activities.

Some change practitioners may refer to this activity as a "change impact assessment." However, that term is ambiguous because it does not clarify what *level* of change it is assessing. Since this is only Phase 2, and the detail design (which will determine the specific end-user impacts) has not yet been created, it is possible only to determine some of the broader *organizational impacts* at this time.

2.09.01 – Complete a current state/future state gap analysis

The differences between the current state analysis and the future state design are documented utilizing a rather simple format.

Table 8.3. *Sample Current State/Future State Template*

Current State (As is)	Future State (To be)	Change Impact
Component A		
Component B		
Component C		

2.09.02 Determine the effect of change impacts on the organization

When determining the impacts to the organization, several areas need to be considered:

- *Impacts on workflows* – Will this change radically alter workflows, or will the workflows basically stay the same?
- *Impacts on jobs and staffing levels* – If certain job roles become obsolete, can the existing employees be retrained? Will there be new tasks added to existing jobs (job enlargement), or will new people need to be hired? Are the changes expected to be so radical that current job classifications become obsolete?
- *Impacts on organizational structure* – If there are major changes to how individuals do their jobs, there may be major changes to the organizational structure as well.
- *Changes in skill sets* – If the change will require a major shift in required skills sets and competencies, then a robust training program needs to be planned for and properly funded.

Depending on the outcome of the organizational impact analysis, additional work streams, tracks, or activities may need to be introduced into the project plan. For example, if major impacts to job classifications are expected, then organizational design activities will need to be woven into the project plan.

The information derived from the organizational impact analysis will also help determine who many of the Tier 3 change recipients groups will be, and if there are additional stakeholder groups that may need to become project contributors.

2.09 Outputs/Deliverables

- Description of anticipated organizational impact for each alternative
- Updated stakeholder map

Activity 2.10 – Select Recommended Solution

Now that three or more solution options have been tested, it is time for the team to recommend one. Before doing so, though, it is important that the solution process be aligned with the project directives previously enunciated, and that the process have enough rigor in it to ensure that the recommendation is fully defensible.

Depending upon the type of solution being considered, there are various processes for decision making, product/vendor ranking, and solution evaluation to consider. Most of them involve some type of weighted evaluation process by a cross-section of stakeholders.

2.10.01 Evaluate and compare alternatives

The previous activities should provide the team with enough information to make an "apples to apples" comparison of each of the solutions.

In the simplified example below, three solution options are being compared with one another based upon three different criteria. (NOTE: Real-world examples may be much more complex.)

Table 8.4.   *Example of alternative evaluation*

Objective	Solution A	Solution B	Solution C
Budget	$500,000	$400,000	$600,000
Time to implement	Completion by end of Q3	Completion by end of Q3	Completion by end of Q2
Degree of functionality	Exceeds user requirements	Meets user requirements	Meets user requirements

As you can see, there is really no clear-cut "winner" in the above example; it is really about deciding upon the different "trade-offs" between the three. If the team wants the least expensive option, it should go with Solution B. If it wants something implemented by Q2, then it should go with Solution C. If it wants something that has all the bells and whistles, then it should go with Solution A.

How does a team determine which trade-offs are acceptable and which are not? This is why Activity 2.03.02 is so important. After all, it is not really up to the project team to decide want it wants, but rather to follow the guidance offered by project governance.

2.10.02 Choose the recommended solution option/alternative

Although it may seem like a matter of semantics, within the Emergence One Method, the project team does not actually choose the best option/alternative. Rather, it makes a recommendation to the appropriate governance committee, which then formally decides which option to go with.

2.10.03 Test for decision quality

Once the solution has been chosen, it is best to test the quality of the decision making process utilized thus far, since this is a major decision point in the project life cycle. Good decision quality is essential.

When testing for decision quality, first decide upon the quality criteria. (Some common decision making standards are listed below.) The project team should determine which ones are relevant to the project, and add in any others they see fit. It is usually best to limit the decision quality assessment to no more than six well-chosen, non-redundant criteria.

- Have we thoroughly considered all other options and alternatives?
- Did we involve all the right stakeholders in the process?
- Did we have access to and utilize all available up-to-date information, both positive and negative?
- Were the trade-offs between positive and negative equally considered?
- Was the reasoning utilized to reach the decision clear, rational, and free of bias?
- Was the decision making process influenced by any strong personalities?

After the project team agrees on what the criteria or standards should be, have each core project team member rank each one from one (low) to five (high). The decision-quality assessment does not weigh one criterion against another; instead, all of the criteria listed are important to ensure decision quality. If any one element receives a score of three or less, then the project team may want to consider doing some additional work in that area. Only when *all of the scores* are four or better can the team confidently claim that there was adequate quality in the decision making process.

2.10.04 Vet the recommendation with key stakeholders

Since this is one of the most important recommendations the project team will make, it is wise to vet the proposed recommendation with relevant stakeholders before moving forward. Regardless of the alternative chosen, the recommendation will most likely carry substantial political ramifications for many people in the organization. Therefore, it is best to explore some of the arguments for or against the recommendation so that they can be mitigated (it possible) prior to Phase Gate 2. The stakeholder analysis tool may need to be updated after this activity.

2.10 Outputs/Deliverables

- Documentation of the selection process, including any relevant flowcharts, evaluation criteria, ranking/scoring sheets, etc.
- Summary presentation of the selection process (for stakeholders outside of the immediate project team)

- Results from the decision quality assessment tool
- Documentation of the reasoning behind selecting the recommended solution option
- Updated stakeholder analysis tool

Activity 2.11 – Prepare for Phase 2 Phase Gate

Phase Gate 2 is often one of the most difficult of the five Phase Gate sessions the team will experience. The reason for this is that Phase Gate 2 is the point at which the organization is truly being asked to commit to investing in the development of an opportunity solution that, most likely, will have major impacts on the company. Therefore, the project team needs to make sure there are no shortcuts taken in preparing for this session.

2.11.01 Refine/update critical project documents

For Phase 2, refining and updating includes the following:

- *Business Case and Scope* - Now that a solution option/alternative has been selected, the team needs to determine how it will affect the business case and scope. If there is enough information to make the decision, any "Undecided" scope items should be placed in either the "In Scope" or "Out of Scope" column. Cost estimates should also be further refined, as should the metrics for business value realization.
- *Project Roadmap* – Update the project roadmap accordingly.
- *The Risk Management Log* – Have there been any new risks identified during the course of Phase 3 activities? If so, revise the risk management log.

2.11.02 Assess Phase Gate readiness

Some of the questions the team members need to ask themselves for a Phase Gate 2 meeting are as follows:

- Is our business case still strong? Has anything changed, or has anything new been learned in Phase 2 since we last refined our business case? Are we aware of any external events that could impact the business case?
- Did we involve all the right stakeholders during the formulation and testing of our project options/alternatives?
- Did we really challenge ourselves to consider all of the possible options/alternatives, including potential solutions, which may not be

on anybody's radar screen or for which there may not be adequate political support?

- Did we apply enough rigor to the process of selecting the recommended solution option? Will we be able to adequately support and defend our recommendation?
- Did we do enough Phase 3 planning to provide the Project Review Board with a good sense of our objectives and planned activities?

2.11.03 Design the Phase Gate 2 event

The meeting structure and roles will most likely be similar to those of Phase Gate 1, with the project manager leading the meeting and the change lead facilitating. However, more questions and concerns are typically raised during Phase Gate 2 than Phase Gate 1, so a longer meeting may be required.

2.11.04 Create and distribute pre-read material

The pre-read package for Phase 2 should contain similar material to the Phase Gate 1 materials but be updated to reflect Phase Gate 2 needs.

2.11.05 Conduct a Phase Gate preparation session

For Phase 2, the Phase Gate preparation session will be similar to the Phase Gate 1 preparation session.

2.11 Outputs/Deliverables

- Phase Gate 2 meeting agenda
- Phase Gate 2 pre-read package
- Phase Gate 2 presentation and meeting material
- Phase Gate 2 project team preparation material

Activity 2.12 – Conduct Phase Gate 2 Session

The stakes are a little higher for Phase Gate 2 than they were for Phase 1. The outcome of this phase will most likely have the organization commit significant amounts of money and resources to the remaining project phases. Therefore, this Phase Gate meeting will likely have a different level of intensity and focus than the Phase Gate 1 meeting. It is recommended that the project manager discuss the overall recommendations, that the change lead discuss the potential organizational impacts and what they will mean going forward, and that project team subject matter experts be available to answer any of the more technical questions.

Phase Gate 2 will have several key questions that need to be adequately answered:

- Have we considered all of the viable options?
- When considering different options, did we "think outside the box" or did we stay mainly within our comfort zone and skill sets? Did we invite any "outsiders" in, to shake up our thinking?
- Did we choose the right solution?
- Is the business case still strong enough to support moving forward with the solution option the team has chosen?
- Did we do all that we could to make sure that the budget for Phase 3 is accurate and not overblown?

After all of the concerns are answered, the Project Review Board should go through the standard set of Phase Gate questions that were first introduced at Phase Gate 1:

- Has all the work been completed in a satisfactory manner? Are we confident we won't have to rework anything?
- Do we have alignment on the scope/purpose/objectives for the next phase of work?
- Is there still a sufficient business case for proceeding?
- Do we have the right resources in place for the next project phase?
- Are there any concerns about the high-level plan for the next phase?
- Do we need to modify our governance structure/project processes for the next phase?

There should now be another documentation sheet to capture the decision or recommendations from Phase 2.

At the conclusion of the meeting, the team should debrief and document any concerns, recommendations, or outstanding items.

2.12 Output/Deliverable

- Documentation of Phase Gate 2 project decision/recommendations

Activity 2.13 – Communicate Outcomes/Next Steps

Provided that the team has been given the green light to proceed to Phase 3, and that there are no outstanding issues coming out of the executive debrief meetings, the change resource should help draft a closing Phase 2 communication. Ideally, the project sponsor should distribute the message if this is a high-level project. For smaller projects, the project manager should suffice. The communication should include results of the Phase Gate 2 meeting and an overview of the plans for the next phase.

Most of the recipients of this communication will be Tier 1 and 2 stakeholders: senior leaders and key decision makers as well as the various project contributors with whom the team has interacted. Since it will still take a bit of time to design and build out the solution, it may be premature to communicate to Tier 3 stakeholders, who will be the change recipients in Phase 5 (and who are probably receiving communications about other company initiatives that are closer to their deployment phase).

It is important to gather any feedback after communicating the results of Phase Gate 2. If high-level stakeholders are making it known that they strongly disagree with the outcome of Phase Gate 2, their objections need to be addressed prior to wrapping up this phase. If members of the Project Triad cannot resolve any outstanding concerns or objections, then a member of the Project Review Board may need to intervene to make his or her thinking regarding the project more visible.

Do not let outstanding issues fester, carrying over into Phase 3.

2.13 Outputs/Deliverables

- Communication regarding outcome of the Phase Gate 2 session
- Communication regarding an overview of Phase 3 plans

Activity 2.14 – Phase 2 Wrap-up

Phase 2 is closed out in a similar manner as Phase 1.

2.14.01 Document lessons learned, pertinent observations, and outstanding needs

Anything that can benefit the execution of the Phase 3, or outstanding issues arising from the debriefing session or other activities, should be documented.

2.14.02 Celebrate and Acknowledge the Team

A successful Phase 2 is reason to celebrate. It is one of the most difficult phases to get through when it comes to senior-level stakeholder buy-in and support. Make sure that team members are recognized for their contributions.

2.14 Outputs/Deliverables

- Documentation of lessons learned, pertinent observations, and outstanding needs

Conclusion of Phase 2

For more information...
Templates, detailed examples, and process tools relating to Phase 2 of the Emergence One Method can be downloaded for free (though some material may require a small licensing fee) from: **www.emergenceone.com**

Chapter 9

Phase 3: Detail Design

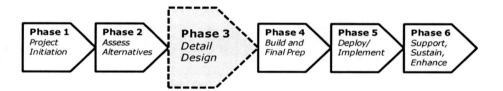

Introduction to Phase 3

Now that the project team has assessed several alternatives for the path forward, it is time to start to further refine and detail the option/alternative that was chosen. While some project teams tend to "hunker down" in this phase, there is actually a greater need for stakeholder involvement and management than ever before.

One of the main reasons why projects fail to deliver their expected bene-fits is that the actual design of the initiative does not always capture the true needs of the customers throughout the organization while remaining true to the vision and the business case set forth by executives. Perhaps no other phase represents as much of a balancing act between the different layers of the organization as Phase 3.

While creating detailed designs may require a lot of "pen and paper" work, it also requires that there be active stakeholder engagement: listening to various needs, wants, desires, and fears regarding the change architecture. If not, the initiative team runs the risk of designing a solution that will only partially satisfy the needs of the various stakeholder groups. There is also a danger that both the timeline and the budget will need to be expanded if the design process gets drawn out owing to conflicting requirements, vacillation, and inadequate cooperation by those who should be project contributors.

In order to stay on time, within budget, and according to spec, and to facilitate ongoing organizational adoption, these human dimensions need just as much careful consideration as do the design elements.

NOTE: In a number of methodologies, the design phase is combined with the development phase. Because the Emergence One Method recommends a Phase Gate to review and approve project designs before expending time and resources to build the solution, the design and development are two separate phases.

Phase 3 – Detail Design				
#	Activity			Subtask
3.01	Conduct Phase 3 Startup Activities	3.01.01		Identify the needs/expectations of Phase 3 stakeholders
		3.01.02		Update and review iterative documents
		3.01.03		Finalize Phase 3 plan/approach
3.02	Develop Tier 3 Communication/Engagement Plan	3.02.00		None
3.03	Engage/Align/Mobilize Key Stakeholders	3.03.01		Engage key stakeholders
		3.03.02		Align key stakeholders
		3.03.03		Mobilize key stakeholders
3.04	Kick Off Phase 3 Team	3.04.00		None
3.05	Gather Detailed Requirements	3.05.01		Determine objectives and level of rigor
		3.05.02		Identify and prepare participants
		3.05.03		Prepare the project team
		3.05.04		Conduct requirements-gathering sessions
		3.05.05		Update documentation and stakeholders
3.06	Finalize the Business Case and Scope	3.06.00		None
3.07	Conduct Project Health Checks	3.07.01		Conduct project health check

Phase 3 – Detail Design			
		3.07.02	Conduct project team health check
		3.07.03	Remediation planning
3.08	Develop Future State Designs and Change Control	3.08.01	Develop designs
		3.08.02	Develop and communicate a change-control process
		3.08.03	Vet design drafts
3.09	Analyze Impacts on Tier 3 Stakeholders	3.09.01	Conduct a gap analysis
		3.09.02	Determine degree of impact
		3.09.03	Develop key performance indicators/metrics
		3.09.04	Determine plan to meet organizational adoption challenges
3.10	Review/Refine Designs; Freeze Scope	3.10.01	Review designs
		3.10.02	Refine designs
		3.10.03	Freeze scope
3.11	Prepare for Phase Gate 3 Session	3.11.01	Refine/update critical project documents
		3.11.02	Assess Phase Gate readiness
		3.11.03	Design the Phase Gate 3 event
		3.11.04	Create and distribute pre-read material
		3.11.05	Conduct a Phase Gate 3 preparation session
3.12	Conduct Phase Gate 3	3.12.00	None
3.13	Communicate Outcomes/Next Steps	3.13.00	None
3.14	Phase 3 Wrap-up	3.14.01	Document any lessons learned and other pertinent information
		3.14.02	Celebrate and acknowledge the team

Activity 3.01 – Conduct Phase 3 Startup Activities

Phase 3 startup activities include the following:

1   Identify the needs and expectations of Phase 3 stakeholders.
2   Update and review iterative documents.
3   Finalize the Phase 3 project plan and schedule; align the project team on the Phase 3 plan/approach.

3.01.01 Identify the needs/expectations of Phase 3 stakeholders

In Phase 2, the activities centered on designing two or more solution options and then presenting the recommended solution to the Project Review Board for approval.

In Phase 3, the team will engage in more detailed design work. In order to do that successfully, they will need to work with various subject matter experts from the business to learn the ins and outs of how things are done today (current state analysis) and what the detailed requirements will be for the future state. Refer back to the stakeholder map (created in section 1.02.04) as a starting point for identifying Phase 3 stakeholder groups. Update the stakeholder map accordingly.

Table 9.1.   *Common needs/expectations of Phase 3 stakeholders*

Major Stakeholder Groups	Stakeholders Prominent in Phase 3	Common Needs and Expectations *During Phase 3*
TIER 1 Stakeholders: Senior Leaders/ Key Decision Makers	**Company Executives and Project Governance**	• Will the project team take the time to listen to what this organization needs, or will they just design what *they* want? • Are cost estimates going to stay pretty close to expectations? • Will the designs have any unintended consequences? • Will this project create business value or simply create change? • Are the designs flexible enough to account for any unexpected shift in business strategy or direction we may need to make?
	Project Sponsor	• Will my colleagues start to lose interest because they assume the project is now on auto pilot? • Will the project team keep making progress, or will they get lost in a maze of design details? • Is the project manager adequately overseeing the scope, budget, and timeline? • Will I have a chance to review design ideas before they are etched in stone?
	Project Review Board Members	• When can we expect Phase Gate 3 to happen? • Will what looks good on paper work as expected in the real world? • Are we going to have a chance to review designs before being asked to render a verdict on them?

Major Stakeholder Groups	Stakeholders Prominent in Phase 3	Common Needs and Expectations *During Phase 3*
TIER 2 Stakeholders: Project Contributors	Phase 3 Project Team	• If I hear different opinions on how the design should look, whom should I listen to? • How do I know that the requirements I'm hearing about are the best ones for the organization? • Is the feedback we are hearing on designs valid, or are the design elements just low-value "nice-to-haves" that clutter the scope without adding value? • How is this cross-functional, multi-disciplinary team going to function as one? • How do we integrate the multiple work streams?
	Corporate Governance Representatives	• Is the project team cognizant of corporate standards, policies, and procedures as they begin their designs?
	Business/Process Owners	• How do I make sure the needs of my department/work unit are adequately represented? • Will the designs lead to something that is clunky or difficult to implement? • How can I utilize this initiative to my advantage, or at least stay safe from its negative impacts? • Will I have the opportunity to veto or reject any proposed designs?
	Support Organizations (for example, HR, help desk, procurement)	• How will the initiative affect the different support services I provide to internal customers? • Who will fund the necessary changes my support organization may need to make in order to accommodate this change?

Major Stakeholder Groups	Stakeholders Prominent in Phase 3	Common Needs and Expectations *During Phase 3*
TIER 3 Stakeholders: Change Recipients	Impacted Employees	• I'm hearing something about a new initiative. What is it all about, why is the company doing it, and how might it affect me?
	External Customers, Vendors, and Suppliers	• What kind of changes is the organization designing, and how will they impact us? • Will the changes that the organization is designing force us to modify anything on our end?

NOTE: This is a generic assessment of stakeholder needs and expectations. Depending upon the scope and nature of the project, as well as the hierarchical structure of the company, there may be other stakeholder groups, or other needs and expectations, involved in Phase 3.

3.01.02 Update and review iterative documents

The following iterative documents need to be reviewed and may need to be updated:

- The Business Case and Project Scope Document
- The Project Roadmap
- The Lessons Learned Document
- The Executive Stakeholder Analysis Document
- The Risk Management Log
- Leadership Action Plans

Once the documents have been updated, they should be combed for potential inputs to other documents that will be completed in Phase 3.

3.01.03 Finalize Phase 3 plan/approach

The primary goal of Phase 3 is to develop the detailed plans that adequately meet the needs of a broad range of stakeholders while remaining true to the business case and scope.

Phase 3 goals and objectives should be clearly understood by all members of the project team. Many team members may be so eager to "start building the house" that they want to take shortcuts in the detail design phase. The goal here is to make sure that designs are well conceived, solidly constructed, and have the buy-in of stakeholders before spending the time and resources building something that may then require rework.

If the initiative is large, there are likely to be different work streams that are executing their activities concurrently. Therefore, developing a strong project plan and realistic project schedule is critical for this phase.

As a reminder, the Emergence One Method tries to avoid having a distinct change management work stream because change management activities are often interwoven or triggered by other team activities. Even when it comes to something as basic as a communication plan, communications are often triggered by project team activities. Therefore, it often makes more sense to tack on a communication distribution at the end of an activity rather than have a separate communication plan that may not synchronize as easily.

3.01 Outputs/Deliverables

- Updated stakeholder map
- Documented list of needs and expectations for key Phase 3 stakeholders
- Updated iterative documents
- Phase 3 project approach and schedule

Activity 3.02 – Develop Tier 3 Communication/Engagement Plan

NOTE: Communications involving the project team and Tier 1 and Tier 2 stakeholders are addressed in earlier phases. Therefore, the scope of this activity will focus on communication and engagement activities aimed at potential change recipients (Tier 3 stakeholders). Communication and engagement activities for Tier 1 and 2 stakeholders are already built into the appropriate Phase 3 activities.

Depending upon the size of the project, communication and engagement with Tier 3 stakeholders are likely to be a more complex affair than with Tier 1 and Tier 2 stakeholders.

It is important that the communication and engagement plan be developed in conjunction with, or soon after, the Phase 3 plan. Like other change management–related activities, communication and engagement activities are driven by the project plan and triggered by the execution of certain project activities. Also, the outputs of project team activities serve as inputs to the development of communications material.

Although communication and engagement planning are two of the most traditional change management activities, the Emergence One Method includes them as joint project management/change management activities.

After all, the project manager needs to be intimately involved in helping to craft, approve, and in many cases, deliver the messages. Also, the project team will be engaging numerous Tier 3 stakeholders throughout the requirements-gathering process.

The elements of a communication and engagement plan are fairly standard, though the actual structure (e.g., the sequence of information columns and rows) can be sliced and diced in a number of ways as preferred.

The essential elements of a communication/engagement plan include:

- **Targeted Audience** – If change recipients within Tier 3 stakeholder groups will be impacted differently, then the targeted audience should be further subdivided.
- **Purpose** - What is the purpose of the communication/engagement activity? Is it to provide general awareness, address rumors or misinformation, or gather feedback? Generally, communication objectives build over time: Awareness --> General Understanding --> Detailed Knowledge. Depending upon the scope and visibility of the project, these three objectives can be achieved from two weeks to several months out.
- **Key Messages** – What key information needs and messages do the stakeholder groups need to have?
- **Media or Format** – Assess in advance which media will be most effective, given the nature of the message, the project, and the culture of the organization.
- **Timing** – Notate the most optimal time to send out this message. Since communications is a strong suit of most change practitioners, many of them jump the gun and communicate too much too soon. It is important for the project manager to make sure that the change lead in charge of communications is cognizant of the need to go at a measured pace. Generally, the more transformative the initiative, the sooner the project manager will want to build awareness within the organization. However, since most organizations generally have several projects being executed at once, it is important not to overload the organization with extraneous information – especially when the actual deployment is several months away.
- **Messenger** – The "messenger" is the person who will be conducting the engagement meeting, signing the bottom of an email announcement, or having his or her name on other project tasks.
- **Additional Roles** – This can take up one or more columns, depending upon preference. Sometimes, many people are involved in one seemingly simple communication, like an email announcement. For instance, a change management resource may compose the

announcement, the project manager may approve it, the project sponsor may attach his or her name to the bottom of it, and an administrative assistant may compile the distribution list and hit the "send" button. In cases like this, it is best to document who will be playing what role.

The communication and engagement plan will be a "living document" and, as such, will be continually updated. Key messages and audience needs will develop as more and more project decisions get made.

In addition to the communication plan, larger initiatives would benefit from having a communications library: a repository of approved, up-to-date presentations available to present to different stakeholder groups or audiences.

Emergence One believes that many change practitioners tend to over-communicate throughout the project, as well as overwork the communication component of a project.

The reason for this is twofold:

1   *The "more is better myth"* – There is a myth within many change management circles that "you can never communicate too much." Sure you can! Communication recipients will tune out excess or redundant information, putting at risk their reception of future communication. This is especially true in evolving organizations that have multiple initiatives happening at once.

2   *Communication consultants are disguised as "change management" consultants* – There are many project communication resources who have deceptively rebranded themselves as "change management" consultants. Outside of communications-related activities, they understand very little of the broad range of activities that true, more experienced change management resources take on. Thus, they spend an inordinate amount of time on many low-impact activities, such as designing over-the-top graphics, writing project newsletters, or developing overwrought slide decks.

Regardless of the exact scope of the communication and engagement plan, some essential "collateral" needs to be developed since it will be frequently utilized by various project team members. This collateral will include a "Project Overview" presentation and a list of Frequently Asked Questions (FAQs).

3.02 Outputs/Deliverables

- Communication and engagement plan for Tier 3 stakeholders

Activity 3.03 – Engage/Align/Mobilize Key Stakeholders

3.03.01 Engage key stakeholders

Referring to the stakeholder map and the executive stakeholder analysis tool, identify any individuals from these groups with whom the project manager or change lead may need to engage. Use the need to debrief key executives on the Phase Gate 2 meeting outcomes as the "ticket" to secure engagement meetings.

With the business case more refined, the solution path selected, and the costs and impacts better defined, there will likely be more intense reactions from key stakeholders. Someone whose interest was initially piqued may now become even more excited about the opportunity. Conversely, don't be surprised if an initial supporter all of a sudden gets "cold feet" once he or she learns more about the costs and impacts. Lastly, be aware that someone who was initially skeptical of the project may become overtly hostile.

Hopefully, if the change lead or project manager periodically checked in with some of the executives during the Phase 2 process, and if the project sponsors have been doing their job of keeping their colleagues informed of the project's general progress and direction, there should be no unanticipated reactions. However, people often times hear what they want to hear. Thus, it is not until they see the hard dollar figures and anticipated impacts the change will have on the organization that they really sit up, pay attention, and let their true feelings be known.

3.03.02 Align key stakeholders

If some of the stakeholders appear resistant to the decisions that were agreed upon at the end of the previous phase, it is important to address these concerns and align these stakeholders behind the project.

This may involve:

- Reiterating the agreed-upon project governance structure;
- Asking them to have faith in the project;
- Providing them with the background material that contributed to the decisions; or
- Engaging a peer who is a strong project support to help turn around any resisters or naysayers.

3.03.03 Mobilize key stakeholders

Mobilizing key stakeholders encourages them to take the necessary steps to visibly support the project, understand and mitigate risks, and help maintain project momentum. It can take a variety of forms:

- Providing them with coaching based upon the leadership action plans that were created or updated.
- Assigning them specific responsibilities, such as speaking at or attending a requirements-gathering session or speaking at a town hall, and formalizing these into the project plan.
- Inviting them to sit in on a project team meeting to get firsthand knowledge of the specific project issues and risks.

3.03 Outputs/Deliverables

- Phase Gate 2 debriefing material
- Updated executive stakeholder analysis tool
- Updated leadership action plans (if necessary)
- Updated Phase 3 approach and schedule (if necessary)

Activity 3.04 – Kick Off Phase 3 Project Team

NOTE: On large change projects, additional resources (usually subject matter experts [SMEs]) are often brought in at the start of Phase 3. If so, there should probably be a kick-off of the broader Phase 3 project team; if not, this activity may be skipped.

Now that the solution path has been decided (at the end of Phase 2), it is time to design the details of the solution/change driver. Most of the Phase 2 project team members will probably continue on to Phase 3, providing the project with some continuity and allowing Phase 2 team members to build on their work from the previous phases. However, if the project is large and complex, it will probably need a broader team of SMEs to work on the solution designs.

Typically in Phase 3, the project manager leaves on-boarding the new team members to the work stream leads (if there are any on the project). While seemingly efficient, this approach poses several problems, since work stream leads tend to do the following:

- Typically focus on the needs and objectives of their particular work stream rather than providing the proper context and "big picture" view team members need to have of the project.
- Insufficiently describe the purpose and practices of the other project work streams.
- Omit the proper amount of instruction regarding the team's operating standards.

- Fail to provide team development activities that would allow new team members to interact with those on other work streams.

The likely result of having work stream leads orient new team members is that each work stream, lacking an understanding of the big picture as well as the work and value of the other work streams, will work in a more silo fashion (see Chapter 4 for more detail on the Silo Approach). Therefore, instead of developing a well-integrated, high-performing team (with several integrated work *streams*), the project will now be made up of several independent teams that will have a difficult time coming together later down the line to produce one integrated solution.

Do keep this from happening, the change management resource should revisit the Phase 2 project team kick-off material and update it for Phase 3.

3.04 Outputs/Deliverables

- Project team kick-off agenda for Phase 3
- Updated project pre-read materials
- Relevant project on-boarding information
- Outline and instructions for the team development activity (optional)

Activity 3.05 – Gather Detailed Requirements

NOTE: Although "requirements gathering" is a term commonly associated with IT development projects, Emergence One employs this terminology and many of the same key activities as a means of ensuring that customer needs and expectations are properly considered during any type of change initiative.

Many project teams assume they know what the customer wants. This is one of the biggest mistakes a project team can make.

Business requirements gathering is a process of clarifying and documenting the information and process requirements the business needs. It serves as the foundation of subsequent work because requirements serve as critical inputs into development, testing, training, and deployment/implementation activities. Strong user requirements will lead to improved customer satisfaction, higher rates of organizational adoption, and better business value realization.

Because requirements gathering is one of the first engagement events involving stakeholders from Tier 3 (change recipients), there are just as many "change management" opportunities within this activity as there are pure design opportunities.

3.05.01 Determine objectives and level of rigor

When determining the objectives for this activity, it is important to consider both design objectives as well as objectives relating to stakeholders and project risk management.

While most traditional project management methodologies look at the requirements-gathering process only as a means to gather inputs to project design, the Emergence One Method incorporates additional activities and objectives.

Primary objectives:

1   Gather the necessary inputs to project design needs.
2   Positively position the value of this initiative with participants.

Secondary objectives:

3   Record any outstanding issues or risks participants see so that the team can mitigate potential obstacles.
4   Record questions so that the team can compile a FAQ sheet for future communication activities.
5   Develop networking relationships so that the project team can more readily engage the business in any future discussions.

How much rigor to include in the requirements-gathering process depends upon the nature and scope of the initiative.

3.05.02 Identify and prepare participants

Choosing participants for the requirements-gathering sessions must be done with care. On one hand, there needs to be strong representation from impacted employee groups; on the other hand, having too many participants will not only overwhelm the project team, but may result in an avalanche of redundant material. Be sure to select participants that can adequately represent and clearly articulate the needs of *their group,* as opposed to voicing their own exclusive requirements.

Participants need to know what the initiative is about, why they were chosen to participate, what the process will be, how they can best prepare for it, and how it fits into the context of the initiative. The change lead can create and forward material addressing the above subjects to accompany the actual request (which may be made either by the project sponsor, by the project manager, or through the supervisor of the targeted participant).

3.05.03 Prepare the project team

In order to have productive requirements-gathering sessions, not only do the participants need to be prepared ahead of time, but so does the project team.

The change lead, working in conjunction with the project manager, should document the entire process and convert it into team training material.

This training material should include instructions not only on the mechanics of the requirements-gathering and documenting process, but also on many "soft skills" elements.

The training and preparation material may include some or all of the following:

1   An overview and details of the process and the deliverables (such as business requirements documentation); possibly Use Cases and functional requirements.

2   "Rules of Engagement" with the participants, such as: brainstorm, don't validate, stay within scope, defer irrelevant participant questions, etc.

3   A standard "Opening Script" for project team members to follow that reiterates purpose, process, and other key themes.

4   A "Closing Script" to positively position the project and set forth the required next steps.

5   Any supporting project material, such as FAQs or project overviews, that may be needed to competently answer queries or concerns from participants.

6   Material on how to conduct effective interviews and manage different participant personality types.

7   Material on how to identify and document any potential stakeholder management, organizational change, or project risk issues.

3.05.04 Conduct requirements-gathering sessions

When conducting the requirements-gathering sessions, project team members should utilize the guidance received during team training and preparation. It is also important to keep participants within the desired range of details: If the session is too high level, then the participants are just repeating what is in the current scope document; if it is too much in the weeds, then the project team may have a difficult time deciphering the actual requirements.

3.05.05 Update documentation and stakeholders

The process for documenting requirements should have been provided to the team as part of Activity 3.05.03. The goal of this step is to develop requirements with the right amount of quality and detail to reduce any possible ambiguity or misinterpretation. Applying a quality assurance (QA) check is often helpful. Project governance also may mandate sign-offs on completed requirements.

In addition to documenting the requirements, other documents should be updated as well. These include the risk management log and any updates to the list of FAQs.

Project team members may also want to debrief the change lead on any pertinent observations about participants' perceptions and attitudes toward the initiative.

Finally, relevant project stakeholders should be updated on any pertinent information that may have come out of the requirements-gathering session. The change lead should also draft a follow-up note, thanking participants for their time and advising them what the next steps will be (e.g., a review of completed designs or an opportunity to be part of a pilot group).

3.05 Outputs/Deliverables

- List of the most optimal participants
- Orientation material for participants
- Team preparation and support material
- Documented business requirements
- Updated risk management log
- Updated FAQ list

Activity 3.06 – Finalize the Business Case and Scope

Now that detailed business requirements have been documented and validated, the project team can finalize the business case and scope. Any scope items that have been languishing in the "Undecided" column should now be put either in or out of scope.

Whether or not there should be "scope freeze" (when there are no more changes to the scope) depends upon the nature of the project and directions from project governance. Generally, at this point in the project life cycle, there should not be any more major scope changes. However, minor changes to specific requirements may be allowed until sometime in Phase 4. Keep in mind, though, that numerous minor changes can have a cumulative effect and cause a major shift in project direction.

Any major scope changes from this point on should be presented to the appropriate governance body.

3.06 Deliverables/Outputs

- Updated business case
- Updated project scope document
- Updated project roadmap
- Updated project plan and schedule

Activity 3.07 – Conduct Project Health Checks

NOTE: Health checks can be conducted at any point in the project life cycle. Since the next few activities tend to be labor intensive, Emergence One recommends this as a good point within the project life cycle to conduct a health check.

While some project teams may consider a project health check to be an optional activity, the Emergence One Method stresses the proactive identification of issues and risks that may affect project quality, momentum, or success. The duration of this activity is rather short, but it can go a long way toward uncovering any issues that may impede the journey to total project success: on time, within budget, according to spec, adopted throughout the organization, and realizing business value.

A project health check can either look at the health of the entire project (beyond what is usually examined during the Phase Gate reviews) or just examine the overall health and efficiency of the project team.

3.07.01 Conduct project health check

Having a project health check conducted by an unbiased, outside resource will contribute to the integrity of the project. This resource should assess the following areas of the project:

- Scope
  - Is the scope well defined?
  - Was there proper justification for scope changes?
  - Were the right stakeholders consulted beforehand?
  - Were the project plan, schedule, cost estimates, and resource needs updated?
  - Etc.
- Time
  - Has the project schedule been accurate, or have there been frequent changes?
  - Are various milestones noted along the timeline?
  - Etc.
- Cost
  - Is there a reliable cost-tracking system in place?
  - Are costs being allocated to the correct cost centers?
  - What is the process for differentiating between capital costs and operating costs?
  - Etc.

- Stakeholder Management
  - Have all relevant stakeholders been identified and engaged during the right periods?
  - Is there a process for measuring stakeholder support along with methods for increasing their support?
  - How frequently do stakeholders seek out the project team to voice their needs and expectations, as opposed to the project team proactively identifying and mitigating these issues?

Other areas for a project health check may include governance, risk and issue management, metrics, resources, and quality.

3.07.02 Conduct project team health check

A project team health check has a smaller scope than a project health check but can usually be conducted by the change lead involved in the project.

The project team health check looks at the qualities that make up a high-performing team. It does this by measuring the attitudes and perceptions of *project team* members (not the project manager). Project team members are asked to rate on a five-point scale a series of statements, from "Strongly Disagree "(1) to "Strongly Agree" (5):

- I have a good picture of what we hope to achieve by implementing this change.
- I believe we have the right people with the right skill sets in place on this team.
- The officers/managers are providing the resource support necessary for us to realize our objectives.
- The manager of this project/process team has been communicating a clear understanding of how to get the job done.
- If I make a suggestion about this change effort, I know it will be given serious consideration.
- I am recognized for my contributions as part of this process team.

By gathering metrics in specific areas critical to high performance, the change lead can analyze the results and target *specific* areas for improvement rather than simply providing generic talking points or team development training.

3.07.03 Remediation planning

Regardless of what type of health check is conducted, a remediation plan should be developed and put in place for any identified deficiencies. It is important to try to identify and address the *root cause* of any identified issue rather than applying a general solution. For instance, if a team member is unclear on his roles and responsibilities, then instead of simply telling him what he should be doing, it is preferable to find out whether the project manager is adequately defining *and communicating* team roles and responsibilities.

3.07 Outputs/Deliverables

- Project/project team health check tool
- Project/project team health check results
- Remediation plan

Activity 3.08 – Develop Future State Designs and Change Control

3.08.01 Develop designs

At this point, the project team has received inputs from a variety of stake-holders, including project executives and decision makers (who provided input on project scope and direction); project contributors (who provided inputs on project requirements and organizational integration/compliance); and change recipients/customers (who provided inputs into more detailed requirements). Now it is time for the project team to start working on designs.

Before starting design work, it is important to review the stakeholder map one last time. This is done to verify that all relevant stakeholder groups have had an opportunity to provide input to the project.

Most likely, with diverse stakeholder inputs, the project will not be able to incorporate every need, wish, and desire that has been voiced. It may turn out that there are some contradictory requirements or other project requests that simply cannot be integrated. Therefore, the project team needs to stay true to the project scope and the directions provided by any governance committees.

3.08.02 Develop and communicate a change control process

Depending upon the type of initiative, the design process may involve several iterations. While it may not be necessary to fully freeze the scope during the iterative process, for certain projects (such as ERP and other IT projects), freezing the scope gives the project developers a level of stability with which to work. If the scope is frozen, any change to a requirement should just be thought of as a new requirement.

In any case, what will be most important is to have a good change control process in place.

Most professionals do not fully understand the change management implications of this activity. They think that they can simply "lock down scope" and send any late-breaking requests back to the sender. However, there are some issues with doing this:

- There will be stakeholders (who may have a degree of political backing) who expect the project team to be accommodating. When the project team is not, it may create some resistance to project adoption.
- Some late-breaking requests are legitimate (e.g., a requirement may have been missed, customers didn't fully understand their needs). However, by simply holding hard and fast to a lockdown deadline, the team may miss the chance to add in some truly valuable design elements.
- There may have been a recent external event, or some type of internal shift, that may create a legitimate need for change.

On different types of projects, such as technology and quality management systems, "scope freeze" or "lockdown" is usually handled by a *change control* process so that changes are considered and introduced in an organized manner.

3.08.03 Vet design drafts

Before finalizing project designs, they should be vetted by key project stakeholders. The vetting process is not the same as the testing or review process: when vetting project designs, one is looking at the *initial drafts and direction* of the project designs, not the final product.

When vetting the designs, it may be beneficial to have the change lead accompany team members. Project team members should try to capture any feedback about how these plans might impact the organization and any concerns stakeholders may have regarding these impacts.

3.08 Outputs/Deliverables

- First iterations of future state designs
- Documented change-control process
- Communication material regarding the change-control process
- Documented issues and concerns regarding design impacts

Activity 3.09 – Analyze Impacts on Tier 3 Stakeholders

The difference between the Tier 3 impact analysis and the organizational impact assessment (Activity 2.09) is that the former analyzes the change that will impact most individual Tier 3 stakeholders, whereas the latter assesses organizational changes.

Although there are different styles of change impact analysis, the Emergence One Method promotes a project-centric model that integrates human elements (e.g., employee motivation and competence) with organizational structural support elements (e.g., organization design, policy changes, modification to job roles and performance management systems). Both sets of elements help facilitate and sustain change adoption.

3.09.01 Conduct a gap analysis

Similar to the organizational impact assessment in Activity 2.09, the team should look at the difference between the employees' current state and the future state. The difference is that the employee gap analysis, instead of looking at what the organizational change impact will be, looks at the impact of change on individuals: what they "do now" versus what they will "need to do."

Table 9.2. *Tier 3 Stakeholder Analysis Example*

Tier 3 Stakeholder Group	Area of Change	What They *Do Now*	What They *Need to Do*
Stakeholder Group A	Desktop	Utilize different desktops with various configurations	Transfer to new HP desktops with standardized configuration
	Operating System	Utilize Microsoft Vista	Adopt MS Windows 7
	Business Applications	Utilize MS Word 2007	Adopt MS Word 2010
Stakeholder Group B	Procurement	Order from catalog	Adopt Ariba eProcurement
	Goods received	File paper receipts	Key in receipts

3.09.02 Determine degree of impact

Determine degree of impact on change recipients' motivation and required competencies. Now that there is a better idea of the specific changes for the individuals within each work group, the next step is to determine how much of a challenge each particular change brings when it comes to employee motivation and competency requirements.

This can be accomplished by asking two fairly simple questions:

- Will the initiative clearly benefit the impacted individual, or does it provide more of an esoteric organizational benefit that is less likely to be motivating?
- Does the change require a major shift in required competencies or skill sets, or will these be fairly easy for the impacted employee to pick up?

When assessing motivational challenges, keep in mind:

- **The degree of "What's In It for Me?"** (WIIFM)– The more WIIFMs that come with the change, the less of a motivational challenge there will be.
- **The user's perceived "ease" of the required change** – Employees are more motivated to adopt a change if it does not appear be too difficult to master. The more complicated the change, the less likely employees will be motivated to embrace it.
- **The level of confidence in the training and support to be provided** – Employees often fear change. However, they will be more motivated to embrace it if they know the organization will be doing all it can to provide them with the necessary training and support.
- **Whether the culture supports "team players" or mavericks** – Even when project teams make a mediocre communication effort, employees generally know that, in order to be a good team player and not get on the wrong side of the organization, they should support the changes that accompany any new projects. After all, they get paid to do a job, and part of that job requires that they accept direction from their managers and the organization.

When assessing competency development changes, keep in mind:

- **How much training or competency development is required?** – The greater the amount of training or competency development, the greater the challenge will be to teach the required skill sets.
- **How much of the new skill can be applied to other situations?** – If a new skill can be applied to a variety of situations, and is not unique to one esoteric process, the end-user will generally be more eager to learn it. As a result, learning retention is stronger.

This is especially true when it comes to IT implementations. Emergence One frequently works with companies that are implementing new technology. E1 has found that there is a less of a challenge to get people to learn a new application such as MS Office, which can be used in a variety of situations, both at work and at home. In contrast, it may be difficult to get them on board with a more narrowly focused technique that applies solely to a unique work function.

Once the challenges are identified, rate them as high, medium, or low. The higher the challenge in either one of these areas, the more attention will need to be paid. This will form the basis of the Tier 3 stakeholder management plan (which should be integrated with the remaining project activities outlined in the Emergence One Method).

3.09.03 Develop key performance indicators/metrics

Key performance indicators (commonly referred to as KPIs) are required not only to measure the performance of those in impacted roles, but also to help define and align expectations. KPIs should be based upon measures that are important to the organization and should align with some of the business realization goals set forth in the business case. Metrics for measuring performance objectives should be specific, measurable, achievable, realistic, and time-bound (SMART).

3.09.04 Determine plan to meet organizational adoption challenges

Outdated change management approaches look at organizational adoption challenges solely as "change management issues," not something the entire project team should be engaged in. This is wrong. For instance, choices that design and migration teams make can facilitate organizational adoption just as much as any change management program that narrowly focuses only on training and communication.

Once the change lead has finished conducting and analyzing the change results, he or she should share these results with the appropriate project stakeholders, who will use this information as inputs for additional activities.

For instance:

- **Project Decision Makers** - The results may be useful for determining how best to bundle or deploy changes so as not to overload employees all at once.
- **IT Migration Teams** - High ratings may indicate the availability of attractive work-arounds. Teams may need to consider shutting down or "roadblocking" these avenues.
- **Design Teams** - High ratings may indicate design complexity. The appropriate teams may need to consider simplifying the employee experience.
- **Training Team** – A high "competency challenge" rating will require more robust training; a low competency challenge rating may require only a job aid.

- **Communications** – High "motivational challenge" ratings will require more persuasive messaging. Low ratings may indicate an "easy win" that is useful for promoting the change.

In addition, high ratings in either category may mean that structural changes are necessary to help facilitate change adoption, such as the following:

- Changes to compensation and other rewards systems;
- Mandating that certain policies or procedures be followed;
- Changing the reporting relationships and design of the organization;
- Increasing or decreasing business unit funding, dependent upon compliance metrics;
- Shutting down system or process work-arounds; and
- Taking disciplinary action against those who do not exhibit the required work behaviors.

There are many things that can increase an employee's motivation to make a change, such as visible and vocal sponsorship, clear and compelling communications, enhancing the usefulness of an application or work tool, increasing rewards and recognition, or limiting the availability of work-arounds.

There are also numerous ways to increase competency development. Although some project methodologies place much emphasis on traditional classroom-type training as the only means to develop the required skill sets and competencies, depending upon how difficult the competency development challenge is, there are many other ways to achieve this objective:

- Computer-based training
- Detailed communications (may include attachments)
- Coaching
- On-the-job training
- Job aids
- Process summaries or "cheat sheets"
- Electronic or virtual classrooms
- Net meetings
- Computer "pop-up" instructional windows
- Automatic workflow notifications

Regardless of the method chosen, there should at least be a training/competency development strategy for change initiatives that rate high for competency development challenges. The components of a typical training strategy are shown below.

Table 9.3. *Common Training Strategy Components*

Common Training Strategy Components	
Audience Identification	*Who needs to be trained?*
Training Needs Assessment (TNA)	*What do they need training on?*
Training Infrastructure	*What sort of training infrastructure do we need to support the training?*
Training Delivery Options	*How can we best deliver the training?*
Content Development	*How can we best develop the training?*
Deployment	*How can we best deploy the training?*
Evaluation and Modification	*How can we best evaluate and modify training effectiveness?*
Audience Identification	*Who needs to be trained?*

3.09 Outputs/Deliverables

- Change impact analysis results
- Tier 3 organizational adoption plan, which may include activities to facilitate motivation, address competency development needs (training strategy), and recommendations to modify organizational structural elements

Activity 3.10 – Review/Refine Designs; Freeze Scope

3.10.01 Review Designs

Once the plans are completed, they should be reviewed with the appropriate stakeholders. This step will most likely include the stakeholders who were engaged as part of the requirements-gathering exercise. It is important for them to receive validation that their requirements have been captured. However, they may need to be reminded that they are to focus on *reviewing* the plans that were created, not necessarily *enhancing* them (unless their recommendations will truly add value and not conflict with project scope).

In addition to vetting the plans with design participants, an informal vetting of key Phase Gate 3 proposals should take place before the team undertakes more formal Phase Gate planning. There should be senior level support for the team's designs. If not, the team should take remedial actions. The executive stakeholder analysis tool should also be updated if necessary.

3.10.02 Refine designs

Design plans may need to be refined based upon the outcomes of both the change impact analysis (Activity 3.09) and the review session described above.

3.10.03 Freeze scope

It is also important to consider locking down the scope at this point, since accommodating late-breaking design requests will likely affect the budget, timeline, and the "build" activities of Phase 4. The change lead may wish to communicate the lockdown of scope.

3.10 Outputs/Deliverables

- Updated project designs
- Communication regarding scope freeze

Activity 3.11 – Prepare for Phase Gate 3

The activities to prepare for the Phase Gate 3 meeting will follow a similar process to Phase Gate 2.

3.11.01 Refine/update critical project documents

The business case and scope documents should have been finalized earlier in Phase 3. There are other documents that may need updating, including the following:

- *The Stakeholder Map* – Have any new stakeholder groups been identified during the course of Phase 3 activities?
- *The Project Roadmap* – Update the project roadmap accordingly.
- *The Risk Management Log* – Have there been any new risks identified during the course of Phase 3 activities?

3.11.02 Assess Phase Gate readiness

Some of the questions the team needs to ask itself for a Phase Gate 3 meeting are as follows:

- Is our business case final and no longer subject to revision? Given the time frame between when the business case was first developed and where we are now, is the business case still compelling and strong enough to invest in Phase 4 (and most likely Phase 5 and 6, since projects are less likely to be canceled after Phase 3)?

- Did we involve all the right stakeholders in our requirements-gathering sessions?
- Were our design activities able to find additional business value without significantly adding to scope?
- Are our designs feasible? Should the build and final prep phase go smoothly based upon our design?
- Are there political support and momentum around the designs we are proposing?
- Did we do enough Phase 4 planning to provide the Project Review Board with a good sense of our objectives, planned activities, and anticipated costs?

3.11.03 Design the Phase Gate 3 event

The meeting structure and roles will most likely be similar to those of Phase Gate 2, with the project manager leading the meeting and the change lead facilitating. Even though the team may have been expanded during Phase 3, only the core project team should attend the Phase Gate meeting.

3.11.04 Create and distribute pre-read material

The pre-read package for Phase 3 should contain similar material to the Phase Gate 2 materials but be updated to reflect Phase Gate 3 needs.

3.11.05 Conduct a Phase Gate 3 preparation session

By now, the core project team (or those who will be attending the Phase Gate meeting) should know the drill when it comes to preparing for the meeting. As a matter of fact, now that the team has more experience with the various personalities on the Project Review Board, they may be a bit defter when it comes to identifying potential questions and points of contention.

3.11 Outputs/Deliverables

- Phase Gate 3 meeting agenda
- Phase Gate 3 pre-read package
- Phase Gate 3 presentation and meeting materials
- Phase Gate 3 project team preparation material

Activity 3.12 – Conduct Phase Gate 3

The Project Review Board will no doubt want to discuss any issues they have with the design. In addition, an engaged Project Review Board will most likely ask several of the following questions:

- Now that the business case has been finalized, will it be worth the time and expense to actually build this solution?
- Will we be able to actually build and implement these designs? How do we know they will work in the real world?
- Are the cost estimates correct? Have we considered options that will save us money?
- How do we know the design will generate business value as opposed to simply changing the organization?
- Does this design present any outstanding risks?
- Were all the right stakeholders involved? Did they have any specific concerns or recommendations and, if so, how did you deal with them?
- How did you reconcile any conflicting requirement requests?
- How will you deal with scope change requests in Phase 4?

While receiving a green light to proceed is always a great outcome, getting a "Proceed" recommendation or decision at Phase Gate 3 is especially encouraging. Most projects that are green-lighted in Phase 3, barring some unforeseen event, will eventually get implemented. There might be a "rework" required at the end of Phase 4 owing to a lack of organizational readiness, but since the business case has now been finalized and accepted, it is doubtful that the project will be killed (so long as the schedule and budget are maintained within tolerable limits).

3.12 Outputs/Deliverables

- Documentation of Phase Gate 3 project recommendations

Activity 3.13 – Communicate Outcomes/Next Steps

Regardless of whether or not Phase Gate 3 was a success, the change lead should draft communications regarding the outcome of the session to all of the stakeholders involved in Phase 3. The communication should ideally be sent by the project sponsor, especially if a broad number of stakeholders were involved. The audience and methods of dissemination for this communication should already have been documented as part of Activity 3.02.

At this point, the team may need to communicate with some of the Phase 3 stakeholders who may be involved in requirements-gathering and design reviews.

It is important to gather any feedback after communicating the results of Phase Gate 3. If there are high-level stakeholders who are making it known that they strongly disagree with the outcome of Phase Gate 3, then their concerns need to be addressed prior to wrapping up this phase. If members of the Project Triad cannot resolve any outstanding concerns or objections, then a member of the Project Review Board may need to intervene to make his or her thinking on the project more visible.

Outstanding issues should *not* be carried into Phase 4.

3.13 Outputs/Deliverables

- Communication regarding outcome of the Phase Gate 2 session, along with an overview of Phase 3

Activity 3.14 – Phase 3 Wrap-up

Phase 3 is closed out in a similar manner as Phase 2.

3.14.01 Document any lessons learned, pertinent observations, or outstanding needs from Phase 3

Anything that could benefit the execution of Phase 4, or outstanding issues arising from the debriefing session or other activities, should be documented.

3.14.02 Celebrate and acknowledge the team

Phase 3 can be long and tedious. Gaining the organization's commitment to support the project into Phase 4 (often the longest and most expensive phase) is quite an accomplishment. If the team is indeed given a green light to proceed to Phase 4, a well-deserved team celebration is in order.

3.14 Outputs/Deliverables

- Documentation of lessons learned, pertinent observations, and outstanding needs

Conclusion of Phase 3

For more information...
Templates, detailed examples, and process tools relating to Phase 3 of the Emergence One Method can be downloaded for free (though some material may require a small licensing fee) from: **www.emergenceone.com**

Chapter 10

Phase 4: Build and Final Prep

Phase 1 — Project Initiation
Phase 2 — Assess Alternatives
Phase 3 — Detail Design
Phase 4 — Build and Final Prep
Phase 5 — Deploy/ Implement
Phase 6 — Support, Sustain, Enhance

Introduction to Phase 4

Phase 4 is where the solution and all the peripheral support materials are developed and tested.

An important aspect of this phase is that "Final Prep" refers to the completion of the solution, deployment plans, and support material. Activities that directly involve Tier 3 stakeholders, such as training, are considered to be part of Phase 5 deployment/implementation (occurring just before the deployment of the solution/change driver)..

Project expenses during Phase 4 generally tend to peak because this phase usually requires the organization to procure materials and resources required to build out the initiative. Development of required training materials, along with the actual training of support staff (such as help desk personnel), can also take an unexpected chunk of the project budget unless they were properly planned for in Phase 3.

Owing to the high costs associated with this phase, it is important that nothing impede the momentum or effectiveness of the project team. This phase needs to have a well-managed project plan, properly trained and focused resources, and clearly defined roles and responsibilities for its participants. It will also require the effective management of stakeholder anxiety, which may manifest itself in any number of ways, including asking for additional modifications to scope, requesting deferments, or engaging in covert activities designed to get decision makers to delay or even abandon the project.

Lastly, the deployment planning process that occurs in Phase 4 needs to be conducted as rigorously as the project planning process was in Phase 3. This means creating and validating deployment plans with relevant project stakeholders; identifying possible deployment risks; and developing the necessary contingency plans to ensure that an acceptable level of productivity is maintained during the transition.

Phase 4 – Build, Final Prep				
#	Activity			Subtasks
4.01	Conduct Phase 4 Startup Activities		4.01.01	Identify the needs/expectations of Phase 4 stakeholders
			4.01.02	Update/review iterative documents
			4.01.03	Finalize Phase 4 plan/approach
4.02	Engage/Align/Mobilize Key Stakeholders		4.02.01	Engage key stakeholders
			4.02.02	Align key stakeholders
			4.02.03	Mobilize key stakeholders
4.03	Kick Off Phase 4 Team		4.03.00	None
4.04	Build the Solution/Change Driver		4.04.00	None
4.05	Develop Initial Deployment Plan and Implementation Support Material		4.05.01	Engage Tier 3 stakeholders
			4.05.02	Develop the initial deployment plan
			4.05.03	Build training and implementation support material
4.06	Conduct Project and/or Team Health Check		4.06.01	Conduct project health check
			4.06.02	Conduct project team health check
			4.06.03	Remediation planning
4.07	Test and/or Pilot Solution; Refine		4.07.01	Determine objectives and level of rigor
			4.07.02	Identify and prepare participants

Phase 4 – Build, Final Prep			
		4.07.03	Prepare the project team
		4.07.04	Conduct testing sessions
		4.07.05	Gather inputs for deployment planning
		4.07.06	Update documentation and stakeholders
		4.07.07	Refine/rework solution (if needed)
4.08	Finalize Training and Deployment Support Material	4.08.01	Finalize training and deployment support material
		4.08.02	Update leadership/management action plans
4.09	Vet and Finalize Deployment Plan	4.09.00	None
4.10	Conduct High-Level Readiness Assessment	4.10.01	Develop the readiness assessment tool
		4.10.02	Conduct readiness assessment
		4.10.03	Review results; address outstanding issues
4.11	Prepare for Phase Gate 4	4.11.01	Vet Phase Gate deliverables with key stakeholders
		4.11.02	Assess Phase Gate readiness
		4.11.03	Design the Phase Gate 4 event
		4.11.04	Create and distribute pre-read material
		4.11.05	Conduct a Phase Gate 4 preparation meeting
4.12	Conduct Phase Gate 4	4.12.00	None
4.13	Communicate Outcomes/Next Steps	4.13.00	None
4.14	Conduct Phase 4 Wrap-up	4.14.01	Document any lessons learned, pertinent observations, or outstanding needs
		4.14.02	Celebrate and acknowledge the team

Activity 4.01 – Conduct Phase 4 Startup Activities

Phase 4 startup activities mirror those of the previous phase:

1   Identify the needs and expectations of Phase 4 stakeholders.
2   Update and review iterative documents.
3   Finalize the Phase 4 project plan and schedule; align the project team on the Phase 4 plan/approach.

4.01.01 Identify the needs/expectations of Phase 4 stakeholders

The two main deliverables of Phase 4 are to build the solution or change driver and create a deployment plan. In order to complete these two activities, it may be necessary to reach further into the organization in order to engage the end-users/employees who will be most affected by the change. The project team will need these change recipients' input to test the solution and provide feedback for the deployment plans.

Table 10.1. *Common needs/expectations of Phase 4 stakeholders*

Major Stakeholder Groups	Stakeholders Prominent in Phase 4	Common Needs and Expectations *During Phase 4*
TIER 1 Stakeholders: Senior Leaders/ Key Decision Makers	**Company Executives and Project Governance**	• Will the project team work effectively and efficiently, or are they going to blow the budget? • Have we accounted for all the anticipated costs, or are we going to be hit with some last-minute surprises? • Are the deployment plans going to consider current operational needs and productivity levels, or are they going to be completely centered on the change?
	Project Sponsor	• Is the success of the project overly dependent on external resources and vendors? • How do I know if the project team is working effectively? • Are people going to be coming to me to insist on last-minute modifications? • Is the project manager overseeing the scope, budget, and timeline adequately? • How do I know that the organization will adopt this change? • Is the team considering all the necessary components to pull off a successful deployment?
	Project Review Board Members	• When can we expect Phase Gate 4 to happen? • How much of a role will I need to play after Phase Gate 4, once the solution is deployed or the change is made?

Major Stakeholder Groups	Stakeholders Prominent in Phase 4	Common Needs and Expectations *During Phase 4*
TIER 2 Stakeholders: Project Contributors	**Phase 4 Project Team**	• Do we have enough resources for this phase, or will we all be working 80-hour weeks? • Will this project work as expected, or are we going to get kicked back to the design phase? • How do we maintain momentum and buoyancy during this long and challenging phase?
	Support Organizations (e.g., HR, help desk, procurement)	• What is the project team expecting from my organization in terms of deployment coordination or support? • How can I best accommodate any unique project support needs while maintaining a proper level of service to other internal customers?
	Business/Process Owners	• How do I make sure the needs of my department/work unit are adequately represented? • Is the project team considering the unique needs of my people as the team prepares for deployment? • How can I provide my people with more information? • Will the organizational impacts affect my ability to deliver? • Is the deployment plan sensitive to my needs to maintain a certain level of productivity?

Major Stakeholder Groups	Stakeholders Prominent in Phase 4	Common Needs and Expectations *During Phase 4*
TIER 3 Stakeholders: Change Recipients	Impacted Employees	• Why are they doing this? Is it really necessary? • How will this change impact me and my job? • What will be expected of me? • Are they planning to train me and give me the new skills I'll need to be successful? • What other kind of support will I get from the organization? • Will I still be able to use a work-around if this new [system, process, etc.] doesn't work?
	External Customers, Vendors, and Suppliers	• Can we build and test any integration requirements with the organization within the timeline they have set? • Will we get preferential treatment if we bend over backwards to support their organizational initiative?

NOTE: *This is a generic assessment of stakeholder needs and expectations. Depending upon the scope and nature of the project, as well as the hierarchical structure of the company, there may be other stakeholder groups, or other needs and expectations, involved in Phase 4.*

4.01.02 Update/review iterative documents

The following iterative documents need to be reviewed and may need to be updated:

- The Business Case and Project Scope Document
- Communication and Engagement Plan
- The Project Roadmap
- The Lessons Learned Document
- The Executive Stakeholder Analysis Document
- The Risk Management Log
- Leadership Action Plans

Once the documents have been updated, they should be combed for potential inputs to other documents that will be completed in Phase 4.

4.01.03 Finalize Phase 4 plan/approach

The primary goal of Phase 4 is to build the solution along with any peripheral support tools and documentation that will be required for successful deployment. Apply any lessons learned from the previous phase or elsewhere while finalizing the Phase 4 plan and project schedule.

All members of the project team should clearly understand Phase 4's goals and objectives. This is an expensive phase to operate, both in terms of man-hours and materials. Mistakes can be costly; therefore, it is important to have a solid, well-thought-out plan along with clear roles and responsibilities.

4.01 Outputs/Deliverables

- Updated stakeholder map
- Documented list of needs and expectations for key Phase 4 stakeholders
- Finalized business case and scope
- Updated iterative documents
- Phase 4 project approach and schedule

Activity 4.02 – Engage/Align/Mobilize Key Stakeholders

The need to engage, align, and mobilize key stakeholders continues to be of primary importance for each new phase. This is especially true in Phase 4, when it is important that time and material not be wasted building a solution that all stakeholders do not fully support.

4.02.01 Engage key stakeholders

Since Phase 4 will involve deployment planning, a wider range of individuals from the business (operations) may need to be included in this activity. The project manager and change lead can use the talking points debrief from the Phase Gate 3 meeting as leverage to secure engagement meetings with the key stakeholders from previous phases. For stakeholders who become key to Phase 4 success, gaining their understanding and support for the upcoming deployment can be the catalyst for securing engagement meetings.

After engaging key stakeholders, be sure to update the executive stakeholder analysis tool.

4.02.02 Align key stakeholders

If some of the stakeholders appear resistant to the decisions that were agreed upon at the end of Phase 3, it is important to address their concerns and align these stakeholders with project objectives. It is also important to get key stakeholders from operations aligned around project and deployment design efforts.

4.02.03 Mobilize key stakeholders

Within Phase 4, mobilizing key leaders can require them to undertake any of the following:

- Understanding and addressing any dissension that colleagues may have
- Ensuring that the project team gets the necessary resources as soon as they need it; and
- Beginning to positively position the project with others throughout the organization

The change lead should be able to provide additional thoughts and ideas on the type of actions key stakeholders can take to maintain project momentum, direction, and acceptance.

Any information coming out of the engagement sessions that could have an effect on the project plan should be relayed to the project manager.

4.02 Outputs/Deliverables

- Phase Gate 3 debriefing material
- Updated executive stakeholder analysis tool
- Updated leadership action plans (if necessary)
- Updated Phase 4 approach and schedule (if necessary)

Activity 4.03 – Kick Off Phase 4 Team

NOTE: On large change projects, additional resources (usually subject matter experts [SMEs]) are often brought on at the start of Phase 3. If so, there should probably be a kick-off of the broader Phase 3 project team; if not, this activity may be skipped.

For Phase 4, additional project resources are often brought in to build not only the solution, but also the peripheral support material as well (such as the training manual and troubleshooting guides).

It is important to orient any new team members to all of the project essentials: scope, purpose, business case, project team charter, project plan and schedule, etc. Most important is to ensure that the new project team resources understand the project designs they need to realize and to further assess that the right resources to do this have been secured. Now is not the time for on-the-job training.

4.03 Outputs/Deliverables

- Project team kick-off agenda for Phase 4
- Updated project pre-read materials
- Relevant project on-boarding information
- Outline and instructions for the team development activity (optional)

Activity 4.04 – Build the Solution/Change Driver

Building the "solution," that is, what you will be deploying, is at the heart of the change project. This activity is most likely to be one of the longest in any of the project phases. As such, it needs to be properly managed. While the project manager can help oversee the project tasks, the change lead can help manage some of the group dynamics that may impact project momentum and quality.

For some projects, this activity will most likely be one of the longest activities of the project life cycle. It can involve scores of subcontractors and multiple tasks that will be reflected in a large segment of the project schedule. This work is generally overseen by the project manager.

If the solution requires multiple work streams, then there needs to be an *integration plan* put in place. The integration plan will monitor the work and progress of the different work streams to help ensure that the timing of various integration points is properly synchronized. The plan will also help ensure that the outputs of the various work streams will be compatible, thereby contributing to the total solution.

4.04 Outputs/Deliverables

- The solution/change driver in a tangible form

Activity 4.05 – Develop Initial Deployment Plan and Implementation Support Material

While the solution is being built, it may be feasible to start working on the initial deployment plan and any required training and implementation support material. Depending upon the nature and scope of the initiative, these two activities (especially the latter) can be time-consuming and labor-intensive. Emergence One consultants have typically found that these activities tend to be under-scoped and under-budgeted by most organizations.

4.05.01 Engage Tier 3 stakeholders

Although a subset of Tier 3 stakeholders may have already been engaged during requirements-gathering and design review sessions, it is often helpful to engage a broader set of these stakeholders before developing the deployment plan.

For larger initiatives, this engagement is often accomplished in employee focus groups. In the opinion of Emergence One, employee surveys are a great way of gathering "nice to have" information but often fail to yield the critical insights necessary for developing a truly effective deployment plan. Nor do surveys achieve many of the other objectives listed below.

The engagement sessions with Tier 3 stakeholders have multiple objectives:

- To provide additional, more personalized information regarding the initiative;
- To gather inputs for the deployment plan (e.g., timing, desired level of support, issues that can facilitate or hinder employee motivation);
- To gain awareness of potential work-arounds and other avenues for non-compliance (Note: this is very important for the project team to have but, unfortunately, is often overlooked by many change practitioners); and
- To position the initiative so that engagement participants will return to their workplaces with a positive impression of what is to come and hopefully start an informal "buzz" regarding the initiative.

It is important that the people facilitating these engagement sessions stay focused on the above objectives and handle any complaints or concerns in a positive manner.

The change lead often moderates these engagement sessions with support from other core and extended team members as necessary. However, it is essential for the change lead to debrief the project lead on any potential system or process work-arounds so that the project manager can decide whether or not to roadblock these avenues. The change lead should also debrief the project sponsor about any issues regarding stakeholders' needs to see more visible senior-level leadership.

4.05.02 Develop the initial deployment plan

The deployment plan will contain several key elements to facilitate the successful deployment and implementation of the solution and the subsequent changes it causes.

The project team should seek the input of any corporate support organization that will also be involved in deploying and supporting the initiative.

Some of the more common elements of a deployment plan are as follows:

Table 10.2. *Common deployment planning components*

Project Y Deployment Planning Guide	
Component	Description
Deployment Strategy and Schedule	Will the change be rolled out in a phased manner, based upon geographic location and/or degree of change, or will the organization go with a one-shot "big bang" approach? How will the organization continue to meet ongoing operational needs while absorbing change? Will parallel systems or work-arounds remain active, or will they be turned off?
Roles and Responsibilities	What will be the specific roles and responsibilities for members of the Tier 1 and Tier 2 stakeholder groups?
Logistic	If the change driver requires the movement or installation of something tangible, how will the logistics be managed?
Contingency Plans	What are the contingency plans if all does not go according to plan? What events will trigger a contingency plan?
Support	What kind of support, both tangible (such as reference manuals) and intangible (such as management encouragement), should be made available?
Reward and Consequences	Should there be rewards and consequences to go along with the new performance expectations or compliance requirements?
Metrics	How does the team know that the deployment is progressing as planned and that the implementation is taking hold? What are some objective measures of progress and success? (NOTE: When designing metrics to evaluate deployment/implementation progress, it is important to utilize metrics that can be quickly gathered and analyzed so that problems and "hiccups" can be promptly identified and addressed.)

Project Y Deployment Planning Guide	
Cost Allocations	How are the costs of deployment and implementation going to be allocated? Will corporate absorb all of the costs, or will affected business units and locations be expected to pick up a share of the expenses?
Additional components?	*Add description if needed.*

This activity is just the start of the deployment and implementation plan. In later activities, the team will be able to gather deployment plan inputs from the soon-to-be-impacted stakeholders: namely the end-users/employees as well as their managers and supervisors. The inputs of these stakeholders will be critical when crafting an effective deployment plan.

4.05.03 Build training and implementation support material

Regardless of the solution or change driver, it will most likely need supporting material built to accompany its deployment and implementation.

Determining what sort of training and implementation support material will be required is based upon the anticipated organizational and end-user/employee impacts that were previously determined.

Training and implementation support material may include the following:

- *Training Materials* – These may be comprised of student guides, instructor manuals, and computer-based training modules (CBTs).
- *Additional Competency Development Materials* – These may include job aids, "cheat sheets," memory joggers, and quick reference manuals.
- *System/Process Documentation* – Many teams develop strong processes but fail to adequately document them, causing problems for users who are unfamiliar with the new processes. Flow charts and other forms of system documentation should be developed.
- *Help Desk and Support Manuals* – Project teams should never assume that training is the be-all and end-all of change competence. Impacted employees may need to request assistance from a help desk for any competency development challenges or troubleshooting needs.
- *New Policies and Procedures* – If there will be new policies or procedures put in place that will help promote change compliance, they will need to be approved and promoted by the appropriate corporate compliance governance committees.

- *HR Support* – If the change driver will require modifications in employee behaviors, those may need to be reflected in new or revised job role descriptions, career ladders, performance reviews, employee remuneration, organizational design and staffing support levels, and other components of the HR apparatus. (NOTE: Because HR is generally slow to modify their systems, changes to the HR apparatus may need to begin sooner rather than later.)
- *Management Action Plans* – Management action plans (MAPs) are similar to leadership action plans but are written for frontline managers and supervisors or those responsible for overseeing a majority of Tier 3 stakeholders (change recipients). MAPs outline how managers can support and promote change and how best to deal with any resistance that may occur. MAPs also provide additional information on the project, such as FAQs, where to go for additional support, and what new policies and procedures may accompany the change. MAPs can be especially useful for promoting organizational adoption and business value realization since centralized planning and control (which often accompanies large projects and initiatives) lacks the effectiveness and responsiveness that local management can provide.
- *Additional Communication Material* – Besides building the solution, one of the main objectives of Phase 4 is to prepare the material necessary for deployment. This material will most likely include various communications customized to each unique stakeholder group identified in the stakeholder map.

Many of the above material and information can be placed upon a project information intranet site, specifically designed for end-users/employees and separate from the project team site. Note that many company intranet sites need to conform to company standards or meet design and usability standards. Therefore, the project team will need to engage these stakeholders in a timely manner.

4.05 Outputs/Deliverables

- Engagement session preparation material
- Documentation of engagement session outputs
- Initial draft of the deployment/implementation plan
- Deployment/implementation support material
- Project intranet site

Activity 4.06 – Conduct Project and/or Team Health Check

Health checks were first introduced as a recommended activity in Phase 3. They are a means to maintaining project momentum, quality, and completeness.

4.06.01 Conduct project health check

Project health checks are recommended again in Phase 4 because mistakes here can be extremely costly – threatening not only the budget, but the project timeline as well. It is recommended that outside resources be utilized for the project health check.

4.06.02 Conduct project team health check

Since Phase 4 can be labor-intensive, having a high-performance team in place will greatly enhance task completion during it. It is usually best to have the change lead conduct an assessment of the project team, share the results with the project manager, and then employ targeted team development activities to improve performance in the areas identified as substandard.

4.06.03 Remediation planning

Regardless of whether one or both types of health checks are conducted, a remediation plan should be developed and put in place for any identified deficiencies.

4.06 Outputs/Deliverables

- Project/project team health check tool
- Project/project team health check results
- Remediation plan

Activity 4.07 – Test and/or Pilot Solution; Refine

NOTE: This activity is critical to IT and some process reengineering projects. For other projects, this activity may be replaced with a stakeholder vetting session.

Before the project team can embark on subsequent phase activities, such as finalizing the training material and deployment plans, they should first test or pilot the solution. This step helps to ensure that no additional changes or modifications need to be made to the solution. It also helps to ensure that training material, deployment plans, and project documentation adequately reflect the actual solution that will be deployed.

4.07.01 Determine objectives and level of rigor

When determining the exact structure of this activity, the project team should ascertain the following:

- Can the solution be tested beforehand? If so, how rigorous does the testing process need to be?
- Will participants be testing a fully built solution or some type of prototype?
- How can the testing process adequately capture and reflect real-world usage or application?
- Will it, and should it, be piloted with a (non-critical) stakeholder group after it has been tested?
- Will it be a temporary pilot program, where the change is halted and results are analyzed and refined before being redeployed, or will it be a pilot program that continues straight into the operational phase?

Similar to some of the stakeholder and risk management activities associated with Phase 3 requirements gathering, additional objectives may stretch beyond the primary need to test the integrity or veracity of the solution. Such long-range objectives include the following:

- Positively positioning the value of this initiative with participants.
- Recording any outstanding issues or risks that participants see so that the team can mitigate any potential obstacles.
- Recording questions so that a FAQ sheet can be compiled for use in pre-deployment and deployment/implementation activities.
- Developing networking relationships with an additional set of stakeholders.

4.07.02 Identify and prepare participants

When choosing participants for testing, include representatives from all of the impacted stakeholder groups. If piloting, choose stakeholder groups that are not as critical to operations as are the core business groups.

Regardless of their level of understanding regarding the project, participants will need to know why they were chosen for the test or pilot group and how their feedback will be utilized. The change lead can create the necessary materials to explain.

4.07.03 Prepare the project team

Project team members involved in testing or pilot group deployment should also be cognizant of the many stakeholder management and organizational change needs that may exist or arise as a result of the process.

The team should be trained in several areas:

- "Rules of Engagement" with participants (e.g., observe how users navigate around a system glitch rather than jumping in and providing them with the correct path).
- An "opening script" that gives an overview of the testing process.
- A "closing script" that positively positions the project and the required next steps.
- Any supporting project material, such as updated FAQs or project overviews, that may be needed to competently answer queries or concerns from participants.
- Training material on how to document outcomes and results in a standardized manner.
- Material on how to document project risk related to stakeholder management, organizational change, or other issues.

4.07.04 Conduct testing sessions

If the testing session or pilot program does not go smoothly, it is critical that project team members reassure participants that any identified issues will be further explored and addressed. After all, the purpose of testing and piloting is to identify and correct issues *before* deploying the solution to the broader organization.

4.07.05 Gather inputs for deployment planning

Once formal testing has been completed and the participants have gained greater insights into the solution, the change lead should facilitate a session to gather inputs for deployment planning.

Here are some questions he or she could pose:

- How do you think this solution will be received by the organization?
- Are there any potential deployment risks that the deployment planning team should be aware of?
- If you wanted to utilize a work-around, what would you do?
- How much training and communication support do you think change recipients will require?
- Would any other type of deployment/implementation support be beneficial?

Information gathered during this session can serve as one source of inputs for the deployment plan.

4.07.06 Update documentation and stakeholders

The project team should document any relevant results and feedback. The project manager and change lead can review the findings and then update the necessary project documents, such as the risk log.

The change lead should also draft a follow-up note, thanking participants for their time and informing them how their feedback will be utilized.

4.07.07 Refine/rework solution (if needed)

Depending upon the outcome of the testing session or pilot program, the solution may need to be further refined or reworked.

4.07 Outputs/Deliverables

- List of the most optimal participants
- Orientation material for participants
- Team preparation and support material
- Documented testing results
- Updated risk management log

Activity 4.08 – Finalize Training and Deployment Support Material

Now that the actual solution has been tested, refined, and possibly piloted (as mentioned in the previous activity, piloting may be delayed until later in this phase), the next activity is to finalize any training and peripheral support material that may be required.

4.08.01 Finalize training and deployment support material

Since the change driver or solution may have been refined or reworked in the previous activity, it is important that all training materials, support manuals, etc., be updated to reflect any last-minute modifications.

4.08.02 Update leadership/management action plans

Leadership and management action plans should be developed or updated not only for key executives, but also for influential business unit leaders and department heads. Leadership action plans should contain a deployment support package that includes all the critical information regarding the deployment plan, for example, timeline, key contacts, available support, and key talking points on the solution's purpose and benefits.

Leadership action plans should be consistent with any roles and responsibilities outlined in subtask 4.05.02, "Develop the initial deployment plan."

4.08 Outputs/Deliverables

- Updated training and deployment support material
- Updated leadership action plans

Once upon a time...
Getting Ready for Rio

Emergence One once had a client whose project involved the rollout of some fairly minor process changes to a global workforce located in various countries around the world. Although the process changes were fairly minor, some members of the project team (from the internal side) strongly believed that the *only* way to accomplish this was to fly around the world to certain key cities (very attractive cities, by the way, such as Rio de Janeiro, London, Cape Town, and Singapore) and conduct training sessions. And since most of the participants worked at factory locations away from these key cities, they too would be asked to fly to one of these very attractive "training hubs."

When Emergence One suggested that there were less expensive and time-consuming solutions to achieving the project objectives, we were met with strong resistance. All the team could think about were the beaches in Rio, the food in Singapore, etc. They were not interested in hearing about video conferencing and other distance-learning methods, or doing a "train-the-trainer" session with a smaller group of regional managers instead.

Despite the resistance, Emergence One was able to put together a business case for two alternative solutions. To make a long story short, although this did not curry favor with some of our internal colleagues on the team, we did save the company over $100,000, as well as a lot of unnecessary travel time for the affected employees.

Activity 4.09 – Vet and Finalize Deployment Plan

Before finalizing the deployment plan, the project team should informally vet it, not only with project governance, but also with key stakeholders from the affected business units.

It is especially important to get buy-in from business unit leaders before proceeding. If any major issues are raised at this point in Phase 4, then the project sponsor (or other relevant high-level stakeholder) needs to be called in to alleviate any concerns.

Vetting the deployment plans serves two purposes: it helps the deployment team incorporate fresh ideas into the deployment plan and it raises their understanding of any potential risks or barriers. It also serves a communication/engagement purpose by giving project stakeholders a preview of how the initiative will be rolled out in Phase 5.

4.09 Outputs/Deliverables

- Updated deployment plan
- Updated stakeholder analysis tool

Activity 4.10 – Conduct High-Level Readiness Assessment

There are two pre-deployment assessments recommended in the Emergence One Method. One occurs here in Phase 4, and is entitled a "High-Level Readiness Assessment." This focuses on items that will most likely require a time-consuming fix (e.g., the solution is still not ready, training material has not yet been fully developed, entrenched stakeholder resistance issues will take time to mitigate). In Phase 5, there is a "Go/No Go Assessment" that is conducted shortly after activities to prepare the organization. Its purpose is to evaluate these activities' effectiveness.

4.10.01 Develop the readiness assessment tool

For Phase 4, the high-level readiness assessment helps to ensure that all the components for a successful kick-off of Phase 5 are in place. The change leader, working in conjunction with the project manager, can design and lead this assessment activity.

As far as organizational assessments are concerned, there are as many "readiness assessments" available as there are flavors of ice cream. Most project managers assess *technical* readiness. Conversely, most change leads assess *psychological* or *emotinal* readiness. Since E1 is an integrated methodology, it combines both aspects into one readiness assessment.

The readiness assessment should ascertain whether or not all the elements of the deployment and implementation plan are fully developed and ready to go. For example:

- Have all the tangible elements of the initiative been procured, and are they ready to be distributed according to schedule?
- Has all the training material been finalized and produced in sufficient quantity to meet the needs of all the targeted participants?
- Is all related support material ready to be distributed to the relevant stakeholders?

- Has there been any identified resistance to this initiative, and if so, what is the source of this resistance? Can it be mitigated during the early part of Phase 5?

The actual training (skill development) of impacted employees will commence in the first half of Phase 5. Managers and supervisors who have a role in facilitating or championing the change effort will also be trained or given guidance at the start of Phase 5.

4.10.02 Conduct the readiness assessment

Since the assessment involves looking at areas that are traditionally considered to be the purview of project management as well as change management, both the project lead and the change lead should work collaboratively on this activity.

4.10.03 Review results; address outstanding issues

Once the data have been collected from the readiness assessment, review the results and address any outstanding items prior to conducting the Phase Gate 4 session.

The decision to proceed to Phase 5 will be formally made at the end of the Phase Gate 4 session. However, if the organization is obviously not ready for this change, the team may need to either rework some of the previous activities or initiate specific activities to address any deficiencies they have noted.

4.10 Outputs/Deliverables

- Readiness assessment tool
- Readiness assessment results

Activity 4.11 – Prepare for Phase Gate 4

The activities to prepare for the Phase Gate 4 meeting will follow a similar process to the one for Phase Gate 3.

4.11.01 Vet Phase Gate deliverables with key stakeholders

The team should informally vet key Phase Gate 4 proposals before undertaking more formal Phase Gate planning. They should consider any actionable feedback and update the executive stakeholder analysis tool accordingly.

4.11.02 Assess Phase Gate readiness

The following are some questions the team needs to ask themselves for a Phase Gate 4 meeting:

- Will the solution, as built, deliver the expected business value as laid out in the business case?
- Did we involve all the right stakeholders when it came to reviewing/testing the solution and developing the deployment plans?
- Were there any discrepancies between what was designed and what was actually built?
- Have we accounted for all the variables that can affect deployment and implementation? Should the deployment and implementation phase go smoothly?
- Has most of the political resistance been mitigated?

4.11.03 Design the Phase Gate 4 event

The meeting structure and roles will most likely be similar to those of Phase Gate 3. The Phase Gate 4 meeting is liable to last longer than the Phase Gate 3 meeting, since inevitably, numerous questions will be asked about deployment.

4.11.04 Create and distribute pre-read material

The pre-read package for Phase 4 should contain the following:

- A cover letter outlining the agenda and the objectives. Phase Gate 4 has two main objectives: discovering whether the solution "works" and if the deployment plans are adequate.
- Background on the Phase 4 project team and their activities.
- Details regarding the deployment/implementation plan and any contingency plans.
- An understanding of any organizational adoption challenges that may emerge and how the project team plans to address them.
- Any anticipated challenges that may be confronted when building out the designs into something more tangible.
- The high-level plan for Phase 4, including the cost, plus or minus a certain percentage.

4.11.05 Conduct a Phase Gate 4 preparation meeting

The Phase Gate 4 preparation meeting should include all core team members and follow a structure similar to what was outlined in previous phases.

4.11 Outputs/Deliverables

- Phase Gate 4 meeting agenda
- Phase Gate 4 pre-read package
- Phase Gate 4 presentation and meeting materials
- Phase Gate 4 project team preparation material

Activity 4.12 – Conduct Phase Gate 4

The Project Review Board will need to have confidence that whatever the project team built will work as expected when deployed in the organization. The Board will most likely also want to talk in depth about the deployment and implementation plans and present a number of what-if scenarios to the team.

In addition, the Project Review Board may ask a variation on several of the following questions:

- Does the solution represent the agreed-upon designs that came out of Phase 3, or have additional design modifications been made in this stage?
- Has the solution be tested or piloted? What degree of confidence do you have that it will work on the organizational/enterprise level as opposed to in a limited test environment?
- Did the project stay on time and within budget? If not, why?
- What will be the metrics going forward?
- Are the impacted managers and department heads onboard with the change, and are they willing to support its successful deployment?
- What are the deployment risks and how are you going to address them?
- Were all the right stakeholders involved? Did they have any specific concerns or recommendations and, if so, how did you deal with them?
- How did you reconcile any conflicting requirements requests?
- How will you deal with scope change requests in Phase 4?

If a green light is given to proceed to Phase 5, there is no turning back. If any doubts persist about the reliability of the solution or the thoroughness of the deployment plans, then it is better for the project team to be given a "rework" verdict than to rely on luck.

4.12 Outputs/Deliverables

- Documentation of Phase Gate 4 project recommendations

Activity 4.13 – Communicate Outcomes/Next Steps

Regardless of the outcome of Phase Gate 4, any stakeholder who was involved in, or previously communicated to, during Phase 4 should receive an update on the project's status and next steps.

If the Phase Gate was a success, and the project team will be starting Phase 5 deployment and implementation, then it is time to build awareness of the impending deployment to all Tier 3 stakeholders. (For large or highly visibly projects, "awareness"-level communications may have already commenced.)

Because of the impending deployment/implementation, the activity of "communicating out" can be more intensive than in previous phases. However, not every detail about the initiative needs to be communicated at this time. After all, the initial activities of Phase 5 also include communication activities, and any project-induced changes will not hit the organization until the mid-point of Phase 5.

4.13 Outputs/Deliverables

- Communication regarding outcome of the Phase Gate 4 session
- Details regarding the Phase 5 deployment/implementation

Activity 4.14 – Conduct Phase 4 Wrap-up

Phase 4 is closed out in a similar manner as Phase 3.

4.14.01 Document any lessons learned, pertinent observations, or outstanding needs from Phase 4

Anything that can benefit the execution of Phase 5, or outstanding issues arising from the debrief session or other activities, should be documented. Because the next phase of the project is deployment/implementation, it is especially important that anything documented here be considered when finalizing the Phase 5 approach (Activity 5.01.03).

4.14.02 Celebrate and acknowledge the team

Phase 4 often involves a large number of project resources working long hours. In Phase 5, the core project team will be relying on the support of numerous Tier 1 and Tier 2 stakeholders to successfully deploy and implement the initiative. Therefore, as a goodwill gesture, the team may want to consider inviting some of these stakeholders to join in the celebration of concluding the pre-deployment prep work.

4.14 Outputs/Deliverables

- Documentation of lessons learned, pertinent observations, and outstanding needs

Conclusion of Phase 4

For more information...
Templates, detailed examples, and process tools relating to Phase 4 of the Emergence One Method can be downloaded for free (though some material may require a small licensing fee) from: **www.emergenceone.com**

Chapter 11

Phase 5: Deploy/Implement

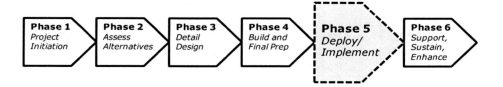

Phase 1 — Project Initiation
Phase 2 — Assess Alternatives
Phase 3 — Detail Design
Phase 4 — Build and Final Prep
Phase 5 — Deploy/ Implement
Phase 6 — Support, Sustain, Enhance

Introduction to Phase 5

During Phase 5, the solution or "change driver" is deployed and implemented. This phase is also the first test of how well the organization will absorb the organizational impacts that accompany the deployment/implementation. The ability to sustain and enhance the change during Phase 6 will be the second test.

In Phase 5, all the efforts around planning, designing, building, engaging stakeholders, contingency planning, and so forth get to prove their worth. As such, Phase 5 is characterized not so much by project team deliverables, but more by the activities the project team helps to coordinate and monitor.

Many well-designed organizational initiatives have turned into failures because of a botched deployment effort. This is because so many elements go into a good deployment plan: managing logistics; conducting effective training; providing timely support to deal with glitches, breakdowns, and frazzled employees; ensuring clarity around new roles and responsibilities; and managing naysayers who love to pontificate on how corporate "just doesn't get it."

Despite the challenges, if the project team has been diligently applying the Emergence One Method throughout the project life cycle, Phase 5 should run fairly smoothly. And if this milestone is reached, the project is just one phase away from realizing the business value and other benefits that started the organization down this path of change to begin with.

Phase 5 – Deploy/Implement			
#	Activity		Subtasks
5.01	Conduct Phase 5 Startup Activities	5.01.01	Identify the needs/expectations of Phase 5 stakeholders
		5.01.02	Update and review iterative documents
		5.01.03	Finalize Phase 5 plan/approach
5.02	Engage/Align/Mobilize Key Stakeholders	5.02.01	Engage key stakeholders
		5.02.02	Align key stakeholders
		5.02.03	Mobilize key stakeholders
5.03	Kick Off Phase 5 Project Team and Deployment/ Implementation Partners	5.03.01	Design the kick-off event
		5.03.02	Conduct the event
5.04	Prepare the Organization	5.04.01	Prepare support organizations
		5.04.02	Prepare managers and supervisors
		5.04.03	Prepare change recipients
5.05	Conduct Final Go/No Go Assessment	5.05.01	Develop Go/No Go assessment tool
		5.05.02	Conduct the assessment
		5.05.03	Determine next steps
		5.05.04	Communicate next steps
5.06	Deploy Solution/Change Driver	5.06.00	None
5.07	Evaluate Deployment/ Implementation Effectiveness	5.07.01	Gather metrics
		5.07.02	Analyze and evaluate metrics
5.08	Stabilize the New Current State	5.08.01	Determine necessary interventions for stabilization
		5.08.02	Identify and roadblock work-arounds
5.09	Develop High-Level Phase 6 Plan	5.09.00	None

Phase 5 – Deploy/Implement			
5.10	Prepare for Phase Gate 5	5.10.01	Vet Phase Gate deliverables with key stakeholders
		5.10.02	Assess Phase Gate readiness
		5.10.03	Design the Phase Gate 5 event
		5.10.04	Create and distribute pre-read
		5.10.05	Conduct a Phase Gate 5 preparation meeting
5.11	Conduct Phase Gate 5	5.11.00	None
5.12	Communicate Outcomes/Next Steps	5.12.00	None
5.13	Conduct Phase 5 Wrap-up	5.13.01	Document any lessons learned, pertinent observations, or outstanding needs
		5.13.02	Document subject matter expertise
		5.13.03	Determine "off-boarding" plan for project team members
		5.13.04	Archive project documentation
		5.13.05	Celebrate and acknowledge the team

Activity 5.01 – Conduct Phase 5 Startup Activities

Phase 5 startup activities are similar to those of the previous three phases:

1 Identify the needs and expectations of Phase 5 stakeholders.
2 Update and review iterative documents.
3 Finalize the Phase 5 project plan and schedule; align the project team on the Phase 5 plan/approach.

5.01.01 Identify the needs/expectations of Phase 5 stakeholders

Phase 5 has an impact on and requires the involvement of perhaps the greatest number of stakeholder groups thus far. As a result, it gives rise to a tremendous variety of stakeholder needs and expectations. Anticipating these needs and expectations will go a long way toward facilitating strong stakeholder management.

Although the stakeholder map was updated in Phase 4, it should be reviewed again for completeness. Include in this iteration of the stakeholder map any groups who are responsible for the coordination and deployment/implementation of the solution.

Table 11.1. *Common needs/expectations of Phase 5 stakeholders*

Major Stakeholder Groups	Stakeholders Prominent in Phase 5	Common Needs and Expectations *During Phase 5*
TIER 1 Stakeholders: Senior Leaders/ Key Decision Makers	**Company Executives and Project Governance**	• When can we start seeing some return on our project investment? • Are the businesses doing their part to make this project succeed, or are they just deferring to the project team?
	Project Sponsor	• Will others in the organization do their part to make this initiative succeed? • What can I do to make this phase succeed?
	Project Review Board Members	• When can we expect Phase Gate 4 to happen? • How confident can we be that, if we approve this project for deployment, it will be a change for the better? • Now that we have implemented the changes, how important is Phase Gate 5? Can I start disengaging?
TIER 2 Stakeholders: Project Contributors	**Phase 5 Project Team**	• Will we get the cooperation we need from the rest of the organization to pull this off? • What are our contingency plans, and what criteria need to be met before we implement them? • Will I still have a job now that my role on this project is coming to an end?

Major Stakeholder Groups	Stakeholders Prominent in Phase 5	Common Needs and Expectations *During Phase 5*
	Business/Process Owners	• Are my operations and performance metrics going to take a hit during this transition? • What do I need to do to make this initiative succeed? • What will be some of the political ramifications of this deployment? Will it shift my level of influence? • Are my front-line people getting all the help and support they need?
TIER 3 Stakeholders: Change Recipients	**Managers and Supervisors**	• How can I best support my people during this time of change? • How can I maintain productivity and keep my people from getting too stressed out? • Will this change have a positive or negative impact on my department? • What's more important, meeting my ongoing targets or adopting this change? • Where do I find the answers to the questions my direct reports are asking?
	Impacted Employees	• How will this change benefit me? • Will I receive the proper amount of training and support to be successful? • What will happen if I continue to do things the way I'm use to doing it? • Will this change have positive or negative impacts? • In the "old world" I was seen as an expert. Now that everyone is being asked to adopt something new, will I lose my importance? • How serious is the organization about the need to do things in a new or different manner?

NOTE: This is a generic assessment of stakeholder needs and expectations. Depending upon the scope and nature of the project, as well as the hierarchical structure of the company, there may be other stakeholder groups, or other needs and expectations, involved in Phase 5.

5.01.02 Update and review iterative documents

The following iterative documents need to be reviewed and may need to be updated:

- The Project Roadmap
- The Lessons Learned Document
- The Executive Stakeholder Analysis Document
- The Risk Management Log
- Leadership Action Plans

5.01.03 Finalize Phase 5 plan/approach

The primary goal of Phase 5 is to deploy and implement the solution within the organization and to quickly mitigate any issues that may arise in the process.

Unlike previous phases, much of the Phase 5 approach was already crafted in the latter half of Phase 4. That plan should be modified based upon:

- Recommendations from the Phase 4 Project Review Board;
- Any new information or stakeholder inputs that have come in since the Phase Gate 4 meeting;
- A review of stakeholder needs/expectations from Activity 5.01.01; and
- A review of the recently updated documents from Activity 5.01.02.

A project schedule (with both start dates and end dates) should then be developed once the plan is finalized. This schedule is absolutely critical for Phase 5 because deployment and implementation activities for most organizational initiatives involve the widest set of Tier 2 stakeholders (project contributors). Everyone must be on the same page regarding the timing and execution of tasks.

(NOTE: The project schedule will be shared with both the core and extended project team members in a later activity.)

5.01 Outputs/Deliverables

- Updated stakeholder map

- Documented list of needs and expectations for key Phase 5 stakeholders
- Updated iterative documents
- Phase 5 project approach and schedule

Activity 5.02 – Engage/Align/Mobilize Key Stakeholders

By the time the project team reaches Phase 5, hopefully, most of the key stakeholders with whom the project team has been working during previous phases should be aligned. The key to Phase 5 is to engage, align, and mobilize a *new* set of key stakeholders: namely, the deployment and implementation partners who will help make this phase a success.

5.02.01 Engage key stakeholders

The set of relevant key stakeholders in this phase is likely to be a bit larger than in previous phases. The reason is that coordinating various deployment- and implementation-related activities is likely to require the cooperation of numerous Tier 2 stakeholders (project contributors).

Reviewing the deployment plan and project schedule can be a catalyst for obtaining engagement meetings with Tier 2 stakeholders. From Tier 2 stakeholders, the project team needs reassurances that the leaders of support organizations have the resources in place to meet deployment and implementation requirements.

5.02.02 Align key stakeholders

For Tier 1 stakeholders, many issues pertaining to the alignment of project objectives and the plan going forward should have already surfaced and been resolved. If not, then it is critical to work on aligning these important stakeholders before commencing deployment activities.

If some of the stakeholders appear to be resisting the roles and responsibilities they had agreed to, as set forth in the deployment plan created in Phase 4, it is important to immediately address their concerns.

Areas that are high risk for misalignment may include:

- The project rollout schedule;
- Exceptions to adherence to project/change requirements;
- Deferrals; and
- Deployment/implementation cost allocations.

5.02.03 Mobilize key stakeholders

Now that the solution is being deployed to the organization, mobilizing key stakeholders will likely require more robust guidance than in previous phases. Most activities should center on preparing the organizational for change by ensuring that the required participants attend training sessions and understand the purpose and scope of the project and their role in its success.

Recommendations for mobilizing key stakeholders in this phase include:

- Developing more robust leadership action plans that outline specific activities (e.g., making a town-hall presentation to Tier 3 stakeholders) along with specific dates and any support material required (e.g., a PowerPoint presentation);
- Speaking with peers in the various support organizations to make sure they are ready and able to lend their assistance for successful project deployment/implementation; and
- Being a visible champion of the initiative by visiting the affected business units and personally voicing support for the project.

The change lead should be able to provide additional thoughts and ideas on what actions key stakeholders can take to maintain project momentum, direction, and acceptance. The change lead should also ensure that actions key stakeholders take align with the (updated) communication and engagement plan.

5.02 Outputs/Deliverables

- Phase Gate 4 debriefing material
- Updated executive stakeholder analysis tool
- Updated leadership action plans
- Updated communication and engagement plan
- Updated deployment plan and project schedule (if necessary)

Activity 5.03 – Kick Off Phase 5 Project Team and Deployment/Implementation Partners

Kick-off activities for those involved in Phase 5 are likely to differ from the core team kick-off activities described in earlier phases.

In order for Phase 5 to succeed, the roles and responsibilities of the core team will need to be separate from those of various deployment and implementation partners. Depending upon the size and scope of the project, this may include coordinating with external product and service vendors and internal support organizations, such as the help desk, HR, and IT.

5.03.01 Design the kick-off event

The goal of the Phase 5 kick-off event is to develop a shared commitment to deployment/implementation success. This unity can be achieved by holding joint project events in which core team members as well as the various deployment/implementation partners are present.

This event will require more than a feel-good team-building session between core team members and deployment/implementation partners. It will require that there be a solid understanding regarding:

- Roles and responsibilities;
- Deployment schedules and timing contingencies;
- Cross-team communications; and
- How best to respond to the concerns and needs of impacted stakeholders.

The concept of *total project success* also needs to be promoted at this event. Deployment and implementation partners will need to understand that the goal of Phase 5 is not simply to deploy or implement something within the organization. Rather, it is to help facilitate the adoption of the change so that change recipients can embrace the solution and utilize it as a catalyst for realizing business value.

5.03.02 Conduct the event

An event that includes deployment/implementation partners and other extended project team members is likely to be more difficult to facilitate than sessions that involve only core team members. One difficulty is that many extended project team members have a sense that they do not owe any allegiance to this project team or the initiative. To them, it is perhaps one of many initiatives that an evolving organization takes on. Therefore, developing a shared sense of ownership for success among these players is likely to be more challenging.

This challenge may manifest itself in having deployment/implementation partners appear to be disengaged during the meeting, feeling like they "know it all," or questioning the deployment plan (even though their superiors may have signed off on the idea during subtask 5.02.02). It is important that the meeting facilitator (who is usually the change lead) manage these inappropriate behaviors accordingly.

5.03 Outputs/Deliverables

- Project team kick-off agenda for Phase 5
- Relevant project on-boarding information

- Deployment plan with updated roles and responsibilities for deployment/implementation partners

Activity 5.04 – Prepare the Organization

Activity 5.03 focused on preparing the project team and the deployment/implementation partners for what they will need to do to make this phase a success. Activity 5.04 focuses on preparing the rest of the organization for the requirements and impacts of the initiative.

5.04.01 Prepare support organizations

Corporate support organizations, such as the help desk, HR, IT, and vendor management, are considered Tier 2 stakeholders (project contributors) within the Emergence One Method. Within many initiatives, success depends upon these stakeholders' willingness to support the project team, the organization, and the end-users/employees. Unless they are willing to "adopt" their role of supporting the initiative, the project may not attain its objectives or may even have its deployment pulled back.

Having the relevant support organizations commit to boosting the initiative should have occurred earlier in the project life cycle. Now that the project team is getting ready to deploy the solution, it is important that the relevant support organizations be properly prepared to play their role. This may include training for help desk personnel or distributing new job descriptions to HR.

Lastly, the company intranet often plays a supportive role during implementation by providing access to both static (e.g., company documents) and dynamic (e.g., project updates) information. A strong end-user/employee-focused intranet site that hosts project information, competency development material, and clear direction on roles and responsibilities can help anchor the organization going forward.

5.04.02 Prepare managers and supervisors

Although managers and supervisors can also be change recipients, at this juncture in the project life cycle, their role is to be responsible for motivating and supporting their direct reports who will be impacted by the initiative.

The role that managers and supervisors play during the deployment of the initiative should have been developed as part of Activity 4.05.02 – "Develop the initial deployment plan." Within that activity, it was recommended that management action plans (MAPs) be developed. MAPs provide guidance to managers and supervisors on how they can best support and promote change or deal with any resistance to it. MAPs also provide project information such as FAQs, what kinds of additional support are available, and what new policies and procedures may accompany the change.

Depending upon the nature and scope of the initiative, it may be enough to simply deploy MAPs to the appropriate personnel. More complex or transformational initiatives may require that managers or supervisors receive training on how best to motivate their employees during times of change.

5.04.03 Prepare change recipients

In order for Tier 3 stakeholders (change recipients, which could include managers, supervisors, and other organizational hierarchy) to adopt change, they need to possess the right set of skills and suitable level of motivation.

Motivation is instilled by employing numerous levers. Deciding which ones to use will depend upon the nature and scope of the initiative, the prevailing corporate culture, and other factors that have been discussed previously. Motivation is usually developed over time; therefore, the Emergence One Method recommends that various activities, such as communication, visible sponsorship, and engagement, occur at points earlier in the project life cycle.

At this point in the project life cycle, it is appropriate to deploy the competency development piece of the equation. A competency development program may or may not consist of formal training sessions. Since the scope of some initiatives may entail nothing more than a simple upgrade or enhancement of an existing system, process, or IT application, the required competency development may be modest. It may require simply a job aid, a short intranet-based tutorial, or peer-to-peer coaching.

Because stakeholders have these information needs, it is important that robust communications accompany the deployment of any competency development program. Too often, participants walk into a training class totally unprepared and flummoxed as to why they were there. The successful deployment of a competency development program is closely linked to the surrounding communications and the support and encouragement of management.

If rolling out a training program, it is important to capture participants' feedback on both the trainer and the training material.

5.04 Outputs/Deliverables

- Training and support material for relevant support organizations
- Updated management action plans and/or training material for managers and supervisors
- Updated communication and competency development material
- Training evaluation forms

Activity 5.05 – Conduct Final Go/No Go Assessment

Now that the organization has been properly prepared in terms of competency development and, hopefully, is motivated, it is time to do one final check to make sure that all the diverse elements of a successful deployment are in place. This is accomplished through the use of a Go/No Go assessment (different organizations use different terms for this) and taking mitigating actions, should the assessment identify areas of concern.

The final Go/No Go assessment differs from the high-level readiness assessment found in Activity 4.10. Specifically, this Phase 5 assessment takes a closer look at how successful the previous activity was (Activity 5.04 – Prepare the Organization). It also conducts a final checklist review of the support and readiness of those helping with the deployment.

5.05.01 Develop Go/No Go assessment tool

A Go/No Go assessment should including the appropriate variations on the following questions:

- Has the training been implemented? Was it well attended? Was it effective?
- Do stakeholders understand why this change is taking place?
- Have the appropriate sponsors and other "change champions" been playing an active role in promoting the importance of this initiative?
- Does the project team and those supporting the project team (project contributors) have everything in place for the deployment, and are they clear on their intersecting roles and responsibilities?
- Is everyone aware of the contingency plans, in case the deployment/implementation does not go as smoothly as expected? Does everyone know what criteria need to be met before triggering the contingency plans?
- Do managers and supervisors have all the required support material? Do they understand their role in mitigating any concerns or anxiety?

Because the Go/No Go assessment tool contains elements typically found in both project management and change management disciplines, it is important that the project manager and the change lead jointly construct the assessment tool.

5.05.02 Conduct the assessment

It is important that the data-gathering process for the Go/No Go assessment be as efficient as possible. Most of the key data for the assessment can be culled from speaking with a number of key stakeholders as well as reviewing the outputs (e.g., training attendance logs and evaluation forms) from previous activities. Long, drawn-out surveys are not necessary.

The Emergence One Method has numerous project checkpoints throughout the phases. It emphasizes an iterative process of identifying risks, engaging stakeholders, gathering feedback, and documenting the outputs of various activities. Therefore, if the project team has been diligently applying the E1 Method, there should be little likelihood that the project team *and the organization* are not ready for deployment.

However, because project teams often take shortcuts throughout a project's life cycle, there is the chance that the project team or organization is *not* ready for deployment. Therefore, Emergence One recommends that the project team take the time to do one final review.

5.05.03 Determine next steps

If the Go/No Go assessment does identify areas that need to be addressed, then the project team (in consultation with project governance and other key stakeholders) needs to decide on next steps.

- Are the issues minor, and will they have only a negligible impact on organizational adoption and business value realization? If so, the project team may wish to proceed.
- Are they mid-level issues that can be addressed concurrently with the deployment/implementation of the solution/change driver?
- Are the issues serious enough that the deployment/implementation should be put on hold until they are fully addressed?

There is also a chance that a system glitch or bug may have been discovered that would require a rework of the solution itself. However, if the Emergence One Method has been faithfully followed, and all the review, testing, and stakeholder engagement activities were properly executed, then this possibility is extremely small. If deployment or organizational readiness issues are found, then the appropriate stakeholders should quickly develop a deployment remediation plan.

5.05.04 Communicate next steps

Regardless of whether it is a "go" or "no go" decision, the organization still needs information as to the exact timing of the deployment, what is expected of its members, a reminder of the anticipated benefits, and where they can find additional information or support if needed.

If the project is delayed, then the project sponsor needs to communicate the reasons for the delay to the affected stakeholders. The change lead can craft a communication that focuses on the positive aspect of the delay (for instance, emphasizing the team's dedication to doing it right rather than doing it fast).

5.05 Outputs/Deliverables

- Go/No Go assessment tool and results
- Documentation of the Go/No Go decision
- Deployment remediation plan (if necessary)
- Communication update

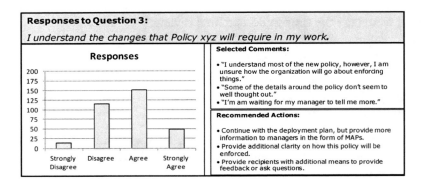

Figure 11.1. *A possible component to a readiness assessment item*

Activity 5.06 – Deploy Solution/Change Driver

Midway through Phase 5 is the deployment of the solution or "change driver." Since a thorough deployment plan has already been created, vetted, refined, and shared with deployment/implementation partners, nothing new should need to be created here.

Keep in mind that there may be more than one deployment taking place. For instance, if deploying a large ERP system, such as SAP or Oracle Applications, not only is the new IT system being deployed, but so are new processes, job classifications, reporting relationships, and so forth.

A successfully deployment at this phase depends not so much on what is being deployed (since that was addressed in previous activities) but on *how* it is being deployed. Specifically, what matters is how well coordinated the different components of the deployment are being managed and how well the various teams are communicating with one another.

Having clear roles and responsibilities is also critical. During deployments, resources are often stretched thin. Therefore, there is not much latitude for people stepping out of their roles.

5.06 Outputs/Deliverables

- Documentation of deployment/implementation progress

Once upon a time...
Coordinating an Assessment Center Process for 1,200 Managerial Candidates
At the tender age of 23, I had the incredible experience of being part of a deployment team for a large-scale assessment center process for evaluating 1,200 state employees who were candidates for promotion. However, since there were only 250 promotions available, the trick was to find the best 250 candidates out of 1,200 pre-qualified applicants in a completely unbiased and legally defensible manner.
The process involved sending multiple groups of eight individuals into different classrooms (a large school building was rented out for the day) to take part in work-related scenarios involving group problem-solving. While the participants were in the classroom interacting with one another, they were being observed and rated by a team of behavioral assessment specialists, who were evaluating their ability to solicit feedback, build consensus, be assertive yet diplomatic in promoting their opinions, and use other negotiation skills.
Part of ensuring that the process was valid and legally defensible was to make sure there was no "contamination" that could give an unfair advantage to one or more participants. For instance, contamination may occur if outgoing participants tipped off incoming participants as to the nature or subject matter of the assessment sessions.
To avoid this from happening, we had to make sure that incoming and outgoing groups never crossed paths – a major logistical challenge. To meet that challenge, we all had our watches synchronized to the second. We also utilized a network of group escorts, each armed with walkie-talkies, providing real-time updates on where each incoming and outgoing group was in the building. It was quite an operation, and to this day, remains one of the most exciting "deployments" of my career.

Activity 5.07 – Evaluate Deployment/Implementation Effectiveness

5.07.01 Gather metrics

Metrics to gauge deployment/implementation effectiveness should have been determined and made part of the deployment plan during Activity 4.05.02 "Develop the initial deployment plan." (Note: The metrics gathered during this activity were for gauging deployment/implementation effectiveness, not business value realization, which will be measured in Phase 6.)

As recommended, it is important to find metrics that can be quickly gathered and analyzed so that problems and "hiccups" can be promptly identified and addressed. As soon as feasible, the project team should begin collecting and analyzing metrics on the effectiveness of the deployment and implementation efforts; more than one type of metric should be utilized.

For instance, if deploying a new IT system, the team should evaluate not just whether the system is "working," but some of the initial user feedback. If users are complaining that the system is "too complicated," that may indicate an issue with the effectiveness of the competency development program.

Be sure to collect any relevant metrics from the support organizations that are also involved in the initiative. For instance, have the project manager collect information on the type and number of help desk tickets that get opened, or ask the change lead to check in with HR regarding any HR-related issues that may have been raised.

5.07.02 Analyze and evaluate metrics

The metrics collected within the previous activities should be analyzed by the project manager, the change lead, and other relevant team members. The reason why several project team members need to be involved in the analysis and evaluation of metrics is that interpreting metrics requires a variety of insights and perspectives.

Metrics may locate a problem but not necessarily provide the root cause for its existence. One of the first steps in evaluating metrics is to generate a sufficient number of alternative hypotheses for the team to consider and explore further. And one of the best ways to generate a variety of alternative hypotheses is to have a variety of viewpoints and perspectives represented. (Note: A great book regarding alternate hypotheses is *Rival Hypotheses: Alternative Interpretations of Data Based Conclusions* by Huck and Sandler.)

5.07 Outputs/Deliverables

- Metrics for determining deployment/implementation effectiveness

Activity 5.08 – Stabilize the New Current State

After analyzing and evaluating the problem areas that may be preventing the new current state from taking hold, it is time to act.

5.08.01 Determine necessary interventions for stabilization

Using the outputs from Activity 5.07, the project team should determine what interventions are necessary to help stabilize the new current state. Previously, some of these interventions may have been described in the "contingency planning" section of the deployment plans; others may be "quick fixes" that are proposed on the spot.

Interventions for stabilization may be temporary or permanent and may include the following:

- Increase staffing levels
- Modify working or reporting relationships
- Deploy a temporary work-around solution
- Delay additional rollouts or push out compliance due dates

Regardless of the intervention deployed, maintaining clear roles and responsibilities is critical when it comes to stabilizing the new current state. Since part of stabilizing the new current state involves responding to mishaps, "hiccups," and frantic requests for assistance, everyone involved should be clear on several points:

- Who needs to respond to which particular issue (for instance, it is inefficient to have four different team members try to respond to the same single issue);
- When a particular issue needs to be escalated; and
- When to personally intervene as opposed to directing the requester to static support material (e.g., a training manual).

One method that Emergence One consultants have used successfully with clients in the past to stabilize the current state is to formulate quick-response teams. These teams can rapidly respond, either in person or by some other means, to any issue that may threaten stability.

All issues, including their resolution status, should be documented in a shared project team repository.

5.08.02 Identify and roadblock work-arounds

Deployment activities may also require the shutdown of parallel systems or the "roadblocking" of process work-arounds that employees may surreptitiously decide to utilize instead of adopting the change, new processes and/or behaviors. Roadblocking can go a long way toward facilitating organizational adoption, if employees know that the only avenue available for completing their work lies within the new state being instituted by the organization.

Some of these work-arounds should have been identified by the project team during Phase 4. Also, more creative work-arounds may not be implemented by end-users/employees until post-deployment. Therefore, additional diligence in identifying work-arounds may be needed at this stage.

Note that not all parallel systems or work-arounds should be disabled immediately. Some project managers may determine that parallel systems and work-arounds for critical tasks should remain accessible while waiting for full adoption to take hold. These are big decisions that should not be made solely by the project team but should involve business process owners as well.

As an alternative, parallel systems and work-arounds may be temporarily roadblocked but easily lifted in case of the need to initiate a contingency plan. Therefore, the project manager or project governance members may recommend shutting down or roadblocking work-arounds later on, sometime in Phase 6.

5.08 Outputs/Deliverables

- Action plans for resolving known issues
- Documentation of newly identified work-arounds
- Agreed-upon strategy for disabling work-arounds
- High-level Phase 6 plan

Activity 5.09 – Create High-Level Phase 6 Plan

A review of the Phase 6 plan is the main deliverable to be submitted for approval in Phase Gate 5, although there are likely to be many questions regarding the effectiveness of the deployment. While high-level plans for the next phase are required for all phases, extra attention must be given to the Phase 6 plan, since this is where business value and ROI are most likely to occur.

Inputs to the Phase 6 plan should come from the project roadmap, data on the effectiveness of the initial deployment and implementation, the identification of work-arounds, and ongoing stakeholder needs that were not adequately addressed in earlier activities.

In addition, the Phase 6 plan should cover the three main elements of that phase:

- *Support* – What else must the organization do to support the change? While much was asked of end-users/employees during Phase 5, it is important that the organization do its part to support the change. Although structural support changes were addressed in previous activities (e.g., modifying performance reviews or readjusting compensation), such changes need to be reevaluated and possibly enhanced in Phase 6.

- **Sustain** – Many times, change recipients are willing to *initially* support or try out a change, only to later revert to previous processes or behaviors. Thus, methods for sustaining the change need to be incorporated in Phase 6.
- **Improve** – Often times, change recipients can find ways to improve upon a solution in ways that project team members never thought of or realized. It is important to encourage these insights and innovations, capture them, and disseminate these ideas or improvements to others in the organization.

Once the high-level plan has been developed, it should be vetted with stakeholders from the business and refined. This is noted in Activity 5.10.01, below.

5.09 Outputs/Deliverables

- High-level Phase 6 plan

Activity 5.10 – Prepare for Phase Gate 5

Many of the clients who utilize the Emergence One Method initially do not understand the need for Phase Gate 5. In their minds, since the project is already deployed and implemented, it is essentially over.

This type of legacy mindset is propagated by many traditional project management methodologies, which see the end point as project delivery as opposed to business value realization. Since projects are designed to "bring about beneficial change," it is critical that the initiative continue into Phase 6: the phase in which business value is often achieved. Conducting Phase Gate 5 sends an important reminder to project stakeholders that there is more work to be done if true business value is to be achieved.

5.10.01 Vet Phase Gate deliverables with key stakeholders

Since Phase 5 is more of an "activity" phase than a planning, designing, or building phase, there are few deliverables that will need to be approved here. The main deliverable for Phase Gate 5 is actually the plan on how the change will be supported, sustained, and enhanced during Phase 6.

Since Phase 6 will transfer the change's operation and ownership from the project team to the business, it is important to vet the Phase 6 plan with business stakeholders.

5.10.02 Assess Phase Gate readiness

The team needs to ask themselves the following questions for the Phase Gate 5 meeting:

- Did the deployment/implementation go according to plan, or were there unexpected delays and challenges?
- Has the future state been stabilized, or is there still more work to be done in this area?
- Have we mitigated major areas of stakeholder resistance? (Minor areas of resistance can be addressed in Phase 6.)
- How can we best call attention to the hard work and talents of our dedicated project team members without appearing too self-congratulatory?

5.10.03 Design the Phase Gate 5 event

The meeting structure and roles will be similar to those of previous Phase Gates, although the project sponsor may wish to play a more active part. After all, his or her responsibilities will be winding down as ownership of the solution is transferred over to the business in the next phase.

5.10.04 Create and distribute pre-read material

The pre-read package for Phase 5 should contain the following:

- A cover letter outlining the agenda and the objectives. The main objectives of Phase 5 are to ascertain that no major remediation work needs be done and that a Phase 6 plan is in place that builds upon the success of Phase 5.
- Background on the Phase 5 project team and their activities.
- A description of any organizational adoption challenges that may still be out there and how the project team plans to address them.
- An overview of the Phase 6 plan.

5.10.05 Conduct a Phase Gate 5 preparation meeting

The Phase Gate 5 preparation meeting should include all core team members and follow a process similar to those of previous Phase Gate preparation meetings.

5.10 Outputs/Deliverables

- Phase Gate 5 meeting agenda
- Phase Gate 5 pre-read package

- Phase Gate 5 presentation and meeting materials
- Phase Gate 5 project team preparation material

Activity 5.11 – Conduct Phase Gate 5

Many Project Review Board members do not understand why Phase Gate 5 is needed since they consider the project to be "over" at this point. Herein lies the danger: the deployment and implementation of an initiative does not necessarily result in ROI or business value realization. Thus, it is essential that the Project Review Board understand and be willing to promote the need for a robust Phase 6.

Some of the Project Review Board questions that may come up in Phase Gate 5 include:

- How did the organization receive the deployment/implementation?
- Were there any unexpected reactions? If so, how were they handled?
- Is the business prepared to take full ownership of the change?
- Did the project stay on time and within budget? If not, why?
- How have the results of Phase 5 been measured?
- Was there a need to implement any contingency plans, and if so, how will they affect the anticipated ROI?
- Is the organization starting to realize any benefits from the solution, or must it wait until Phase 6 for these?
- Is Phase 6 really necessary? If so, is this project team still needed for Phase 6 activities or can the business oversee and manage them all?
- Is any of the funding for Phase 6 going to come from the business, or does corporate need to continue picking up the tab?

Unlike other phases, it is extremely unlikely that the project will not be given a green light to proceed into Phase 6, which will provide opportunities to further support and sustain the initiative. However, for projects that have been poorly designed, lack stakeholder involvement, or have forgone testing, it may be determined that they simply will not work. If so, the project needs to be stopped in its entirety because the associated costs of fixing or reworking the solution would negate the business case and anticipated ROI.

5.11 Outputs/Deliverables

- Documentation of Phase Gate 5 project recommendations

Activity 5.12 – Communicate Outcomes/Next Steps

As is typical at the end of a project phase, the change lead (with inputs from the project manager and project sponsor) should craft a communication covering the results of Phase 5 and an overview of Phase 6 activities.

This is a critical communication to send to the organization. It must reinforce the idea that the project is not "over," and that the organization has a huge role to play in Phase 6 to support, sustain, and enhance the initiative. It needs to emphasize that the goal of the project was not to "implement something" but to achieve business value. And, in order for business value to be realized, Phase 6 needs to be taken seriously.

For larger initiatives, it is especially important that the project sponsor and other high-level executives communicate the need to support, sustain, and enhance the initiative, especially since ownership for the solution is being transferred to the business, and the changes are being absorbed by the organization. Now is the time for project sponsors and business owners to step forward while the project manager slowly fades into the background.

Communication materials should also make mention of the hard work and dedication of various team members.

5.12 Outputs/Deliverables:

- Communication regarding outcome of the Phase Gate 5 session
- Details regarding Phase 6 activities

Activity 5.13 – Conduct Phase 5 Wrap-up

The wrap-up activities for Phase 5 are somewhat more involved than for other phases. After all, many project team members will be rolling off at this point, so it is important to capture their knowledge and expertise before they depart.

5.13.01 Document any lessons learned, pertinent observations, or outstanding needs from Phase 5

Anything that can benefit the execution of the Phase 6, or outstanding issues arising from the debriefing session or other activities, should be documented.

5.13.02 Document subject matter expertise

The Emergence One Method places a great deal of emphasis on documentation throughout the project life cycle. However, if select project team members possess valuable project knowledge or subject matter expertise that has not yet been captured or documented, now is the time to do so.

5.13.03 Determine "off-boarding" plan for project team members

Internal team members who will be rolling off the project at this point possess valuable project skills and in-depth subject matter expertise. If the organization does not find a position within the company to utilize their enhanced skill sets and expertise, then there is a good chance these employees will feel under-recognized or under-utilized. This disaffection puts them at high risk for leaving the company and possibly bringing their expertise over to a competitor.

Plans and ideas for how these individuals can be utilized after rolling off the project should have been discussed during the initial solicitation process. For many internal employees, project assignments are accepted with the implicit understanding that time spent on them will help them advance in their careers. Therefore, the project sponsor should do all he or she can to see to it that these individuals get the recognition and advancement they deserve.

5.13.04 Archive project documentation

The project does not officially end until the completion of Phase 6, when information will be archived. However, it is important to archive project documentation at this point (as well as at the end of Phase 6) so that the information does not get lost as project team members roll off this initiative.

Archiving project information should be done according to organizational standards and in a manner consistent with past practices.

5.13.05 Celebrate and acknowledge the team

Because Phase 6 involves contributors mostly from the business and operational sides of the organization, many project team members will not be continuing on to Phase 6. Therefore, a successful Phase 5 is cause for a large celebration since a successful deployment/implementation is perhaps the biggest milestone for the project team.

5.13 Outputs/Deliverables

- Documentation of lessons learned, pertinent observations, and outstanding needs
- Knowledge capture of project and subject matter expertise
- Off-boarding plan for internal resources
- Archived repository of project documentation

Conclusion of Phase 5

For more information...
Templates, detailed examples, and process tools relating to Phase 5 of the Emergence One Method can be downloaded for free (though some material may require a small licensing fee) from: **www.emergenceone.com**

Chapter 12

Phase 6: Support, Sustain, and Enhance

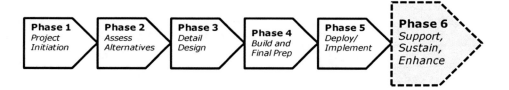

Phase 1
Project
Initiation

Phase 2
Assess
Alternatives

Phase 3
Detail
Design

Phase 4
Build and
Final Prep

Phase 5
Deploy/
Implement

Phase 6
Support,
Sustain,
Enhance

Introduction to Phase 6

Phase 6 is the last phase of the Emergence One project life cycle and, in many ways, the most important phase of all. It is significant because unless the change is supported and sustained, there will be little business value realization or return on investment (ROI). In addition, the opportunity to enhance the deployed solution may offer the organization an even better ROI and additional, unexpected benefits that go beyond anything that was originally stated in the business case.

Despite its importance and potential benefits, this phase is often difficult to execute for a number of reasons. At this point in the project life cycle, many project stakeholders may have developed project or change "fatigue." Project team members (those that remain), many of whom are used to considering deployment and implementation to be their last phase of responsibility, may become psychological and emotionally disengaged from the process, and thus they may only go through cursory motions. Corporate sponsors may not want to fund efforts relating to sustainability or enhancements now that the solution has been implemented, believing that the business should own and fund any activities from this point on. Business owners, on their part, may be eager to get the project team out of the way so they can tinker with and perhaps dilute the impact (and thus the effectiveness) of the initiative. And end-users/employees may now be focusing on the next change or initiative being handed down by an ever-evolving organization eager to enhance various aspects of its operations and corporate infrastructure.

In addition to the above obstacles, the Project Triad may begin to dissolve. The project sponsor begins eyeing other opportunities, the project manager may be assigned to another engagement, and the change lead may now be (falsely) labeled as irrelevant.

Despite these challenges, if the Project Triad did an adequate job of promoting and gaining commitment to a six-phase methodology during the early phases, the organization might take this phase as seriously as it did the previous phases.

The reason so many projects fall short of expectations (as described in Chapter 1) is that they fail to have a robust and well-executed Phase 6. This is the team's opportunity to not only meet expectations, but exceed them as well: this is where the opportunity for total project success will be realized.

Phase 6 – Support, Sustain, and Enhance			
#	Activity		Subtasks
6.01	Conduct Phase 6 Startup Activities	6.01.01	Identify the needs/expectations of Phase 6 stakeholders
		6.01.02	Update and review iterative documents
		6.01.03	Finalize Phase 6 plan/approach
6.02	Engage/Align/Mobilize Key Stakeholders	6.02.01	Engage key stakeholders
		6.02.02	Align key stakeholders
		6.02.03	Mobilize key stakeholders
6.03	Transfer Ownership	6.03.01	Define the transfer
		6.03.02	Agree upon ongoing Phase 6 roles
6.04	Evaluate the New Current State	6.04.01	Collect baseline metrics
		6.04.02	Evaluate employee motivation and competence
		6.04.03	Evaluate structural support

Phase 6 – Support, Sustain, and Enhance			
6.05	Institute Practices to Sustain New Current State	6.05.00	None
6.06	Reevaluate and Remediate	6.06.01	Reevaluate metrics
		6.06.02	Remediation planning
6.07	Identify/Institute Enhancement Opportunities	6.07.00	None
6.08	Perform a Project Review	6.08.01	Validate business value and ROI
		6.08.02	Document any Phase 6 lessons learned, pertinent observations, or outstanding needs
		6.08.03	Consolidate lessons learned from previous phases
		6.08.04	Conduct a project review session
6.09	Phase 6 Wrap-up	6.09.01	Archive project documentation
		6.09.02	Celebrate and acknowledge the team

Activity 6.01 – Conduct Phase 6 Startup Activities

Phase 6 startup activities are similar to those of the previous four phases:

1 Identify the needs and expectations of Phase 6 stakeholders.
2 Update and review iterative documents.
3 Finalize the Phase 6 project plan and schedule; align the project team on the Phase 6 plan/approach.

6.01.01 Identify the needs/expectations of Phase 6 stakeholders

For Phase 6, the stakeholder group with the greatest needs and expectations will be those in the impacted business units.

At this point in the project life cycle, Tier 1 and Tier 2 stakeholders will have fewer outstanding needs. Project governance may be disbanded at this point, and since there is no formal Phase Gate for Phase 6, there is no longer a need for the Project Review Board. So unless previously unidentified groups have been unexpectedly impacted by the initiative, there will likely be no updates to the stakeholder map. An exception to this is when an initiative *directly* impacts external customers.

Table 12.1.   *Common needs/expectations for Phase 6 stakeholders*

Major Stakeholder Groups	Stakeholders Prominent in Phase 6	Common Needs and Expectations *During Phase 6*
TIER 1 Stakeholders: Senior Leaders/ Key Decision Makers	Company Executives and Project Governance	• What proof can the team give me that this was money well spent and that we achieved the benefits that were expected?
	Project Sponsor	• How can I leverage this "win" to gain traction on some additional ideas I may have?
TIER 2 Stakeholders: Project Contributors	Phase 6 Project Team	• Now that the majority of project team members have rolled off, how can we best function with streamlined resources?
	Business/Process Owners	• Do I have everything I need in order to effectively sustain the new state? • How can I maximize the potential of the initiative to save time, ease workloads, and improve quality? • Now that I'm being given ownership of this change, how can I modify it? • Now that the training has already been deployed, how will I keep my people's skills current and train new employees?

Major Stakeholder Groups	Stakeholders Prominent in Phase 6	Common Needs and Expectations *During Phase 6*
TIER 3 Stakeholders: Change Recipients	Managers and Supervisors	• How can I help sustain these new behaviors and prevent my employees from slipping into old behaviors? • Are there any improvement or enhancements I can recommend to make things work even better? • Is my position, or the positions of some of my direct reports, going to become obsolete? • *I'm* having a tough time with transition. Will I look bad if I ask for some additional assistance or support?
	Impacted Employees	• What kind of ongoing training and support will the organization provide? • Am I allowed to make mistakes, or should I revert back to the old tried-and-true way of doing things? • Am I going to work more or have additional responsibilities but no increase in pay or recognition? • Is the organization serious about keeping this initiative going, or is it just the "flavor of the month"? • I have ideas on how to enhance this change; how can I make sure they are considered?
	Customers (if applicable)	• I see that the company is advertising/promoting a change/enhancement to how they do business. Is this enough to keep me from going to a competitor?

NOTE: *This is a generic assessment of stakeholder needs and expectations. Depending upon the scope and nature of the project, as well as the hierarchical structure of the company, there may be other stakeholder groups, or other needs and expectations, involved in Phase 6.*

6.01.02 Update and review iterative documents

The following documents may require review and updating:

- The Lessons Learned Document
- The Executive Stakeholder Analysis Document
- The Risk Management Log
- Management Action Plans

6.01.03 Finalize Phase 6 plan/approach

The primary goal of Phase 6 is to transfer ownership of the changes that were introduced to the organization during Phase 5 to those in the business who will be responsible for maintaining and improving the new current state.

Similar to Phase 5, much of the Phase 6 approach would have been crafted during the latter half of the previous phase. This plan should be modified based upon:

- Recommendations from the Phase 5 Project Review Board;
- Any new information or stakeholder inputs that have come in since the Phase Gate 5 meeting;
- Any feedback that was provided after the phase outcomes and next steps were communicated to the organization at the end of Phase 5; and
- A review of the recently updated documents from Activity 6.01.02.

A project schedule (with both start dates and end dates) should then be developed once the plan is finalized.

6.01 Outputs/Deliverables

- Documented list of needs and expectations for key Phase 5 stakeholders
- Updated iterative documents
- Phase 6 project approach and schedule

Activity 6.02 – Engage/Align/Mobilize Key Stakeholders

Key stakeholders (as opposed to general stakeholder groups) are individuals who have the most influence on the success of the current project life cycle phase.

Because few major decisions need to be made at this point, company executives now play less of a key role in influencing success (however, they may still need to play a role in celebrating the success of the initiative or encouraging its sustainability). Since one of the milestones of Phase 6 is transferring ownership of the change to business operations, most of the key stakeholders will be from this area.

Engaging, aligning, and mobilizing key business stakeholders are the first steps in transferring ownership of the change.

6.02.01 Engage key stakeholders

One of the first major activities of Phase 6 involves transferring ownership of the changes to business owners. These individuals will be accountable for owning any new processes, systems, and other changes while ensuring that they are maintained and sustained.

It is important to engage these individuals to understand their concerns, what kind of support or information they will need, and what actions they will need to take to be successful. These stakeholders will ultimately be responsible for business value realization and maximizing ROI. Therefore, it is important for the change lead to accurate assess their support for sustaining and improving upon the changes that were introduced to their organizations.

After engaging key stakeholders, the change lead should once again update the executive stakeholder analysis tool, since support for Phase 6 activities may wane. Also, if any newly gleaned information could affect the Phase 6 plan, then the project plan and schedule should be updated.

6.02.02 Align key stakeholders

Business owners who will be inheriting the change need to be aligned on their commitment to achieving project goals and objectives (realizing the business case). They also need to agree on the activities required for sustaining and improving upon the initiative.

Because few key decisions are made in this phase, there may not be much on which to align Tier 1 stakeholders. However, all stakeholders must be aligned in one area: the need for the organization to engage in Phase 6 activities. These activities are often thought to be extraneous, when in fact they are crucial to achieving business value and ROI.

It is especially important to align business stakeholders around the project's expectations of realizing business value. Accountability for, and ownership of, realizing business value should be given to appropriate stakeholders and process owners. (These decisions are sometimes crafted as part of Phase 4 deployment planning activities and communicated by project governance to the appropriate project stakeholders in Phase 4 or 5.) For large initiatives, such as the implementation of a SAP, Oracle, or other ERP systems, there may be dozens of process owners.

6.02.03 Mobilize key stakeholders

Mobilizing the key business stakeholders is sometimes a bit more difficult than mobilizing executives and project execution stakeholders. The reason for this is that business people are typically more comfortable with managing the status quo than with leading change.

Although the MAPs that were developed and distributed in Phase 5 may provide some foundation, they may be too generic to offer specific guidance to the change owners. Therefore, the change lead may need to coach a few of the higher-level business owners on what will be expected of them in Phase 6, such as gathering metrics, making staffing-level changes, and sponsoring user groups and communities of practice.

6.02 Outputs/Deliverables

- Phase Gate 5 debriefing material
- Updated executive and management stakeholder analysis
- Updated leadership and management action plans
- Updated communication and engagement plan
- Updated Phase 6 plan

Activity 6.03 – Transfer Ownership

Since the solution was deployed and stabilized during Phase 5, it is now time for the project team to transfer ownership of the new current state to the appropriate business and operations owners/operators. This transition requires the transfer not only of accountability and ownership, but of all relevant project documentation as well.

Ownership transfer is a critical step toward full organizational adoption. Even though the end-users/employees may have initially adopted the solution and the subsequent changes that came along with it, it is up to business owners and operators to sustain that adoption. If not, the organization risks backsliding into the old way of doing things. Although disabling legacy systems and work-arounds can prevent some backsliding, instead of maximizing the benefits of the change (thereby increasing business value and ROI), the organization is in danger of curtailing all potential benefits.

The importance of transferring ownership lies not only in a formal declaration of who is now responsible or accountable (although documentation of accountability does help to build commitment) but also in the change in attitude and sense of ownership as well. The initiative now goes from being viewed by the business as *"their* project/initiative" (meaning corporate or the project team's) to *"our new way of working."*

6.03.01 Define the transfer

When transferring ownership of the solution or change driver, consider the following areas:

- *Delineate Ongoing Roles and Responsibilities* – If an initiative has been transferred from corporate to one or more business units, there should be a clear understanding of what corporate will or will not support from this point forward. For an IT initiative, this may include such things as ongoing support and maintenance, upgrades, training and help desk support, and access to source code. Items such as these are often covered in some type of *service level agreement*, or SLA. It is important to establish ownership and accountability for business value realization as well. Unless someone will be held accountable for realizing business value, it is unlikely to occur.
- *Documentation and Knowledge Transfer* – Along with the transfer of responsibilities comes the transfer of all associated documentation and knowledge produced during the creation and deployment of the solution. Note that, in order to maintain the integrity of the solution, certain elements may not be transferred over. These might include such things as source code (see next bullet point).
- *Parameters Around Customizing or Modifying the Solution* – Emergence One consultants often see problems in the areas of customization or modification. E1 once worked with a client that had a virtual nightmare on its hands as it was about to undertake the upgrade of a popular business application it had deployed three years earlier. When it originally deployed the system, it deployed one configuration to numerous "semi-independent" locations and regions around the world. However, when it came time to upgrade to the new release of the software, corporate IT was shocked to find out that many of the locations had customized the software to their liking. So instead of upgrading one common system, the company had to understand all the customizations and modifications that had been made across the globe, immensely complicating their solution.
- *Ongoing Issues and Risks* – It is not enough to transfer ownership. When ownership is transferred, all the risks and ongoing issues are transferred as well. Therefore, make time to review the updated risk management log and any ongoing issues and risks.

6.03.02 Agree upon ongoing Phase 6 roles

Now that the solution/change driver has been officially transferred to the business, the new owners/operators tend to dismiss the remaining project team members. This is a mistake. There are still a number of Phase 6 activities that project members (especially the change lead and certain team members who possess subject matter expertise) can assist with. In fact, the historic knowledge these team members possess will most likely prove invaluable to the completion of Phase 6 and business value realization.

6.03 Outputs/Deliverables

- Documentation of ownership/accountability
- Agreed-upon service level agreement (if necessary)
- All relevant project documentation (including ongoing issues and risks)
- Phase 6 roles and responsibilities

Activity 6.04 – Evaluate the New Current State

Before the new current state can be sustained for the long term, it needs to be properly supported. Although previous project team activities tried to predict the type and amount of support needed, those predictions were more theoretical. Now that the new current state is operating in the real world, with its broader and more inclusive set of change recipients (as opposed to focus group participants), a more accurate assessment of organizational adoption and ongoing support needs can be made.

6.04.01 Collect baseline metrics

Although the organization has had limited time to work with the changes and extract business value from its initial efforts, appropriate business and ROI metrics should be collected. This will give business owners and those responsible for realizing business value a baseline from which to determine whether their subsequent Phase 6 efforts have yielded measurable results.

Along with business value and ROI metrics, employee performance metrics should be collected.

In order to have validly measure progress, the same set of metrics will need to be collected at a future point in time by utilizing the same process and measurement tools.

6.04.02 Evaluate employee motivation and competence

Organizational adoption by end-users/employees (Tier 3 stakeholders) is the result of their motivation to work with the introduced changes and their ability (competency) to do so. Supporting both of these elements is the appropriate *structural support*: for instance, the right policies and procedures, an effective organizational design, or easy access to subject matter experts. If employees are poorly motivated, or if the workforce has not developed the required competencies, then business value is unlikely to be realized.

There are many ways of evaluating motivation and competency levels. On smaller initiatives, anecdotal feedback from managers and supervisors may be enough. For larger initiatives, pulse surveys and skills testing may be required.

However, assessing motivation with a survey can be difficult. Many surveys that Emergence One consultants have reviewed ask numerous questions to measure informational knowledge (e.g., *"I know what the objectives of this project/change are"*) or beliefs or feelings (*"I feel that these changes can help me do my job more efficiently"*). Questions of this nature assume that people are motivated to adopt an initiative's changes because they know the initiative's objectives, because it will help them do their job more efficiently, or because they believe they will be rewarded for compliance. The problem with this approach is that employee motivation is a much more complex issue. What may be "motivating" to one employee may not be motivating to another. Some people may be motivated by extrinsic rewards (e.g., a year-end bonus); others may be motivated by intrinsic rewards (praise from their manager); and still others may be motivated simply because they pride themselves on being a good "team player."

Therefore, when working with clients, Emergence One consultants find it best to keep questions clear, simple, and direct: *"How motivated are you to make this change part of your (daily/weekly) activities? Why or why not?"* These two simple questions usually provide 90% of the required actionable information that gets to the heart of motivational challenges. While an intricate 20-30 page questionnaire may provide a lot of "nice to have" information, when you strip it all away, not that much additional information is available to guide a different course or direction.

6.04.03 Evaluate structural support

A fully functional future state requires more than just having motivated, competent employees. It also requires that the right structural support elements are in place:

- Having the right policies and procedures that will support the change;
- Implementing tailored reward and recognition systems;
- Optimizing staffing levels and other organizational design features;
- Streamlining certain review and approval processes; and
- Establishing job descriptions, classifications, and career paths that reflect the new current state.

271

Assessing the need for, and designing, appropriate structural support was covered in earlier phases. For Phase 6, the project team should determine how well these support structures have been deployed and communicated to the affected stakeholders, and whether or not they are sufficient to support current objectives.

6.04 Outputs/Deliverables

- Baseline metrics
- Metrics on employee motivation and competence
- Assessment of structural support effectiveness

Activity 6.05 – Institute Practices to Sustain New Current State

Although the new current state was "stabilized" as part of Phase 5's activities, many of those interventions were likely only temporary fixes (for example, the provisional reassignment of resources and personnel).

In Phase 6, the organization is given the opportunity to institute additional "post-deployment" practices that will help sustain the new current state. These post-deployment practices will depend in part upon the following:

- The outputs of the previous activity (Activity 6.04: Evaluate the New Current State);
- The scope and nature of the initiative;
- Company culture and existing norms; and
- The availability of resources.

Some of these post-deployment practices may include the following:

- ***Implementing Alerts and Other Feedback or Reporting Mechanisms*** – Depending upon the nature and scope of the initiative, there may be opportunities to implement alerts and other feedback/reporting mechanisms when something within the new current state dips below optimal levels. These mechanisms may include alerts for stalled workflows; monitoring requests for overtime or temporary staffing; IT usage reports; or finding out when help desk tickets suddenly spike.
- ***Eliminating Workarounds*** – The elimination of work-arounds was first discussed in Phase 5. However, many project teams choose not to eliminate or roadblock workarounds until the new current state is in a sustaining mode.

- *Upkeep and Maintenance of Documentation* – This practice relates to a broad range of relevant documentation, e.g., system documentation and change control, training and end-user documentation, and issue and risk management.
- *Ongoing Skill Development* – Although most of the affected employees should have been trained as part of Phase 5 activities, processes should be put in place to ensure that new or transferred employees also develop the needed skills and competencies required to maintain the new current state. Training and other competency development materials will need to be updated to reflect any post-deployment changes.
- *Ongoing Communication and Engagement Activities* – It is important to keep communicating the need to maintain the new current state and highlight some of the benefits and improved efficiencies that have resulted from it.
- *Creation of "Change Networks"* – Change networks are groups of employees (sometimes referred to as change advocates, champions, diplomats, or leaders) who are responsible for promoting and supporting the change among their colleagues. They use their informal peer influence instead of the formal, hierarchical power of executive-level change sponsors. As such, they can create grassroots support for the initiative and identify any issues or concerns that management might overlook. Emergence One consultants often have had great success with change networks, provided that the organization assigns these roles to individuals who are influential and have the respect of their peers. Unfortunately, many times organizations try to pawn off under-utilized personnel into this role, a practice that rarely yields positive results. The change lead can be an excellent resource for crafting this program.

6.05 Outputs/Deliverables

- Alerts and other feedback mechanisms
- Updated documentation
- Process for ongoing skills development
- Communication and engagement plan (owned by the business, not the project team)
- Change network training material

Activity 6.06 – Reevaluate and Remediate

Baseline metrics were collected as part of Activity 6.04. Now that the organization has had some time to work with the change, it is time to reevaluate how the change is impacting the organization, performance metrics, and the ROI.

6.06.01 Reevaluate metrics

In order to reassess metrics in a valid manner, the same metrics from Activity 6.04 must be measured again using identical instruments and processes.

If negative gaps exist, then the organization may:

1 Be backsliding into old, less efficient behaviors;
2 Not have the necessary skills, competencies, or motivation to operate effectively in the new current state;
3 Be dealing with a technical or structural support issue that is not working as intended; or
4 Some combination of the above.

As a reminder, metrics can often tell a person what is not working but not necessarily be able to diagnose *why*. It is important to accurately diagnose the reason something is happening so that the appropriate remediation steps can be taken.

If the metrics show little change or improvement from the last time they were looked at, this is an indication that the initiative has stalled. If it has stalled at a suboptimal level, then remediation planning will also be required. If it has stalled at an acceptable performance level, then the project team should proceed to Activity 6.07: Identify/Institute Enhancement Opportunities.

6.06.02 Remediation planning

Once the problem has been accurately diagnosed, either the project team, an *ad-hoc* business team, or the relevant support organization will need to address the root causes of the identified issues.

Depending upon the nature of the issue, remediation can take several forms:

- *Better Issue and Risk Management* – A problem may have occurred because the organization took its eyes off the ball when it came to proactively identifying and mitigating risks or ignored current, ongoing issues. Better issue and risk management can help alleviate future concerns.
- *Remedial Training* – If the problem is a lack of required skills and competencies, there may be a need for remedial training. Training programs are notorious for evaluating their own success based upon the subjective opinions of participants rather than measuring specific, applicable skill development.

- *A Repair, Rework, or Customization of the Solution* – Whereas training teams are notorious for not measuring the true effectiveness of their programs, project teams are notorious for doing an insufficient job of gathering customer requirements. If this area is deficient, the solution may need to be reworked or customized to fit local needs; a decision that can carry serious ramifications and should include a review by project governance. However, at times, new technology (for example, a new release of an IT application) simply does not work as intended owing to a bug or poor coding. In that case, a technical fix should suffice, although acknowledging the glitch and the subsequent repair would require communicating appropriately to stakeholders.
- *A Review of Structural Support and Other Peripheral Changes* – As described elsewhere, successful change does not rely solely on the motivation and competence of end-users/employees but also upon changes to the existing infrastructure and other organizational support elements. Stronger policies and procedures may need to be put in place, along with more robust reward and recognition programs, more efficient organizational design, or increased technical support.

6.06 Outputs/Deliverables

- Evaluation of metrics, noted gaps
- Remediation plans

Is It a Technical Problem or a Behavioral Problem?
Metrics can tell you what is happening but not always provide you with the reason.
For instance, the project manager may determine that the reason a new IT system is not being fully utilized is that procurement did not purchase enough user licenses to meet demand. Therefore, the apparent solution is for the organization to go out and buy more user licenses.
On the other hand, the change lead may have a totally different take on the lack of utilization. According to the change lead, the reason may be behavioral, that is, there may be little motivation or incentive for the employees to utilize the new system.
However, the project sponsor, considering both technical and behavioral elements, might determine that the problem is a combination of both. Because there is low intranet bandwidth in some locations, users have been hesitant to log off. The number of licenses the company bought would be sufficient only if users logged off when they were supposed to (a behavioral issue), though part of what was driving that behavior was the technical, low-bandwidth issue. Therefore, the solution to this problem would require both technical and behavioral interventions.

Activity 6.07 – Identify/Institute Enhancement Opportunities

For this activity, "enhancement opportunities" do not refer to meeting remediation needs but to identifying opportunities that will take the organization to the next level of operational efficiency, effectiveness, and business value. (The concept a making a project a "strong success," as opposed to simply meeting expectations, was described in Chapter 1.)

Some of these practices can be developed by motivated process owners or Phase 6 team members; others may occur organically.

- *User Groups* – Sometimes a process owner or motivated "super-user" may decide to form a "user group" that the organization may or may not have officially sanctioned. The purpose of a user group is to share best practices, alert others to potential issues and solutions, share success stories, and support each other in the execution of their work responsibilities. They may meet anywhere from once a week to once a quarter. In some circles, user groups may be referred to as "communities of practice."
- *Governance Boards or Steering Committees* – When user groups grow in influence and coalesce around an agreed-upon set of "best practices," the company may decide to elevate their status by formalizing their roles as guardians or purveyors of best practices. As such, their role may be to mandate and ensure compliance with an established set of practices or principles, or they may merely become recognized "advisors."
- *Conferences and Workshops* – A few years ago, a large client of Emergence One International implemented a nearly complete suite of SAP applications. Since then, they have been holding regular "SAP User Group" conferences for all of their internal users, with topics customized to getting the most out of the company's ERP system. They found this approach to be much more beneficial than paying for users to attend generic, off-site workshops.
- *Reward and Recognition Programs* – Emergence One consultants regularly recommend that change recipients not be treated as passive recipients but as potential sources of innovative ideas and creative thinking. But in order to tap into this potential wealth of ideas, the organization first needs to create and communicate about an appropriate incentive program.
- *Newsletters and Other Communications* – Newsletters that regurgitate ongoing news provide little value. However, newsletters and other communications that boldly tout enhancements to the new

current state, along with directions on how to enact these enhancements throughout the company, can start to bring the organization to the next level.

6.07 Optional Outputs/Deliverables

- Charter for the creation of user groups and similar associations
- Conference materials
- Reward and recognition programs
- Newsletters and other communications

What is $100,000 worth?

When working for a large firm, a colleague of mine once had an idea that she calculated would save the company over $100,000 each year. When I asked her why she didn't submit her idea to the company leadership, she said "it just wasn't worth it."

The reason why she said so is that the company had a program in place to encourage cost savings or efficiency improvement ideas from employees. However, the program only paid a flat fee for any idea or suggestion that, if implemented, demonstrated a positive ROI. The payout was $1,000 – regardless of how much savings the company could achieve!

My colleague thought her $100,000+ idea was worth more than "a measly thousand bucks" and thus never submitted it. If the company had granted an exception for her, they would need to grant it to everyone else. That was not a path the company was willing to go down. In the end, the company held on to its $1,000 flat-fee policy, and my colleague held on to her $100,000 idea.

Activity 6.08 – Perform a Project Review

Now that the initiative is comfortably in a sustaining mode, with the business taking ownership for the new current state, it is time to conduct a project review prior to wrapping up Phase 6 and the overall initiative.

6.08.01 Validate business value and ROI

The most important items to review are: Did the project achieve the expected business value, ROI, and other elements that were put forth in the business case? In order to answer that question, review the business case (which was finalized during Activity 3.06) and the associated metrics.

6.08.02 Document any Phase 6 lessons learned, pertinent observations, or outstanding needs from Phase 6

In previous phases, a similar activity was always a subset of the "Phase Wrap-up." Since wrap-up for Phase 6 simply involves disbanding the remaining project team members, after once again archiving all project information (and holding the celebration Emergence One always insists on!), documenting Phase 6 lessons learned occurs a little earlier.

6.08.03 Consolidate lessons learned from previous phases

Lessons learned from all the prior phases should have been documented near the conclusion of each phase. Now that the project is coming to the end, all lessons learned material (including the recently developed lessons from Phase 6) should be consolidated into a user-friendly format. This material should be placed in a location where it can be easily accessed by future project teams.

6.08.04 Conduct a project review session

It is important that the project review consist not just of the remaining project team members but involve other key players: the appropriate stakeholders from the business, the project sponsor (even if he or she has been only minimally engaged in Phase 6), members of a corporate project or program office (if one exists), and key executives.

6.08 Outputs/Deliverables

- Evaluation of business value and ROI
- Lessons learned documentation (from all project phases)
- Project review document

Activity 6.09 – Phase Wrap-up

6.09.01 Archive project documentation

Project documentation was first archived at the end of Phase 5. The reason for doing so is that valuable project documentation sometimes gets lost during the transfer-of-ownership activities in Phase 6.

The project team should augment the project documentation repository that was created at the end of Phase 5 with relevant Phase 6 documentation. This documentation should also include the outputs of the previous activities.

Archiving project information should be done according to organizational standards and in a manner consistent with past practices.

6.09.02 Celebrate and acknowledge the team

Although the bulk of the project team may have rolled off at the end of Phase 5, the remaining team members who stuck it out all the way through to the end of Phase 6 deserve special recognition (and maybe a pretty good rockin' party as well!). Cheers for a job well done!

6.09 Outputs/Deliverables

- Archived repository of project documentation containing additional Phase 6 material

Conclusion of Phase 6

For more information...
Templates, detailed examples, and process tools relating to Phase 6 and all of the other Emergence One project phases be downloaded for free (though some material may require a small licensing fee) from:
www.emergenceone.com
Emergence One also certifies project professionals in the Emergence One Method. Information on certification and other training opportunities can also be found on the company website.

The "Next Evolution" of the Emergence One Method

As reviewers and implementers of the Emergence One Method have no doubt noticed by now, the methodology is quite extensive and comprehensive.

We here at Emergence One, along with our publisher, have done our best to perfect the final product. But as we tell our clients, one can never achieve perfection, only strive to continually improve and evolve.

As such, we are asking for your help in evolving the Emergence One Method. We welcome any suggestions or recommendations that will help us improve the applicability and effectiveness of the methodology, streamline or enhance the various activities and processes, and eliminate any discrepancies or unnecessary redundancies.

Your contributions will be acknowledged if the need arises for an updated edition of this book. In the meantime, we will post an erratum or any necessary additions of this book on the Emergence One website.

For more information on how to contribute to the ongoing evolution of the Emergence One Method, please visit our website at *www.emergenceone.com.*

References

Anderson, L. A., and Anderson, D. *The Change Leader's Roadmap: How to Navigate Your Organization's Transformation.* The Practicing Organization Development Series, Rothwell, W. J., Sullivan, R., and Quade, K. (eds.). San Francisco: Pfeiffer (Wiley), 2001.

Bagozzi, R. P. "The Legacy of the Technology Acceptance Model and a Proposal for a Paradigm Shift." *Journal for the Association for Information Systems.* 2007;8(4):244-254.

Baron, R. A., and Byrne, D. *Social Psychology: Understanding Human Interaction.* Fifth Edition. Boston: Allyn and Bacon, 1987.

Bell, C. R. *Managers As Mentors: Building Partnerships for Learning.* San Francisco: Berrett-Koehler Publishers, 1996.

Black, J. S., Gregersen, H. B., and Mendenhall, M. E. *Global Assignments: Successfully Expatriating an Repatriating International Managers.* San Francisco: Jossey-Bass, 1992.

Blanchard, K., Carew, D., and Parisi-Carew, E. *The One Minute Manager Builds High Performing Teams.* Rev. ed. New York: William Morrow, 2000.

Block, P. *Flawless Consulting: A Guide to Getting Your Expertise Used.* Second Edition. San Francisco: Pfeiffer (Wiley), 1981.

Bossidy, L., and Charan, R. *Execution: The Discipline of Getting Things Done.* New York: Crown Business, 2002.

Brammer, L. M., and Shostrom, E. L. *Therapeutic Psychology: Fundamentals of Counseling and Psychotherapy.* Fourth Edition. Englewood Cliffs, NJ: Prentice-Hall, 1982.

Brickley, J. A., Smith, C. W., and Zimmerman, J. L. *Designing Organizations to Create Value: From Strategy to Structure.* New York: McGraw-Hill, 2003.

British Journal of Social Work. Editorial review of *On Death and Dying.* Grief & Bereavement Arena. http://www.bereavementarena.com/books/On-Death-and-Dying-isbn9780415463997.

Buckingham, M., and Clifton, D. O. *Now, Discover Your Strengths.* New York: The Free Press, 2001.

Burke, W. W., and Litwin, G. H. *"A Causal Model of Organizational Performance and Change."* *Journal of Management.* 1992;18(3):523-545.

Cameron, E., and Green, M. *Making Sense of Change Management: A Complete Guide to the Models, Tools & Techniques of Organizational Change.* London: Kogan Page, 2004.

Carr, D. K., Hard, K. J., and Trahant, W. J. *Managing the Change Process: A Field Book for Change Agents, Consultants, Team Leaders, and Reengineering Managers.* New York: McGraw-Hill, 1996.

Chuttur, M.Y. "Overview of the Technology Acceptance Model: Origins, Developments and Future Directions." Indiana University, USA. *Sprouts: Working Papers on Information Systems.* 2009;9(37). http://sprouts.aisnet.org/9-37. Accessed on April 20, 2011.

Clayton, M. *The Innovator's Dilemma: The Revolutionary Book that Will Change the Way You Do Business.* New York: Harper Business Essentials, 2003.

Cleland, D. I., and Ireland, L. R. *Project Management: Strategic Design and Implementation.* Fourth Edition. New York: McGraw-Hill, 2002.

Cohen, A. R. *The Portable MBA in Management.* New York: Wiley & Sons, 1995.

Davis, F. D. Perceived Usefulness, Perceived Ease of Use, and User Acceptance of Information Technology. *MIS Quarterly.* 1989;13(3):319-340.

DeLuca, J. R. *Political Savvy: Systematic Approaches to Leadership Behind-the-Scenes.* Berwyn, PA: Evergreen Business Group Publications, 1999.

Doane, M. *SAP Blue Book: A Concise Business Guide to the World of SAP.* Michael Doane, 1998.

Englund, R. L., and Bucero, A. *Project Sponsorship: Achieving Management Commitment for Project Success.* San Francisco: Jossey-Bass, 2006.

Englund, R. L., Graham, R. J., and Dinsmore, P. C. *Creating the Project Office: A Manager's Guide to Leading Organizational Change.* San Francisco: Jossey-Bass, 2003.

Flannes, S. W., and Levin, G. *People Skills for Project Managers.* Vienna, VA: Management Concepts, 2001.

Frame, J. D. *The New Project Management: Tools for an Age of Rapid Change, Complexity, and Other Business Realities.* San Francisco: Jossey-Bass, 2002.

Friedman, R., and James, J. W. "The Myth of the Stages of Dying, Death and Grief." *Skeptic Magazine.* 2008:37-42. http://www.grief.net/Articles/Myth%20of%20Stages.pdf.

Galbraith, J., Downey, D., and Kates, A. *Designing Dynamic Organizations: A Hands-On Guide for Leaders at All Levels.* New York: AMACOM books, 2002.

Garland, R. *Project Governance – A Practical Guide to Effective Project Decision Making.* London: Kogan Page, 2009.

Gergen, K. J., and Gergen, M. M. *Social Psychology.* New York: Harcourt Brace Jovanovich, 1981.

Goldstein, N. J., Martin, S. J., and Cialdini, R. B. *Yes! 50 Scientifically Proven Ways to Be Persuasive.* New York: The Free Press, 2008.

Hammer, M., and Champy, J. *Reengineering the Corporation: A Manifesto for Business Revolution.* New York: Harper Business, 1993.

Hammer, M., and Stanton, S. A. *The Reengineering Revolution: A Handbook.* New York: Harper Business, 1995.

Harrington, H. J., Conner, D. R., and Horney, N. L. *Project Change Management: Applying Change Management to Improvement Projects.* New York: McGraw-Hill, 2000.

Harvard Business Review on Change. Boston: Harvard Business School Press, 1998.

Hesselbein, F., Goldsmith, M., and Beckhard, R. (eds.). *The Leader of the Future.* San Francisco: Jossey-Bass, 1996.

Huck, S. W., and Sandler, H. M. *Rival Hypotheses: Alternative Interpretations of Data Based Conclusions.* New York: Harper & Row, 1979.

Hunter, D., Bailey, A., and Taylor, B. *The Art of Facilitation: How to Create Group Synergy.* Tucscon, AZ: Fisher Books, 1995.

Hunter, D., Bailey, A., and Taylor, B. *The Zen of Groups: The Handbook for People Meeting with a Purpose.* Tucscon, AZ: Fisher Books, 1995.

Jue, A. L., Marr, J. A., and Kassotakis, M. E. *Social Media at Work,* San Francisco: Jossey-Bass, 2010.

Kerzner, H. *Project Management: A Systems Approach to Planning, Scheduling, and Controlling.* Tenth Edition. San Francisco: Wiley, 2009.

Kidder, L. H. *Selltiz Wrightsman & Cook's Research Methods in Social Relations.* Fourth Edition. New York: Holt, Rinehart and Winston, 1981.

Knutson, J. (ed.). *Project Management for Business Professionals: A Comprehensive Guide.* New York: Wiley & Sons, 2001.

Kotter, J. P. *Leading Change.* Boston: Harvard Business School Press, 1996.

Kubler-Ross, E. *On Death and Dying: What the Dying Have to Teach Doctors, Nurses, Clergy and Their Own Families.* London: Routledge, 1973.

Leonard-Barton, D., and Deschamps, I. "Managerial Influence in the Implementation of New Technology." *Management Science.* 1988; 34(10):1252-1265.

Loehr, J., and Schwartz, T. *The Power of Full Engagement: Managing Energy, Not Time, Is the Key to High Performance and Personal Renewal.* New York: The Free Press, 2003.

Lucas, H., Ginzberg, M., and Schultz, R. *Information Systems Implementation: Testing a Structural Model.* Norwood, NJ: Ablex Publishing, 1990.

Merlyn, V., and Parkinson, J. *Development Effectiveness: Strategies for IS Organizational Transition.* The Ernst & Young Information Management Series. New York: Wiley & Sons, 1994.

Miller, V. A. *The Guidebook for International Trainers in Business and Industry.* Madison, WI: American Society for Training and Development; New York: Van Nostrand Reinhold Co., 1979.

Morris, R. A., with McWhorter Sember B. *Project Management That Works: Real-World Advice on Communicating, Problem Solving, and Everything Else You Need to Know to Get the Job Done.* New York: AMACOM books, 2008.

Muchinsky, P. M. *Psychology Applied to Work: An Introduction to Industrial and Organizational Psychology.* Second Edition. Chicago: The Dorsey Press, 1987.

Natemeyer, W. E. (ed.). *Classics of Organizational Behavior.* Oak Park, IL: Moore Publishing Co., 1978.

Nokes, S. *The Definitive Guide to Project Management, 2nd Edition.* London: Financial Times/Prentice Hall, 2007.

Oracle Method. *Organizational Change Management: Method Handbook.* Release 1.1.0. May 1996. Redwood City, CA: Oracle Corp., 1996.

Oracle Method. *Project Management: Method Handbook.* Release 2.0. November 1996. Redwood City, CA: Oracle Corp., 1996.

Oracle Method. *Project Management: Process and Task Reference.* Release 2.0. November 1996. Redwood City, CA: Oracle Corp., 1996.

Perkins, D. N. T. *Leading at the Edge.* New York: AMACOM books, 2000.

Peter, L. J., and Hull, R. *The Peter Principle: Why Things Always Go Wrong.* New York: William Morrow and Co., 1969.

Phillips, J. J., and Phillips, P. P. *Show Me the Money: How to Determine ROI in People, Projects, and Programs.* San Francisco: Berrett-Koehler Publishers, 2007.

Pinto, J. K., and Millet, I. *Successful Information System Implementation: The Human Side.* Second Edition. Newtown Square, PA: Project Management Institute, 1999.

The Price Waterhouse Change Integration Team. *Better Change: Best Practices for Transforming Your Organization.* Chicago: Irwin Professional Publishing, 1995.

Project Management Institute. *A Guide to the Project Management Body of Knowledge (PMBOK® Guide)*--Fourth Edition. Newtown Square, PA: Project Management Institute, 2008.

Robinson, D. G., and Robinson, J. C. *Performance Consulting: Moving Beyond Training.* San Francisco: Berrett-Koehler Publishers, 1995.

Rothwell, W. J., Sullivan, R., and McLean, G. N. *Practicing Organization Development: A Guide for Consultants.* San Diego, CA: Pfeiffer & Co., 1995.

Schein, E. H. *Career Dynamics: Matching Individual and Organizational Needs.* Reading, MA: Addison-Wesley Publishing Co., 1978.

Schein, E. H. *The Corporate Culture Survival Guide: Sense and Nonsense about Culture Change.* San Francisco: Jossey-Bass Publishers, 1999

Schein, E. H. *Process Consultation Revisited: Building the Helping Relationship.* Reading, MA: Addison-Wesley/Longman, 1999.

Schuler, R. S. *Personnel and Human Resource Management.* Second Edition. St. Paul, MN: West Publishing, 1984.

Shafritz, J. M., and Whitbeck, P. H. (eds.). *Classics of Organizational Theory.* Oak Park, IL: Moore Publishing Co., 1978.

Smith, M. E. (ed.) *An Introduction to Performance Technology.* Vol. 1. Washington, D.C.: National Society for Performance and Instruction, 1986.

Stix, G. "The Neuroscience of True Grit." *Scientific American.* March 2011;304(3):29-33.

Taylor, J. *A Survival Guide for Project Managers.* Second Edition. New York: AMACOM books, 2006.

Thorndike, R. L., and Hagen, E. P. *Measurement and Evaluation in Psychology and Education.* Fourth Edition. New York: Wiley & Sons, 1977.

VA Office of Information and Technology. *IT Project Management Guide.* Release 2.0. March 2005. Washington DC: US Department of Veteran Affairs, 2003

Weiner, B. *Human Motivation.* New York: Springer-Verlag, 1985.

Weisbord, M. R., and Janoff, S. *Future Search: An Action Guide to Finding Common Ground in Organizations & Communities.* San Francisco: Berrett-Koehler Publishers, 1995.

Weiss, J. W., and Wysocki, R. K. *5-Phase Project Management: A Practical Planning and Implementation Guide.* New York: Basic Books, 1992.

Worchel, S., Cooper, J., and Goethals, G. R. *Understanding Social Psychology.* Fourth Edition. Chicago: The Dorsey Press, 1988.

Zaltman, G., Duncan, R., and Holbeck, J. *Innovations and Organizations.* New York: Wiley & Sons, 1973.

Index

P

About the Author

Thomas Luke Jarocki is an accomplished "roll-up-your-sleeves" project manager and change leadership professional. He has logged nearly 25,000 hours working side by side with various project teams for clients throughout the United States, Latin America, and Europe. With more than two decades of direct, on-the-ground experience, Thomas has gained the practical know-how and real-world insights often missed by researchers and other academic theoreticians.

He has worked with numerous Fortune 500 companies, including Apple, Motorola, Chevron, McDonalds, HP, McKesson, Cisco Systems, Kellogg's, PepsiCo, Applied Materials, and Microsoft. He has worked with them in the areas of project and program management, organizational/behavioral change management, strategy implementation, project/change leadership, IT User adoption, ERP systems integration, training, and communications.

Before becoming the Managing Director of Emergence One International, Ltd., Thomas was the Managing Principal of Organizational Change for Oracle's ERP consulting practice later advancing to another key position with a Big Five consulting firm. Originally from New York, he earned a Master's degree in Organizational Behavior from Columbia University and served on the Social Sciences faculty in the University of Maryland, European Division.

Besides his consulting work, Thomas's dynamic presentations have made him a popular speaker and workshop leader with both domestic and international audiences. He is a member of the Project Management Institute and actively promotes a more rigorous approach to managing the human and organizational change factors critical to project success.

When not traveling, he resides in the San Francisco Bay Area with his lovely wife and his two joyously rambunctious children.

About Emergence One International

Emergence One International, Ltd. was founded in the Silicon Valley/San Francisco Bay Area in 2001 to provide corporate clients with a more seamless approach to managing project requirements, facilitating change adoption, and achieving business value realization.

Emergence One provides a variety of targeted solutions for project planning, execution, and workplace deployments, including:

- Project management/change management consulting services,
- Project team resources,
- "Enhanced Advantage" tools, templates and process guides,
- Organizational adoption and business value realization strategies,
- Augmentation of existing project methodologies,
- Project management/change management workshops, and
- Customized training based upon the Emergence One Method.

The company also certifies project professionals in applying the Emergence One Method to various projects, change initiatives, IT implementations, and strategy deployments.

For more information on Emergence One International, or to download additional process tools and project templates, visit www.emergenceone.com.

CPSIA information can be obtained at www.ICGtesting.com
Printed in the USA
LVOW10*2300101113

360564LV00002BC/11/P